Writing Lives in the Eighteenth Century

Aperçus: Histories Texts Cultures

Editor: Kat Lecky, Bucknell University

Aperçus is a series of books exploring the connections among historiography, culture, and textual representation in various disciplines. Revisionist in intention, *Aperçus* seeks monographs as well as guest-edited multi-authored volumes, which stage critical interventions to open up new possibilities for interrogating how systems of knowledge production operate at the intersections of individual and collective thought.

The series has recently come under the leadership of a new editor interested in medieval, Renaissance, early modern, and Restoration texts and contexts. Particular areas of interest include but are not limited to:

1) premodern conceptions and theorizations of race, ethnicity, gender, and sexuality in art, literature, historical artefacts, medical and scientific works, political tracts, religious texts, etc.

2) negotiations between local, national, and imperial intellectual spheres;

3) the cultures, literatures, and politics of the excluded and marginalized;

4) print history and the history of the book;

5) medical humanities;

6) the cross-pollination of humanistic and scientific modes of inquiry.

We welcome projects by early-career scholars; we will not consider unrevised dissertations. Please send a proposal and letter of inquiry to Professor Katarzyna Lecky at kat.lecky@bucknell.edu.

For a full list of *Aperçus* titles, please visit our website at www.bucknelluniversitypress.org.

Writing Lives in the Eighteenth Century

EDITED BY TANYA M. CALDWELL

Bucknell University | University Press

Lewisburg, Pennsylvania

Library of Congress Cataloging-in-Publication Data

Names: Caldwell, Tanya, 1969- editor.
Title: Writing lives in the eighteenth century / edited by Tanya M. Caldwell.
Description: Lewisburg, Pennsylvania : Bucknell University Press, 2020. | Series: Aperçus: histories texts cultures | Includes bibliographical references and index.
Identifiers: LCCN 2019049028 | ISBN 9781684482269 (paperback) | ISBN 9781684482276 (hardback) | ISBN 9781684482283 (epub) | ISBN 9781684482290 (mobi) | ISBN 9781684482306 (pdf)
Subjects: LCSH: Biography as a literary form—History—18th century. | Europe—Biography—History and criticism. | Autobiography—History—18th century. | Autobiography in literature. | Biography in literature.
Classification: LCC CT21 .W77 2020 | DDC 808.06/692—dc23
LC record available at https://lccn.loc.gov/2019049028

A British Cataloging-in-Publication record for this book is available from the British Library.

∞ The paper used in this publication meets the requirements of the American National Standard for Information Sciences—Permanence of Paper for Printed Library Materials, ANSI Z39.48-1992.

www.bucknelluniversitypress.org

Distributed worldwide by Rutgers University Press

Manufactured in the United States of America

For Greg Clingham, for his tireless work
of changing lives through print

Contents

Writing Lives in the Eighteenth Century

Introduction

The Art of Writing Lives

TANYA M. CALDWELL

Those parallel circumstances and kindred images to which we readily conform our minds are, above all other writings, to be found in the narratives of the lives of particular persons; and therefore no species of writing seems more worthy of cultivation than biography, since none can be more delightful or more useful, none can more certainly enchain the heart by irresistible interest, or more widely diffuse instruction to every diversity of condition.

—Samuel Johnson, *Rambler* 60 (October 13, 1750)

The study of individual men can never fail to be an object of the highest importance. It is only by comparison that we come to know any thing of mind or ourselves.

—William Godwin, "Of History and Romance" (1797)

L..d! said my mother, what is all this story about?—
A Cock and a Bull, said Yorick—And one of the best of its kind, I ever heard.

—Laurence Sterne, *Tristram Shandy* (1759)

At the end of the eighteenth century, William Godwin insisted that the most satisfying way to study "the machine of society" is through "study of the individual." Such an endeavor, he elaborates, provides an intimate knowledge of "the operation of human passions," through the ages, both on the public stage and in the closet.[1] Godwin's fascination with the individual and humankind is likewise reflected in Samuel Johnson's encomium on the pleasurable and didactic elements (the *dulce et utile*) of biographical writing in *Rambler* 60 quoted above. The ubiquity of the individual's life as subject for writers is most evident in the titles and subjects of so many examples of the eighteenth-century novel.

Recent scholarship on the emergence of celebrity during this period equally arises from interest in the individual as a force that transformed political and social landscapes in the eighteenth century.[2] James Boswell and Samuel Johnson are still most closely associated with "revolutionizing," as Leo Damrosch remarks, "biography as the art of bringing people to life in all their idiosyncrasy and depth" (2).[3] Both celebrity studies and treatments in the second decade of the twenty-first century of Boswell and Johnson reflect the forces that facilitated the rise of the individual as a formidable power while destabilizing traditional notions of genre and rendering emerging ones ambiguous. The essays in this collection investigate the self-consciousness of their roles in history on the part of those in the circle that shaped biography and autobiography as a modern genre.

Constant new publications—new biographies of varying kinds—bespeak ongoing fascination with the figures at the heart of this "Age of Enlightenment." In his very humanized presentation of Johnson to a broad public audience, in *The World in Thirty-Eight Chapters, or Dr. Johnson's Guide to Life* (2018), Henry Hitchings acknowledges what audiences in the eighteenth century and today are interested in: the contours of the daily life of a figure who won fame.[4] Then, as now, Hitchings recognizes, readers are fascinated by the elements of a life and world they can identify with, not one alien to them: "Glossy role models conceal reality from us, rather than helping us to navigate it" (3).

In his conversational style, Hitchings presents an intimate account of the fallible Johnson in order to sketch the minutiae of the daily life for a general twenty-first-century audience—those details that make a celebrity both alluring and marketable.[5] Yet, as James J. Caudle critically examines in the present collection, from the beginning of modern biography Boswell was acutely aware of readers' thirst for the gossipy details that provide contexts for the intellectual achievements—and of the implications for legacy that those details create. In her account here of Isabelle de Charrière, Victoria Warren offers not only an example of a writer who broadens and makes more complex our notions of those at the heart of life writing as it emerged into the modern world but also exactly those kinds of domestic details that twenty-first-century readers are increasingly interested in. Lisa Berglund's chapter complements both Caudle's and Warren's focus on intimate detail as a feature of modern biography in presenting the scrutinizing as well as the female perspective of Hester Thrale Piozzi. Berglund considers Piozzi's recognition of the world's easier acceptance in the Johnson-Piozzi correspondence of "Dr. Johnson's ill health, or his querulous complaints of not receiving letters" than a mother's concern for "little Sophy's headache" or the "slippery Bowels of an old pious Lady long since dead." Yet Piozzi "warns her readers" that "none but domestick and familiar events can be expected from a private correspondence." Peter Sabor provides revealing details of the child-parent relationship of an often self-deluded mother.

This collection focuses on the deliberations of those who shaped the age through the presentation of lives on the page and in history and so develops our understanding of the public and private spaces they inhabited. The need for such ongoing work motivates Damrosch's presentation of Johnson for a twenty-first-century audience from a more critical angle than Hitchings's. Damrosch observes that "The Club" met in a tavern and that Johnson viewed a tavern chair as "the throne of felicity," then remarks that the members each spent no more than "a fraction of his time at the Turk's Head," the center of intellectual debate and home of the throne. His book, as such biographical investigation should, consequently, moves outward "to the larger world in which they made their lives" (3). In *The Club* Damrosch shifts focus constantly to the "new contexts" in which these historical characters "keep reappearing" along with others in their spheres (3).

Committed in the way the essays presented here are to rethinking those at the center of eighteenth-century intellectual life, Damrosch too undertakes to develop knowledge of the circle around Boswell and Johnson. He pauses, for example, to reflect on Isabelle de Charrière—but from a Boswellian perspective. He concludes that Boswell rejected her as wife material because "she probably reminded him too much of himself" (107). Warren's vibrant essay in this collection approaches Charrière from Charrière's perspective using Warren's own translations of her subject's prolific works. Warren cites the same passage on Boswell's humorous reaction to her being "much my superior" and his male indignation: "One does not like that." Yet Warren is interested in Charrière's intricate story—her tale of her own achievements and interactions with the great thinkers of the day. Berglund tells Piozzi's story from her perspective as she looked back on her friendship with Johnson. Marilyn Francus and Sabor present Frances Burney in a new light, while Francus also highlights the endeavors in Alicia LeFanu to help shape a still-emerging genre. Todd Gilman realigns the life and legacy of Dr. Charles Burney in the wake of twentieth-century scholarly biography, and Caudle puts the spotlight on those around Boswell competing with him for the "Life" of Johnson.

Another like-minded approach to those who had the power to shape the lives that preserved and helped, as a coterie, to form the history that we must keep reviewing and extending is at the heart of the 2018 edition of *Eighteenth-Century Life* (42, no. 2). This special collection of the journal committed to "Eighteenth-Century Life" focuses on the Burneys as they wrote the age. As Sophie Coulombeau opens her introduction, she quotes the young Frances Burney in her consciousness of having the power in her pen to save "all the Adventures of this Noble family" from the fate of "oblivion" (1).[6] Two of the essays here, by Francus and Sabor (who also contributes to the *Eighteenth-Century Life* volume), examine the writers' determination to "fix," as Francus terms it, family legacy in the emergence of biography, while Francus, Sabor, Berglund, and Caudle directly address awareness in the time of literary legacy and the powers of the biographer to mold history. Gilman reflects in his essay—as Sabor does in his *Eighteenth-Century Life* article—on Dr. Charles Burney's musical legacy. Gilman's case about Burney's reputation not only highlights the power of scholarly biography to cast for generations the way major literary and historical figures are perceived but also stresses the need for ongoing revision of those we feel familiar with.

Writing Lives in the Eighteenth Century began as a panel on life writing at a meeting of the Northeast Association of the American Society for Eighteenth-Century Studies. As I have suggested so far, the papers reflect a return to more traditional methodologies as well as to a seminal intellectual group following a necessary period of scholarship initiated by Felicity Nussbaum in the 1980s. Nussbaum's injunction to rethink whose voices we hear and the nature of public and private—investigations made richer as they conversed with Habermas's notions of public and private—have added to scholarly studies new voices and new ways of thinking about the writing of lives, studies from which these chapters benefit and on which their expansionary investigations build. In another self-declared return to a more traditional scholarly approach, in 2016 Andrea Walkden examined the individual as a powerful social force engendered by the religious, political, and cultural shifts of the Civil War and Interregnum. Her notion of "biographical populism" consequently places modern biography with its broader, less hagiographical processes in the mid-seventeenth century (13–14 and passim).[7] That Walkden makes her case through the examination of texts that are fictional, what she calls "pseudo-biographical," as well as deliberately biographical inadvertently complicates the question of genre as it intersects with eighteenth-century life writing, a crucial element often sidestepped.

The essays here speak to the generic malleability of biography and autobiography in probing the authors' consciousness of their powers to create heroes for the age and to obfuscate just as much as to inscribe for posterity Truth—in a Keatsian sense as it is inextricable from the Beauty of human stories. Caudle provides an overview of Boswell's changing attitudes toward accuracy from his early dabblings in fictional epistles to his emphasis during the publication of the *Hebrides* narratives on truth. Yet for all Boswell's denial of invention, he made heroes—of himself, of Johnson, of their circle—at a moment when celebrity enabled social mobility. Sabor's examination of the efforts of Frances Burney d'Arblay and Alexandre d'Arblay to raise their only son Alexander as an "idol of the world" suggests that, as on the stage of life as much as in the theaters of the time, the creation of a life could be wrapped in illusion. The d'Arblays strove to generate the life of Alexander d'Arblay through letters and social maneuvering. Also emphasizing the creative powers of Frances Burney as well as of Alicia LeFanu, as both undertook to reshape and consolidate family biography, Francus considers that neither novelist achieved remarkable success as a biographer. Warren, meanwhile, outlines the dexterity and ingenuity of Charrière in writing autobiography through forms that allowed her to depict her renegade status in society.

By the end of the eighteenth century, in his essay on "History and Romance" quoted above, Godwin offers an explanation for the phenomenon these essays underscore as he reflects on the arts of discerning and obfuscating truth for the delight and instruction of the audience. Having begun by stressing that individual "Man," as Alexander Pope wrote before him, is "the proper study of Mankind,"[8] Godwin concludes that the writer of the "romance" or "novel" is better positioned to please and improve the "faculties of his reader" because he (or she) "collects materials from all sources, experience, report, and the records of human affairs; then generalizes them; and finally selects, from their elements and the various combinations they afford, those instances which he is best qualified to portray" (300). The historian—or writer of a life—however is confined to the materials left behind: "He must take what [his subjects] choose to tell, the broken fragments, and the scattered ruins of evidence" (297). Godwin concludes, "Nothing is more uncertain, more contradictory, more unsatisfactory than the evidence of facts" (297).

In a period of anonymous and pseudonymous publishing and of novel-loving readers eager to consume cultural events through sensational stories, imaginative auto/biographers could create the history of worlds familiar and far-flung. Readers had no way of knowing the extent to which any narrative about a life was grounded in historical fact. The subjectivity embedded in the presentation of the all-fascinating individual can become particularly problematic at the hands of scholarly biographers, as Gilman demonstrates. Writers directed their fictitious *Lives* (or their "pseudo" biographies to borrow Walkden's term) to various ends, all underscored by the *dulce et utile* that Johnson prescribed for as the emerging genre—or less altruistically for financial gain or self-aggrandizement.

Outstanding obvious examples include Jonathan Swift's manipulation of readers for satirical purposes with the cloak-and-dagger delivery (a scenario repeated throughout the period) of the manuscript of *Gulliver's Travels, or Travels into Several Remote Nations of the World. In Four Parts. By Lemuel Gulliver.* In presenting the "true" memoirs of Captain Gulliver, written by himself, Swift reinforces through satire Godwin's argument, before Godwin did, that more incisive observations can be made about human beings through fiction than through history. Daniel Defoe used his resources as a journalist for profit and amusement to create the sensational Moll Flanders through periodical newspapers before her "Life"—or was it a novel?—appeared in 1722. In other examples, local fame or simply amusement lay behind pseudo *Lives.* A small town like Tiverton in Devon had no way of knowing if its local hero, the gypsy king Bampfylde-Moore Carew, whose "Life" was published continuously through the century from 1745 onward, was real in the Gulliver sense or real in the sense of Martin Dunsford, a local mayor and merchant who took his own life. In the end, *The Life and Adventures of Bampfylde-Moore Carew, the Noted Devonshire Stroller and Dog Stealer; as related by Himself* (first published

1745) has a reality no matter what the historical authenticity of its subject for it enriches the history of Bickley, Tiverton, and the other Devonshire places associated with the gypsy king, connecting them to transatlantic ventures.[9]

In contemplating genre and the simultaneous emergence of biography and the novel and modern stage practices in the eighteenth century as symptomatic of the period's inherent theatricality, we return invariably to Boswell and Johnson.[10] Boswell epitomizes in his presentation of Johnson and himself, as all of the authors in this collection variously address, the making of heroism. Despite Boswell's gradual tendency toward an insistence on accuracy in details recorded, as Caudle explores them, he never loses sight of his role as a writer in creating those figures that would continue to fascinate later ages. His impulses in society and with a pen in his hand are those of an age newly influenced by celebrity—from the court world that Frances Burney experienced firsthand to the closet where, as Madame d'Arblay, she would write her son into an idol.

From Boswell's theatrical farewell to Edinburgh and Arthur's Seat in the *London Journal* (1763), which has an immediate epistolary audience and an imagined public one in posterity, Boswell writes himself a heroic role. His account of his introduction of Johnson to his Edinburgh friends at the beginning of the *Hebrides* reveals how he sees not only himself and Johnson as figures in the period's best narratives but also his goal—in contrast to the historical and anthropological interest of Johnson's account—of writing himself and Johnson into the travel narratives as literary personae. As Boswell recounts Johnson "display[ing]" to Boswell's friends his "contempt of tragick acting," he reflects that he "was of directly contrary opinion to that of Fielding, in his *Tom Jones*, who makes Partridge say of Garrick, 'why I could act as well as he myself. I am sure, if I had seen a ghost, I should have looked in the very same manner, and done just as he did.' For, when I asked him, 'Would not you, sir, start as Mr. Garrick does, if you saw a ghost?' He answered, 'I hope not. If I did, I should frighten the ghost.'"[11] In this scene played out in Boswell's biographical account,

Fielding's literary characters are as real as Johnson's imagined performance onstage. Through the age's spectacles, the genres blend and Boswell's *Hebrides* becomes a literary and historical text for the ages.

The links with the stage in writers' consciousness as they perform to and reflect an inherently performative society are just as evident in the constant awareness of the theater world as they are in the theatrical presentation of the individual, historical or imagined. Sterne offers his novel, which ends after four long volumes with the narrator telling the reader that this has all been a cock and bull story, as *The Life and Opinions of Tristram Shandy* (1759). Like Aphra Behn, Jonathan Swift, and Daniel Defoe (to pinpoint seminal early novelists), Sterne presents his tale, in other words, as a true history of a life, the medium that Johnson calls most "worthy" and compelling. Yet its self-consciousness as a text demands that readers question its authenticity before being told they are dupes. Likewise, a decade earlier, Henry Fielding presents his soon-to-be-iconic novel as *The History of Tom Jones, a Foundling* (1749). His chapters reflect the self-consciousness of the author while Tom Jones, as a hero in the making, outperforms James Boswell, in his presentation of his heroic self at the beginning of his *London Journal*.

Three essential elements of the age, then, link these genres in their formative period and provide common threads running through the essays here. The first is the consciousness on the part of authors, publishers, readers, and all those involved with the theater of the performativity necessary to create stability—or authority. Paula Backscheider, in sketching the processes of the Restoration, calls this "Spectacular Politics": popular opinion and monarchy both shape and are shaped by popular entertainment in a dialectic engagement. Pageants, theater, and other instruments of mass culture simultaneously express anxieties over and a new intimacy with monarchy while they probe the social machine, to use Godwin's phrase.[12] Out of the ensuing dialectic between a cultural obeisance to traditional institutions and the realization of the individual's power evolves the celebrity culture that allows an actor (for example) the social authority once the domain of nobles and monarchs. The second is the authorial instability of the period: plays in performance as much as written lives and novels were subject to constant revision on the part of the author and everyone involved in the final production of text or performance.[13] Finally, dramatists, writers of lives, and writers of the novel were conscious in their choice of subject matter and addresses to audience of the vast expansion of cultural consumers (readers and playgoers) across class, gender, and genre boundaries.[14]

The authors of *Writing Lives* examine their subjects' responses to the challenges and liberties inherent in the generic ambiguity and social possibilities of this new age of the individual. In the "Lives" discussed in this collection and the narratives surrounding them, we see two eminent human impulses at play: love, in various forms, and power. Frequently the two are inextricable. As the authors here demonstrate, the biographer and the autobiographer—in the case of both Piozzi and Charrière—wrangle with passions for their subjects and those who share their stories as they compete with alternative versions and social forces for control over their subjects. When the arena is scholarly biography, as Gilman argues, the stakes are particularly high.

Four of the essays in this collection demonstrate the impact of passion on family biography. Francus notes that by the beginning of the nineteenth century, a number of women writers attempted a genre that constitutes collective biography, yet family biography was still dominated by men. When Frances Burney and Alicia LeFanu set themselves to casting their families' stories and ensuring legacy, therefore, they were unusual not only in their undertaking but also in attempting as women writers of fiction a formal biography that would, in the phrase Coulombeau quotes from the young Frances Burney, save the family name "from the fate of oblivion" (see above). Gilman observes of Burney's treatment of Dr. Charles Burney that she "characterized" her father as "almost saintly," producing a biography that was later easily eclipsed. Francus likewise notes that neither Burney nor LeFanu was able to achieve the success with their biographies that they had with their novels, even as LeFanu highlights her grandmother, Frances Sheridan, as a novelist. The problem in both cases was the novelist's sense of constraint by notions of truth—proving Godwin's point about the greater impact of romance in telling an individual's tale. Sabor highlights the inability of Madame d'Arblay's attempt as an overly fond mother to write her son as a hero because of the way Alexander performed his own life in history.

Boswell's passion for Johnson almost needs no comment and is the motivation behind his tireless pursuit of accuracy that Caudle maps, even as Boswell employed heroic techniques in his major presentations of Johnson (and himself as participant in this heroism) much more adroitly than his contemporary novelists. Damrosch reminds us that "W. H. Auden observed that Boswell's devotion to Johnson was 'as remarkable in its way as Dante's to Beatrice'" and that he saw his task as conveying to future ages the spirit of Johnson that he breathed: "He wrote proudly in the Life, 'When my mind was, as it were, strongly impregnated with Johnsonian aether, I could, with much more facility and exactness, carry in my memory and commit to paper the exuberant variety of his wisdom and wit'" (4). Yet the union of this "odd couple," as Damrosch spins the relationship, has been so compelling to the historical imagination that it overshadows the relationship Johnson had with others. As Berglund considers the correspondence between the two, she reflects that "if love is measured in letters, Hester Thrale had meant more to Johnson than Boswell himself had."

Berglund's key point, however, is that the importance of this correspondence between Piozzi and Johnson for the biographer, as she made it public, was not primarily to ensure Johnson's reputation as Thomas Cadell implored her (and which had greater initial success in that task than Boswell's *Hebrides*). Piozzi aimed to use this mode of life writing to inscribe for posterity her own status in the Johnson/Boswell/Burney circle. She managed, in other words, to make Johnson work for her reputation, as Berglund argues: "Piozzi used *Letters* to compile what is in effect an 'Apology for the Married Life of Hester Thrale'—an exculpatory biography written by Samuel Johnson" (20). Piozzi's assumption of the emerging genre for her own ends has a parallel in the efforts already discussed on the part of Frances Burney d'Arblay and Alicia LeFanu to take control of family biography even if unsuccessfully. Charrière meanwhile carved a niche for herself as a *savante*, in part through a self-written portrait. She also urged other women to write themselves into existence in a compelling enough way that Hélène Cixous would echo her in the late twentieth century. Gilman rounds out the discussion embedded throughout these essays about modes of life writing as power play in his examination of those who assumed control of Charles Burney's legacy—and used newly surfaced documents to recast his reputation as musician and as champion of another idol of the period, George Frideric Handel. All of the discussions, and most pointedly Gilman's, offer a reminder of the importance of continual scholarly revisions.

In examining the processes and hierarchies of those around Boswell and Johnson, these essays continue the reassessments and conversations that already transform scholarship and classroom approaches. While recognizing the importance still of the transformative nature of Boswell and Johnson on life writing, this collection reminds us to keep their achievements in perspective with those around them. Another biographical text with enormous social and political impact was published two years before Boswell published *The Life of Samuel Johnson LLD. Comprehending an Account of His Studies and Numerous Works, in Chronological Order; a Series of His Epistolary Correspondence and Conversations with Many Eminent Persons; and Various Original Pieces of His Composition* (1791). In 1789 had appeared an autobiography as fully entrenched in the political and literary conversations of its time: *The Interesting Narrative of the Life of Olaudah Equiano, or Gustavus Vassa, the African* (1789). Equiano's *Life* played a vital role in parliamentary debates that resulted in the abolition of the slave trade in 1807. Both Boswell's and Equiano's *Lives* constitute a hodgepodge of generically diverse documents as the subjects both represented and transformed their times. Yet, Boswell's Johnson became synonymous with modern biography. Despite its vast popularity in the eighteenth century, Equiano's text did not take on iconic scholarly status until the late twentieth century and has been the focus of the nature of "Life" writing only since the first decade of the twenty-first century. A number of recent articles move beyond the discussions of *The Interesting Narrative* for its perspectives on slavery, abolitionism, and economics, focusing instead on the "Life" element as cultural and self-identity. In the spirit of such realignment are these essays of *Writing Lives in the Eighteenth Century* offered. Their purpose is to continue to advance the discussions of life writing in this period.

Building on Nussbaum's groundbreaking work, a number of articles and books appeared from the beginning of the twenty-first century. Palgrave Macmillan, in particular, has published a number of books of essays that expand thinking about what life writing constitutes generically. Generally, these essays are more inclusive in their subjects and the materials considered auto/biographical. Apart from Richard Bradford's edited collection *Life Writing: Essays on Autobiography, Biography and Literature*, these predominantly focus on gender and life writing, recalibrating our perspective on who was writing lives in the period, just as the recent scholarship on Equiano's autobiography puts it back into the center of eighteenth-century British culture.[15]

Other progressive presses like Broadview have furthered our knowledge of the eighteenth century by profiling—and placing in the classroom—lives once mostly whitewashed or ignored because of the ways in which the novel presented eighteenth-century life. A book that helps us rethink whose voices we hear from the past is Laura Rosenthal's *Nightwalkers: Prostitute Narratives from the Eighteenth Century* (2008). As Rosenthal remarks in her introduction, Samuel Richardson's heroine in *Clarissa* "spends a considerable portion of the novel held captive in a house of prostitution" enabling the author to explore notions of "domestic virtue" and a culture that "saw such houses around every corner" (x–xi). Yet, Rosenthal also observes, through "fictional letters" we "learn very little about what the world might have looked like through the eyes of the prostitutes themselves" (xi). Such an approach is recent. Amy

Culley stresses that not until 1989 with *The Autobiographical Subject* did Felicity Nussbaum break paradigms of thinking about cultural constructions of self and worthy subjects. Nussbaum's introduction of previously "marginalized" voices as she focuses on gender, genre, and class in her probing of the "technology of self" provides a series of categories of life writing that Culley expands upon as she explores women's lives in their different forms as reflections of communities.[16]

Despite these changes in critical approaches and despite its popular appeal, however, life writing has never quite gained the attention in critical colloquies that the stage and the novel have. A quick survey of the Modern Language Association bibliography alone reveals the constantly evolving nature of the story of the novel, an inquiry begun in earnest by Ian Watt in the mid-twentieth century and kicked into high gear by Michael McKeon and others in the 1980s and 1990s. Still attention remains fixed on the fictional element of the lives that the novel is as much concerned with as the biographies and autobiographies of the period.[17] Both genres explore heroism for the age, looking back to ancient models; both investigate the individual's role in society and the creation of family legacies and national history; and both consequently emphasize the private realm as a foundation to the public. Because of critics' interest in domestic spaces, as studies evolve on the novel and the lives performed in public onstage and through the periodicals, women's stories and their multifaceted historical contexts receive much attention. The purpose here is to unfold further the opposite of the novel: the historical lives with their equally performative and staged elements in both public and private modes.

In the spirit of the Aperçus series, these essays offer a series of vignettes that deepen our understanding of a delineated subject. The essays revolve around recognized major male and female figures in the period but present arguments that dismantle traditional privileging of biographical modes. In furthering discussions already begun, the contributors collect materials according to the methodology Godwin attributes to novelists: "from all sources, experience, report, and the records of human affairs"—or letters, memoirs, family biography, and other manuscript materials intended for public and private consumption. Each contributor examines the anxieties and imperatives of the auto/biographer as she or he shapes material into a legacy. The collection benefits from the contributors' diversity of expertise: they are editors, historians, literary scholars, and a musicologist. Much of the discussion here benefits from the work and manuscripts in the Burney Centre at McGill University under the direction of Peter Sabor. As Gilman concludes in his consideration of how the reputation of Charles Burney was drastically altered in the use of new materials, constant vigilance, revision, and self-conscious employment of the kind of archival documents housed at the Burney Centre are vital to our understanding of the lives and modes that encompass the eighteenth century. *Writing Lives* both underscores the importance of the scholarship and furthers it.

Notes

1. William Godwin, "Of History and Romance" (1797), in *Political and Philosophical Writings of William Godwin*, ed. Mark Philip, 7 vols. (London: Pickering & Chatto, 1993), 5:290–301.
2. Jocelyn Harris's recent consideration of Austen from a political, generic, and biographical angle is informed throughout by the "new fangled" concept of celebrity in her time. See Jocelyn Harris, *Satire, Celebrity, and Politics in Jane Austen* (Lewisburg, PA: Bucknell University Press, 2017), xvii.
3. Leo Damrosch, *The Club: Johnson, Boswell, and the Friends Who Shaped an Age* (New Haven, CT: Yale University Press, 2019).
4. Henry Hitchings, *The World in Thirty-Eight Chapters, or Dr. Johnson's Guide to Life* (London: Macmillan, 2018).
5. The minutiae constitute part of a chapter for Andrea Walkden as she attempts to push the beginnings of modern biography to the mid-seventeenth century. Walkden, *Private Lives Made Public: The Invention of Biography in Early Modern England* (Pittsburgh: Duquesne University Press, 2016), chap. 3: "The Life in Miniature," 93–127.

6. Sophie Coulombeau, "Introduction," *Eighteenth-Century Life* 42, no. 2 (2018): 1–11.
7. Andrea Walkden, *Private Lives Made Public: The Invention of Biography in Early Modern England* (Pittsburgh, PA: Dusquesne University Press, 2016).
8. Alexander Pope, "An Essay on Man: Epistle II," in *The Poems of Alexander Pope*, ed. John Butt (New Haven, CT: Yale University Press, 1963), 516.
9. First published Exon, 1745. Authorship also ascribed to Robert Goadley and to Mrs. Goadley. First London edition, 1749.
10. Nussbaum points to the restrictiveness for autobiography of following the usual bookends that begin with Bunyan's *Grace Abounding* (1666) and continue "with Boswell and Gibbon in the 1760s" before finding "fruition in the birthing of a continuous organic self in Wordsworth's *Prelude*" (xi). She and others recognize Boswell's centrality to modern biography as a genre, however. Murray Pittock begins with the idea of Boswell as "first modern biographer" and points to critical work that recognizes the influence on him of the novel and spiritual autobiography. Pittock's focus is Boswell's "creative representation of reality which renders the very modern biography which is held to be Boswell's central achievement both popular and suspect." Pittock, *James Boswell* (Aberdeen: Aberdeen Introductions to Irish and Scottish Culture, 2007), 1.
11. James Boswell and Samuel Johnson, *A Journey to the Western Islands of Scotland and the Journal of a Tour to the Hebrides*, ed. Peter Levi (New York: Penguin, 1984), 175.
12. Paula Backscheider, *Spectacular Politics: Theatrical Power and Mass Culture in Early Modern England* (Baltimore: Johns Hopkins University Press, 1993). See too Backscheider, "Sex, Sin and Ideology: The Drama's Gift to the Genesis of the Novel," *Lumen: Selected Proceedings from the Canadian Society for Eighteenth-Century Studies* 12 (1993): 1–15.
13. As Amy Culley focuses on the nontraditional influences shaping women's life writing, in particular she highlights Paula McDowell's argument that "'man-and-his-work' approaches with their post-Romantic emphasis on individual authors, are not the most useful models for the study of non-elite men's and women's involvement in

the marketplace." Culley, *British Women's Life Writing, 1760–1840: Friendship, Community, and Collaboration* (Basingstoke: Palgrave Macmillan, 2014), 10–11.

14. Probing the usefulness of New Historicism and Foucault's approach, Felicity Nussbaum's groundbreaking study of diaries and journals first broke down traditional boundaries to establish these private modes "as representations of reality rather than failed versions of something more coherent and unified." Felicity Nussbaum, *The Autobiographical Subject: Gender and Ideology in Eighteenth-Century England* (Baltimore: Johns Hopkins University Press, 1989), 28.
15. These include Richard Bradford, ed., *Life Writing: Essays on Autobiography, Biography and Literature* (New York: Palgrave Macmillan, 2010); Amy Culley, ed., *British Women's Life Writing, 1760–1840: Friendship, Community, and Collaboration* (Basingstoke: Palgrave Macmillan, 2014); Daniel Cook and Amy Culley, eds., *Women's Life Writing, 1700–1850: Gender, Genre and Authorship* (New York: Palgrave Macmillan, 2012); Michelle M. Dowd and Julie Eckerle, eds., *Genre and Women's Life Writing in Early Modern England* (Farnham: Ashgate, 2007); Sharon Cadman Seelig, ed., *Autobiography and Gender in Early Modern Literature* (Cambridge: Cambridge University Press, 2006).
16. See note 4 above. Culley underscores Nussbaum's importance at the beginning of both *British Women's Life Writing, 1760–1840* (see p. 3) and in *Women's Life Writing, 1700–1850: Gender, Genre and Authorship*, ed. Daniel Cook and Amy Culley. See pp. 1–2 of the latter.
17. In 1989, in *The Autobiographical Subject*, Nussbaum noted that New Historicism at least brought "a welcome attention to the multiple crossing discursive domains in any given text. It has blurred boundaries between fictional and nonfictional genres such as Swift's Journal to Stella or Fielding's Voyage to Lisbon, sometimes taken as historical truth" (13).

1

Dr. Johnson's Apology for the Married Life of Hester Thrale

Hester Lynch Piozzi's Letters to and from the Late Samuel Johnson, LL.D.

LISA BERGLUND

When approached about writing a memoir of her friend Samuel Johnson, who had died in December 1784, Hester Lynch Piozzi—the former Mrs. Thrale—envisioned a multivolume work of anecdotes, letters, and verses; she proposed to collect and edit this material after returning from her protracted European honeymoon tour with Gabriel Piozzi. Publisher Thomas Cadell feared that public interest in Johnson might decline, and therefore recommended haste, but Piozzi was unwilling to give Cadell access to her private papers. As she wrote to him from Florence on July 18, 1785, "It will be impossible to print the Letters and Verses till my Return to England as they are all locked up with other Papers in the Bank. . . . If you will have the Anecdotes and print them first . . . I am willing to double my diligence, and we may publish the other two Volumes when I get back."[1] Cadell approved the plan, and Piozzi quickly drafted the slim *Anecdotes of the Late Dr. Samuel Johnson*, relying principally on her memory and on *Thraliana*, the six-volume diary she had brought on her travels. By October 20, 1785, she could write to inform Cadell that she had shipped the manuscript via a banker at Leghorn. The book sold out on the day it appeared—famously, when a messenger arrived from the king to purchase a copy, Cadell had to borrow one from a friend. It went into several printings. Rather than waning, in fact, public interest in Johnson was stimulated by comparison of Piozzi's work with James Boswell's *Tour of the Hebrides with Samuel Johnson*, which had been published the year before by Charles Dilly.

The success of their initial publications, and the news that Sir John Hawkins, Johnson's executor, was working on his own biography, prompted both Piozzi, contracted to Cadell for a two-volume octavo edition of letters, and Boswell, commencing work on the *Life of Johnson*, to canvass their acquaintance for Johnsonian correspondence. To be sure, Piozzi's personal collection of letters from Johnson already numbered in the hundreds, so she scarcely needed the nineteen additional letters that she ultimately acquired.[2] (Most notable among them were letters that Johnson had written in the 1750s to Miss Hill Boothby, along with a handful written to Susanna and Sophia Thrale.) As her edition was at the press, on May 1, 1787, Piozzi reflected ruefully on her failure to secure the letters that Johnson had written to her daughter Hester Maria Thrale, known as "Queeney."[3] As she explains in *Thraliana*, there was more at stake than competition with Boswell or Hawkins:

> Johnson's Letters are at Press—may they *but* succeed! If my eldest daughter would have given me hers from him, how it would have helped the Compilation! But perhaps She keeps them for some professed Enemy of mine: it would be droll enough if after refusing them to her Mother She should give them to Sir John Hawkins as a Reward for having insulted me with every unprovoked, & undeserved Abuse. Very likely. . . . I find Mr. Smith one of our Daughters' Guardians told that poor Baby Cecilia a fine staring Tale, how my Husband locked me up at Milan & fed me on Bread & Water, to make the Child

> hate Mr. Piozzi: Good God! What infamous Proceeding was this? My Husband never saw the fellow, so c[oul]d not have provoked him.[4]

As this diary entry indicates, Piozzi had been subjected to relentless scurrilous gossip, in private circles and in the public press, about her decision to wed the musician Gabriel Piozzi, three years after Henry Thrale's death in 1781. She was reproached for leaving her daughters in England while she traveled for two years to her husband's native Italy (Queeney was twenty, and the youngest, "poor Baby Cecilia," entrusted to a governess, was seven). Upon her return, Piozzi was ostracized by her three adult children—Queeney, Susanna, and Sophia—for making what they considered an imprudent and selfish match; she was abandoned by censorious friends like Frances Burney. She was even accused of hastening the demise of the aging lexicographer, as Johnson had died less than six months after she advised him of her plan to remarry. The publication of *Anecdotes* had compounded the criticism in some quarters; her erstwhile friend Hester Chapone was typical in stating that "it was not handsome to repeat things of [Johnson] which she must know would mightily detract from the hyperbolical praise she affects to give him. . . . Defend me, when dead from such friends!"[5]

Arguably, Piozzi stood even more in need of "defense from her friends" than did the late lexicographer. Yet rather than directly challenging attacks on her marriage or her publications, Piozzi took the opportunity afforded by her contract with Cadell to obliquely vindicate her conduct. As her biographers have noted, by publishing Johnson's letters, Piozzi employed Johnson's own words to show the value that he placed on their friendship, as well as to provide a narrative of their relationship that would justify her conduct toward him. Yet Piozzi's project was even more ambitious, more subtle, and more inventive than has been acknowledged. To defend her public reputation, I argue, Piozzi used *Letters* to compile what is in effect an "Apology for the Married Life of Hester Thrale"—an exculpatory biography written by Samuel Johnson.

In *Thraliana*, Piozzi wrote a mock review of her own book, which reveals that she knew exactly what her edition of Johnson's correspondence could accomplish and how it would be received. Indeed, this wryly witty parody is arguably the most insightful review *Letters* ever received. As Piozzi explains,

> I diverted my Friend Mrs. Lewis while at Reading with reviewing my own Book, and imitating the Style of those I expect to abuse it: Here is the Performance, and I question whether my Enemies will do better.
>
> *Monthly Review for April or May 1788.*
>
> Letters to & from Dr Johnson published by H: L: Piozzi.
>
> The Care and Attention with which we have review'd this Work, was rather excited by our long Expectation of it, than repaid by the Instruction or Amusement it affords; let it not however be consign'd to Oblivion without a few Remarks on its Excellencies & Defects, which to say Truth are neither of them numerous, & we should do the Publick double Injury in covering much paper with Criticisme upon what the Rambler himself would call *Pages of Inanity*. For who can it benefit, or who can it please? to hear in one Letter that poor Mrs Salusbury has had a bad night, and that little Sophy's head ach'd all Yesterday? If our fair Editress publish'd this Correspondence to shew with how much Insipidity people famed for their Wit & their Learning might maintain a twenty Years Intercourse by Letter and Conversation; she has succeeded admirably—. . . . The World will however be probably but little interested concerning the slippery Bowels of an old pious Lady long since dead—perhaps the *strong* or *weakly* Constitutions of the living Miss Thrales may be of more Importance to some Men, but our Reviewers are unluckily not among the Number. We shall conclude by confessing that the Correspondence bears every mark of being genuine, that Mrs Piozzi appears very confident of Success, & careless of what may be said concerning her

> Publication; that there are some brilliant Passages, and some solid Reflections scattered up & down the book, but that upon the whole we find eight or ten Shillings very ill bestowed. (*Thraliana*, 2:704–705)

For Piozzi, the potentially problematic elements of her book—those she is sure that the public will condemn—are the domestic details of the Thrale household. Reviewers will be irritated less by the minutiae of Dr. Johnson's ill health, or his querulous complaints of not receiving letters, than by "little Sophy's head-ache" and the "slippery Bowels of an old pious Lady long since dead." Much as she had apologized in *Anecdotes* for producing a "mere *Candle-light* [that is, interior or private] picture of his latter days," in the preface to *Letters* she warns her readers that "none but domestick and familiar events can be expected from a private correspondence."[6] Significantly, the principal "domestick and familiar events" narrated will be those of the Thrale family circle.

As Piozzi expected, some readers objected to the parochial content of the letters, but others enjoyed the opportunity to view Johnson in a homely context. Clare Brant notes in her study of eighteenth-century epistolarity that "the letter is the literary form *par excellence* of the everyday."[7] One discerning reader of *Letters* was Jane Austen. The novelist approvingly quotes Mrs. Thrale's embrace of the mundane in a letter to her sister Cassandra on December 9, 1808:[8]

> "But all this, as my dear Mrs. Piozzi says, is flight & fancy & nonsense—for my Master has his great Casks to mind, & I have my little Children." It is *you* however in this instance, that have the little Children—& *I* that have the great cask—, for we are brewing Spruce Beer again;—but my meaning really is, that I am extremely foolish in writing all this unnecessary stuff, when I have so many matters to write about, that my paper will hardly hold it all. Little Matters they are to be sure, but highly important.[9]

Austen agrees with Piozzi that the "unnecessary stuff" can easily fill many a page, and many a mind, however witty or literary the possessor of that mind might be. And furthermore, for the mistress of a large household, "Little Matters [are] highly important."

The quotidian content of *Letters* was similarly defended by the reviewer for the *Gentleman's Magazine*, who was moved, like Piozzi in her parody of the reviewers, to imitation:

> Johnson himself would have answered those who think it unjustifiable, in some such way as this, perhaps:
>
> "No, sir; I cannot see any harm in the business. Do the Letters deduct from the man's good fame? Do they prove him to be in any respect less a man of virtue, or more a fool? No sir. Then where is the harm? He has written to women as wise men write when they write to women; and he has written to children as wise men write when they write to children.
>
> "Sir, a laurel has its small branches as well as its large ones."[10]

The reviewer could also have made this point by quoting rather than imitating Johnson, who in a letter of July 11, 1770, observes to Mrs. Thrale that "what is nearest us touches us most. The passions rise higher at domestic than at imperial tragedies" (*Letters*, 1:28). In her own defense, moreover, Piozzi happily could cite the approbation of a judge, as she did in a letter written on June 8, 1789, to her friend Sophia Byron (grandmother of the poet): "Sir William Ashhurst said in Conversation one Day at Guy's Cliffe, I hope Mrs. Piozzi will publish *every Scrap* sent to her by Dr. Johnson: so you see I had the *Judge's Advice* in good Time! It was ill worth the while consulting about such a truly unimportant Correspondence to be sure but the World had a Fancy to see how Johnson wrote upon frivolous Subjects,—and now it is seen that he did it better than anyone else."[11] As Piozzi reminds Sophia Byron, Johnson himself was the author of many letters on "frivolous Subjects," willingly discussing the "slippery Bowels of an old pious lady" or, in one of the most entertaining epistles in the collection, reciting "the history of one of my toes." "The history of my head," he ruefully adds, "would be much shorter" (*Letters*, 2:61). Johnson was eager to write of such commonplace details, observes Bruce Redford, the modern editor of his correspondence. "The intimacies of the Johnson-Thrale correspondence were rooted in the domestic world of Streatham Park," Redford writes, adding that Johnson "called the place 'home.' . . . To be away from Mrs. Thrale and the Streatham milieu was to be exiled from the focus, the center."[12] To write of his toes, or her mother, was to return, if only in imagination, home.

Letters to and from the Late Samuel Johnson, LL.D. is a two-volume compilation of 341 letters written by Johnson: 322 of them to Hester Thrale, 5 to Susanna and Sophia Thrale, 7 to Miss Boothby, and 7 to other persons. There are also 27 letters by Mrs. Thrale to Samuel Johnson, and 9 poems and translations by them both. While her letters initially were added to fill up the two octavo volumes promised to the publisher, Piozzi, as discussed below, soon recognized that her side of the correspondence had additional editorial and narrative value. On the other hand, a few significant letters from Johnson that she had retained in her possession were not included: an ambiguous letter in French is omitted, as are both his first cruel letter on learning of her second marriage and her dignified reply.[13] Overall, it is a remarkable collection, representing an average of twenty letters per year, exchanged from August 13, 1765, to July 8, 1784. The correspondence begins with a brief, formal letter of apology to Hester Thrale, in which Johnson regrets his inability to accompany Henry Thrale to join the rest of the family at their annual summer retreat in Brighton; it concludes with a letter in which Johnson bids Hester Piozzi goodbye upon the occasion of her second marriage. At the commencement of their correspondence, Samuel Johnson was fifty-six years old and Hester Thrale was twenty-four; at its end, he was a valetudinarian of seventy-five, and she, after twenty years of marriage and nearly three years of widowhood, a newlywed at forty-three. During the period covered by the letters, Johnson published his edition of Shakespeare, revised the *Dictionary of the English Language*, traveled to the Hebrides with Boswell, and wrote the magisterial *Lives of the Poets*. During the same two decades, Hester Thrale bore eleven children, suffered the deaths of seven (as well as a stillbirth and several miscarriages), hosted a glittering salon, rescued the Thrale brewery from bankruptcy, lost her mother to breast cancer and her husband to stroke exacerbated by depression, and fell in love with and ultimately married the Italian tenor and music teacher Gabriel Piozzi.

For most readers, then and now, the principal appeal of the letters lies in their depiction of Johnson. As Arthur Murphy observes in the *Monthly Review* (1788), "Our business [in reading the letters] was chiefly with Johnson; and after seeing him struggle with illness and morbid melancholy, it refreshes our imagination to hear him say, almost at the close of life, 'Attention and respect give pleasure, however late, or however useless. But they are not useless, even when they are late: it is reasonable to rejoice, as the day declines, to find that it has been spent with the approbation of mankind.'"[14] The correspondence, Murphy explains, offers uniquely intimate insights into Johnson's character and emotional state. Examination of individual epistles for evidence related to Johnson's personality, biography, and literary style, therefore, is the most conventional use made of the letters by modern critics. Another common approach has been to excavate, generally to condemn, Piozzi's minor editorial changes to Johnson's letters and her substantial revisions to her own.[15] Even more common than criticism has been neglect. There is no modern edition of Piozzi's volumes that preserves the letters, Johnson's and hers, as she edited them, in their original order and context. Nor is there an edition of Thrale letters comparable to the Blooms' magnificent edition of the later Piozzi letters.

Most of the letters that Johnson wrote to Mrs. Thrale have been collected in the two modern editions of Johnson's correspondence, those published by Robert W. Chapman, in 1952, and by Bruce Redford, in 1992. The editors intersperse the letters that Johnson wrote to Mrs. Thrale chronologically among those to other recipients and they exclude her letters to him. (There are occasional exceptions. Chapman, for example, includes her superb letter of reproach, penned on July 4, 1784, responding to his attack on her remarriage. Piozzi had omitted this letter from her edition.) Chapman's and Redford's volumes, like any edition of correspondence by a single writer, privilege the author as a monotonic voice, rather than as a collaborative artist. In extracting Johnson's writings from the context of *Letters*, they also privilege an idea of the individual letter—a document extracted from epistolary exchange or a place in an edited collection—as peculiarly "genuine" (this is Chapman's term, to which I will return). The irony of assuming this stance, on the part of an editor, is notable. By contrast, I now propose that we regard *Letters* as a unified narrative, deliberately constructed from "found" epistolary materials to tell a specific story, the story of Mrs. Thrale, her family, and her friendship with Samuel Johnson.

Like *Anecdotes* before it, *Letters* received mixed reviews. In their edition of Piozzi's correspondence, the Blooms mention several positive contemporary reviews, including those in the *World*, the *Gentleman's Magazine*, and the *English Review*, as well as Murphy's *Monthly Review* assessment, discussed above, which praises Piozzi for her "sound philosophy" and ends by observing that her letters "are written with elegance and vivacity, and . . . exhibit a mind enriched with literature, and provided with a plentiful store of images."[16] Meanwhile, the hostile reviewers charged Piozzi with vainglory; the assessment of the *Original Star & Grand Weekly Advertiser* for May 7, 1788, is typical: "Here then we behold *friendship* sacrificed to *vanity*, and the weak ambition of becoming the topick of public conversation prevailing over the most sacred ties. If obligations of the most valuable nature were ever conferred on the Doctor by Mrs. Piozzi, they are all cancelled by this false step."[17] Despite (or perhaps because of) such detractors, the edition sold briskly. Like most of those who had participated in Mrs. Thrale's celebrated salon at Streatham, James Boswell read the letters with eagerness. While he was disappointed to find that the Dr. Johnson in their pages was less magisterial and sententious than he had hoped, he was horrified to discover that, if love is measured in letters, Hester Thrale had meant more to Johnson than Boswell himself had. Another intimate of the Streatham Coterie,

Frances Burney, had been appalled by Piozzi's biography of Johnson, writing to her friend Queeney, "Tis an opportunity for imprudent anecdotes which might endanger indiscretion even in the most cautious & fearful;—She, therefore, *always in*cautious and fearless!—O with how little pleasure, & how much pain shall I ever see her book!"[18] Yet upon reading *Letters*, Burney was forced to confess to Queeney that they enhanced Piozzi's reputation: "I see Her, however, rising from their Contents,—she is more admired, & meets with greater allowances, from these undoubted proofs of how well she stood with so great & good a man."[19] As Piozzi had understood, through his voluminous, intimate correspondence Johnson could be posthumously established as her chief advocate and apologist.

In addition to proving how much Johnson valued her, *Letters* also vindicated her previous characterization of Johnson. The "imprudent anecdotes" that disturbed Frances Burney receive confirmation from Johnson's own pen. For instance, Piozzi records in *Anecdotes* an occasion when Johnson was "lament[ing] in the most piercing terms his approaching dissolution, and conjured me solemnly to tell him what I thought." She advises him that while "no present danger could be expected . . . his age and continued ill health must naturally accelerate the arrival of that hour which can be escaped by none. 'And this (says Johnson, rising in great anger) is the voice of female friendship I suppose, when the hand of the hangman would be softer.'"[20] This depiction of a querulous and self-pitying Johnson is the kind of "unhandsome" account to which Hester Chapone had objected. Johnson's correspondence is full of similar episodes, however, as he shares minute descriptions of his medical issues while reproaching Mrs. Thrale for apparent indifference or silence. A letter dated April 1782, for example, begins, "Madam, I have been very much out of order since you sent me away; but why should I tell you, who do not care, nor desire to know?" and the following letter, dated April 30, 1782, commences, "Dearest Madam, I have had a fresh cold and been very poorly" (*Letters*, 2:237–238). The letters show that the insulting outburst recorded in *Anecdotes* was characteristic of Johnson, even as they also offer repeated expressions of affection, sympathy, and compliment. Typical is a letter of February 17, 1782, that begins, "Dear Madam, Sure such letters would make any man well. I will let them have their full operation upon me; but while I write I am not without a cough" (*Letters*, 2:235). Thus the unattractive portrait sketched in *Anecdotes* was in *Letters* confirmed but softened; as Bruce Redford notes, "Distance creates unhappiness; unhappiness purifies emotion; emotion breeds letters; letters crystallize love."[21] A few letters actually exonerated Piozzi of charges that *Anecdotes* had misrepresented incidents that showed Johnson in a bad light, while also allowing for an innocent yet repentant Johnson. Chief among these is a reference to the story of Johnson rudely ignoring an acquaintance, Mr. Cholmondeley. Evidently, the episode was known years before 1786, when Piozzi recounted it in *Anecdotes*, for in a letter of October 25, 1777, Johnson writes to Mrs. Thrale, "Cholmondeley's story shocks me, if it be true, which I can hardly think for I am utterly unconscious of it; I am very sorry, and very much ashamed" (*Letters*, 2:12).[22] Here, Johnson's phrasing indicates that Cholmondeley had made public an account of his rude behavior, absolving Mrs. Thrale who appears only to have passed along the report of Cholmondeley's complaint. Johnson also manfully apologizes.[23]

During the twenty years of their correspondence, Johnson most frequently wrote to Mrs. Thrale during the summer and fall, when he visited family and friends in Lichfield and Ashbourne while the Thrales undertook more elegant sojourns to Brighton or other resorts. Apart from his 1773 tour of the Hebrides with Boswell, his domestic situation offered little novelty; the uniformity of his summers perhaps explains why, apart from accounts of health troubles and the quotidian details of life with his stepdaughter Lucy Porter or his friend John Taylor, much of his correspondence consists of paraphrases of her letters. For example, in a letter from Ashbourne dated June 14, 1779, he writes,

> Your account of Mr. Thrale's illness is very terrible; but when I remember that he seems to have it peculiar to his constitution,

that whatever distemper he has, he always has his head affected, I am less frighted [*sic*]. The seizure was, I think not apoplectical, but hysterical, and therefore not dangerous to life. I would have you however consult such physicians as you think you can best trust. Bromfield seems to have done well, and by his practice appears not to suspect an apoplexy. That is a solid and fundamental comfort. I remember Dr. Marsigli, an Italian physician, whose seizure was more violent that Mr. Thrale's, for he fell down helpless, but his case was not considered as of much danger, and he went safe home, and is now a professor at Padua. His fit was considered only hysterical. (*Letters*, 2:47–48)

Clearly, in this letter Johnson is repeating what Mrs. Thrale has written to him, about Henry Thrale's recent stroke, the symptoms, his prognosis, and the medical treatment she has arranged. His letter reports, shares, and soothes her anxieties, as it echoes and approves her choice of a physician. This is one of two letters Johnson writes on June 14, 1779, and he writes again three days later. Twice weekly letters, even without the stimulus of a health crisis, are typical of Johnson's stays in Ashbourne; also routinely, these letters tell the story of the Thrale household by reporting and reflecting upon incidents described in letters from Mrs. Thrale not included in the collection. As we read Johnson's letters, therefore, we become deeply immersed in the domestic concerns of Mrs. Thrale and her family, particularly the illnesses and deaths of her mother, husband, and too many children. We also learn to love Hester Thrale, at a distance, as Johnson was obliged to do during their summers apart. His letters depict a woman who is valiant, beset, amusing, exhausted, determined, vexed, whimsical, anxious, and charming—it is a complete, complicated portrait.

Johnson's letters, in other words, present a narrative of Hester Thrale's life during the two decades of their friendship, paralleling her own *Anecdotes of the Late Samuel Johnson, LL.D. in the Last Twenty Years of His Life.* He records the household duties that preoccupied her, sympathizes with her troubles, and approves her conduct as a wife, mother, and friend. For example, in a letter written

October 24, 1772, he responds to news that the brewhouse was in a financial crisis and that she had sought assistance, perhaps unwisely, from her estranged uncle Sir Thomas Salusbury. Johnson writes,

> When you wrote the letter [to Sir Thomas] which you call injudicious, I told you that it would bring no money; but I do not see how, in that tumult of distress, you could have forborn it, without appearing to be too tender of your own personal connections, and to place your uncle above your family. You did what then seemed best, and are therefore not so reasonable as I wish my mistress to be, in imputing to yourself any unpleasing consequences. Your unkle [*sic*] when he knows that you do not want, and mean not to disturb him, will probably subside in silence to his former stagnation of unactive kindness.
>
> Do not suffer little things to disturb you. The brewhouse must be the scene of action, and the subject of speculation. The first consequence of our late trouble ought to be, an endeavor to brew at a cheaper rate. (*Letters*, 1:57)

Now, the story of the danger to the brewery and Mrs. Thrale's efforts to rescue their finances could have been conveyed to readers, as it was originally to Johnson, in a letter written by Mrs. Thrale; or she could have published a first-person memoir. Instead, by producing Johnson's letter, Piozzi secures the services of a biographer and apologist. Johnson's letter makes it clear that Mrs. Thrale was deeply and admirably engaged in the management of her husband's business at this critical moment. Furthermore, his letter not only describes Mrs. Thrale's conduct in writing to her uncle but also voices her emotional state ("tumult of distress"), her motives (placing her family first; doing "what seemed best"), and her self-reproach ("imputing to yourself any unpleasing consequence"). He then absolves her ("you could not have forborn it"; she is "not reasonable" in blaming herself) and assesses the damage as slight (her uncle "will subside in silence"; the "injudicious" letter is a "little thing"). No defense that Piozzi could have made of her conduct could be as powerful and as sympathetic as that conveyed in *Letters*.

Redford's and Chapman's editions of Johnson's correspondence present a man with a diversity of friends, interests, and activities. By contrast, in the narrative of *Letters*, Johnson, as edited by Piozzi, engages intensely and almost single-mindedly in the concerns of the Thrale family. To approximate the cumulative impact of Johnson's "Apology," I have compiled an excerpt gleaned from forty consecutive epistles written by Johnson to Mrs. Thrale, from July 20, 1770, to May 17, 1773 (a period that includes the episode of the brewery failure). In what follows, I list each letter by the number assigned it in Piozzi's edition and briefly quote or describe the content related to the Thrales. Other business in the letters is not summarized, and if Johnson doesn't mention the Thrale family, apart from conventional compliments, I indicate that the letter said "Nothing." For the sake of clarity, members of the Thrale family are referred to by their given names.

> Letter XXVI: Hester is pregnant: "I hope your complaint, however troublesome, is without danger; for your danger involves us all." Mrs. Salusbury was not at home when the London house was burgled, Hester is enjoying Giuseppe Baretti's book (presumably *Familiar Letters*), and the Streatham Coterie has been searching for female names ending in O. XXVII: Johnson plans to visit. XXVIII: Johnson asks Henry to help a friend's son get out of the East India Company service. XXIX: Nothing. XXX: Johnson has visited their house twice but missed them; he offers to attend Mrs. Salusbury if she goes to Bath. XXXI: Nothing. XXXII: Hester is expecting to deliver her child soon. XXXIII: she is still expecting. XXXIV: Nothing. XXXV: she has written to him & included compliments to his step-daughter Lucy Porter. XXXVI: she is reading at home. XXXVII: her baby is overdue; "I return all the compliments, and hope I may add some at last to this wicked, tiresome, dilatory bantling." XXXVIII: her son Harry wrote to Johnson but Queeney did not. XXXIX: they are setting up a laboratory

at Streatham for Johnson. XL: Mrs. Salusbury continues ill, still no letter from Queeney. XLI: Hester wrote to Johnson. XLII: Queeney still has not written. XLIII: Queeney still hasn't written; building on the laboratory continues; "Desire that his builders will leave about a hundred loose bricks. I can at present think of no better place for chymistry [*sic*], in fair weather, than the pump-side in the kitchen garden." XLIV: Henry has written to tell Johnson that Hester has delivered a child, and Johnson accepts his invitation to visit. XLV: she is recuperating. XLVI: she has not written for two posts. XLVII: she has not yet written but he imagines a letter from her.

XLVIII: the Thrales are in financial straits; Hester has written to her uncle for assistance; she is worried by Henry's attempt to brew cheaply; they need to retrench. XLIX: Mrs. Salusbury has had a medical procedure for [breast] cancer; Hester is going to Southwark. L: she is working to repair the brewhouse situation. LI: Henry has been ill, Mrs. Salusbury continues ill. LII: Hester has not written; she is working on resolving the financial situation. LIII: Hester in fact had written but the letter was misdirected; she is at Southwark. LIV: Mrs. Salusbury continues ill, Queeney has not written, they are contracting their expenditures in an attempt to save 1,000 pounds.[24] LV: Mrs. Salusbury's cancer continues; Hester has written to Johnson several times. LVI: he "wish[ed] you had been with me to see" Chatsworth. LVII: Hester has written twice, she continues to retrench. LVIII: Henry is a candidate for Parliament; they are eating mock turtle and "stewed rumps of beef" and "sit with parish officers." LIX: they are canvassing; she is using name cards to keep track of voters at dinner. LX: her mother is dying; Hester is engaged in business negotiations. LXI: her mother is dying; business negotiations continue. LXII: her mother is suffering "weakness of mind" as she faces impending death; they remain at Streatham. LXIII: her mother's health is improving although she has not yet been downstairs; their financial situation has improved. LXIV: Mrs. Salusbury's appetite has improved; Harry is going to boarding school.

LXV: her mother is still alive. LXVI: her mother continues day to day; Hester is advising a young woman [Fanny Plumbe] who is inclined to marry without parental consent. (*Letters*, 1:31–85)

This summary illustrates Johnson's engagement with the Thrales. His interest encompasses both significant events like childbirth, financial emergency, and a campaign for Parliament as well as building projects, reading habits, and word games. Discussing in general the content of *Letters*, Bruce Redford observes that Johnson's "emphasis on 'trifles'"—a word used in *Rambler* 152 to describe the content of familiar letters—"helps to communicate a total identification with the pleasures and pains of his adopted family."[25] This "total identification" manifests itself not just in Johnson's repeating the details of their daily activities, as summarized above, but also in his profound investment in narrating their lives, particularly that of Mrs. Thrale. William McCarthy remarks in his biography *Hester Thrale Piozzi: Portrait of a Literary Woman* that "an account of the contents of *Letters* really belongs in a book about Johnson";[26] however, as my summary shows, the "contents of *Letters*" form a book about the married life of Hester Thrale.

That Johnson as a letter writer functioned as Mrs. Thrale's echo perplexed Arthur Murphy, who admitted, "Had not Johnson left a name, that, since his death, has sounded far and near, it is true that this publication might have been spared. For what can be expected in letters, which conveyed the news from Streatham to Bolt-court in Fleet Street, and from Bolt-court back again to Streatham?"[27] Murphy's image of the circularity of the news neatly conveys the way that Johnson tells Mrs. Thrale's stories back to her. For example, in July and August 1775, a series of twelve letters by Johnson describe both the trivial and the tragic events in the Thrale family, from Queeney keeping ten chickens and Mrs. Thrale squabbling with Baretti to the illness of Sophia and the death of two-year-old Ralph. Presumably, these twelve letters were inspired by at least half as many from Mrs. Thrale and other members of the Thrale family, but none appear in *Letters* to break the flow of Johnson's biographical narrative, even though Johnson reports that

Mrs. Thrale was writing by every post (*Letters*, 1:297). In the last letter of this series, Johnson wonders if Mrs. Thrale keeps his letters, and then adds, "Of this speculation you are perhaps tired, and would rather hear of Sophy. I hope before this comes, that her head will be easier, and your head less filled with fears and troubles, which you know are to be indulged only to prevent evil, not to increase it" (*Letters*, 1:300–301).[28] Johnson could have learned of Sophy's headache, and her mother's "fears and troubles," only from Mrs. Thrale, but letters like these, together with the omission of her replies, convey the impression that he is writing of her children to her, rather than she to him.

More dramatically, some letters do more than repeat her stories; they actually invent her life for her. For example, upon arriving in Lichfield in October 1772, he remarks that "this is to be my home long enough to receive a letter" and goes on to sketch out its contents, "which will, I hope, tell me that you are busy in reformation [that is, retrenching their expenses], that dear Mrs. Salusbury is easy, that all the young people are well, and that Mr. Thrale brews at less expense than fourteen shillings a quarter" (*Letters*, 1:55). Five years later, on October 10, 1777, in a charming and sensually imagined sentence, Johnson fantasizes about Mrs. Thrale's toilette upon her having given up wearing a wig:

> Well, but seriously I think I shall be glad to see you in your own hair; but do not take too much time in combing, and twisting, and papering, and unpapering, and curling, and frizzing, and powdering, and getting out the powder, with all the other operations required in the cultivation of a head of hair; yet let it be combed at least once in three months, on the quarter-day—I could wish it might be combed once at least in six weeks; if I were to indulge my wishes, but what are wishes without hopes, I should fancy the operation performed—one knows not when one has enough—perhaps every morning. (*Letters*, 2:5)

This artful synathroesmus wittily positions Johnson as a hairdresser, hovering above Mrs. Thrale at her dressing table. The scene then becomes more intimate, bringing Mrs. Thrale nearer and nearer as an object of desire. Johnson begins by advising her "not [to] take too much time" in tending to her coiffure, yet as his fancy luxuriates in the "operations required in the cultivation of a head of hair" his admonition of "once in three months" becomes "once at least in six weeks" and finally "every morning," while he confesses in a phrase both amorous and arch that "one knows not when one has enough."

Even while visiting the Hebrides with Boswell, as John Radner has noted, Johnson is almost as preoccupied with imagining Hester Thrale as with reflecting on the scenes before him.[29] The Latin "Ode to Skye" that Johnson included in one letter moves from celebrating that island to envisaging her daily routine at Streatham. Here is the translation by Ellis Cornelia Knight that Piozzi printed in *Letters*:

> How think'st thou of thy absent friend?
> How dost thou? whither dost thou tend?
>   My gentle Thralia say.
> If, pious wife, thy husband's cares
> Thou softly sooth[e]; or infant heirs
>   Watch o'er as mother kind:
> Or, 'mid the charms of letter'd lore
> Thou add new treasures to thy store,
>   And feed thy active mind . . . (*Letters*, 1:180)

Surrounded by the beauties of Scotland, Johnson in his mind's eye returns "home," where he sees Mrs. Thrale thinking of him, supporting her husband, watching over her children, and reading—perhaps reading his letters. Similarly, in a letter written the following year, frustrated at not having heard from her, he imagines her in the country and ventriloquizes: "Now, thinks my dearest Mistress to herself, sure I am at last gone too far to be pestered every post with a letter: he knows that people go into the country to be at quiet [*sic*]; he knows too that when I have once told the story of Ralph, the place where I am affords me nothing that I shall delight to tell, or he will wish to be told; he knows how troublesome it is to write letters about nothing; and he knows that he does not love trouble himself, and therefore ought not to force it upon others" (*Letters*, 1:258–259). This is a witty, sympathetic epistle, in which Johnson echoes her stories, reads her mind, and effectively writes her side of their correspondence as well as his own. Yet this letter, like that vindicating her petition to her uncle about the brewery, also is notable for excusing Mrs. Thrale's conduct toward Johnson by its complete investment in her point of view. In his biography *Hester Lynch Piozzi*, James Clifford writes, "Dr. Burney, in the *Monthly Review*, indicated what might to-day be considered the greatest defect in the *Anecdotes*, when he asserted that the volume had been planned with only one thought in mind, to excuse the author's behavior by showing how difficult it had been to live with Johnson. For we might agree with Mrs. Chapone that 'it was not handsome to tell the World how insufferable the friend she had cherish'd & Courted so long was become to her, & that she went to Bath only to shake him off.'"[30] In this letter, Johnson again emerges as her champion. He himself "tells the World how insufferable" he could be; he agrees that she is "pestered every post with a letter" and that he "forces" the trouble of his friendship upon her. He implicitly apologizes for harassing her, by presenting a comical version of his own conduct, and he absolves her for failing to write to him—even as he begs for another letter.

As explained previously, Piozzi's edition of *Letters* consists of 341 letters by Johnson, interspersed with a mere two dozen or so written by Mrs. Thrale. In her preface, she justifies the inclusion of the latter by suggesting that they serve in lieu of footnotes: "But on revisal of these letters when at last they were collected, some notes began to appear almost necessary; partly therefore to avoid writing what could in that form have given little satisfaction, partly from finding in my own answers to him, a better comment on his meaning than I could *now* have written, I was induced to print trifles not originally intended for the Publick, on whose indulgence I depend for protection" (*Letters*, 1:v). In other words, by printing her letters she can excuse herself from performing the explanatory role of an editor; implicitly, she will intervene in Johnson's epistolary narrative as little as possible. Chapman and other critics have pointed out that Piozzi was more selective with her own letters than those of Johnson; according to the Blooms, "she chose her own letters to [Johnson] with an eye toward lively revision and amplification."[31] She not only culled her letters but also improved the grammar and added pithy phrases from *Thraliana* and elsewhere. In some cases, she combined several shorter letters into one. It is indisputable that the epistles ascribed to Mrs. Thrale and printed in *Letters* are not those that she initially wrote to Johnson; nevertheless, it is misleading to suggest, as Chapman does in the title of his edition of Johnson's correspondence, that only the letters in their initial state are "genuine." The implication, of course, is that the versions published by Piozzi in *Letters* are forged or invented. Rather, I would argue, the revised letters should be approached and understood as compositions to be read as parts of a larger literary work. The original versions of Mrs. Thrale's letters no more undermine the artistic value of her edition of *Letters* than Boswell's diaries negate the account of Johnson that he developed by amplifying and expanding those diaries. More bluntly, if the epistles of *Letters* are fake letters, then much of the *Life of Johnson* is fake biography.

The fact that Piozzi revised her letters, however, should certainly alert readers to the way that she deployed these newly polished epistles in conjunction with the 341 letters of Johnson in her edition. Two kinds of control over Johnson's correspondence are exercised by the Thrale letters. In their original exchange, by writing (or by failing to write, as discussed above), Mrs. Thrale prompts Johnson's letters to her. Her letters provide the material for him to imagine, narrate, and vicariously share her life. Years later, Piozzi distributes the revised letters from Mrs. Thrale throughout the collection as narrative cues; her letters interrupt the series of Johnson's letters, so that she at different moments acts as diversion, monitor, confidante, or muse.

McCarthy argues that Piozzi's edition of the letters "displays a high degree of internal coherence . . . in reading through them we seem to follow the whole progress of the friendship without interruption from its complimentary flourishes through it maturity to its waning. . . . Here not only is Johnson at his best, but here also . . . is epistolary friendship itself at its most attractive. This heightened general appeal is just the effect aimed at by editing such as Piozzi's; to achieve it is the purpose of the principles she followed."[32] While I agree with McCarthy's assessment of the book's "internal coherence" and its narrative arc, I think that the "effect aimed at by editing such as Piozzi's" was more calculated than "heightened general appeal." Except for detailed journal-letters written from the Hebrides, which Johnson planned to use as the foundation for what became *A Journey to the Western Islands of Scotland*, the letters he composed are generally brief, frequent, and personal. In the collection, these modest epistles provide a striking context for the long, infrequent, and more formal letters from Mrs. Thrale. In editing her letters for publication, she took the opportunity to reposition herself in the correspondence. Omitting or combining her letters transformed what had evidently been a more balanced exchange—two or three letters from Johnson for each of hers—to a pattern in which a long series of his letters (as many as forty) would be followed by a single letter of hers. By withholding her letters, she alters the dynamic of the relationship; she makes herself more remote, more serious, and more sought after. Her organization and revision of her own correspondence strengthens the impression that he was pestering her with short letters, while she remained at a dignified distance. True, a careful reader will detect Johnson's references to many letters that she wrote that do not appear in the collection, but because we do not read those letters, they do not significantly disturb our experience of an unequal correspondence. Her infrequent letters therefore become as valuable to us readers as they are to Johnson.

Mrs. Thrale, mixing in the world, raising a large family, apparently too busy to write often, reports on the crowds in London or the vanities of Brighton. It is Johnson who is the domestic storyteller, chronicling the humdrum. The letters by Mrs. Thrale that are included, moreover, are often exceptional, such as her advice to a young man on marrying or her long and amusing account of attending the regatta. She seldom prints letters on ordinary household news, nor does she remark on Johnson's activities (apart from references to his ongoing work on *The Lives of the Poets*), because she presumably omits those of her letters whose contents are echoed in his. Meanwhile, Johnson was absorbing her life into his letters, reciprocating with a biographical account that fully acknowledges her experiences.

Following two centuries of critical attention to Johnson, in which Piozzi's editorial efforts were attacked, ridiculed, or ignored, should we judge Piozzi's project a failure? Is it quixotic to seek to recover the reading experience that she attempted to create with her carefully managed edition? No; on its own terms, in 1788, *Letters* did accomplish the goal that Piozzi had set for herself. She found a way to plead her case before the public without directly answering the charges in the newspapers or by writing an autobiography. Piozzi shrewdly recognized that Dr. Johnson interested people, who therefore wanted to read his letters; Johnson meanwhile, as Boswell discovered to his chagrin, was interested in Mrs. Thrale. From former friends like Frances Burney to contemporary admirers like Arthur Murphy to appreciative strangers like Jane Austen, people who read *Letters* read about her, and they therefore experienced the ways she charmed her acquaintance, managed her finances, and coped with a large and ailing family.

In her letter of October 7, 1773, Mrs. Thrale begins by thanking Johnson for his "descriptive letters" from Scotland. She notes that he will not read her expression of thanks until he has returned to Edinburgh but assures him that the empathetic reciprocity of their correspondence will palliate the delay: "What I am now writing will serve to recal[l] those images with which you were impressed when you wrote to me; and one pleasure of correspondence arises from the recollection of those accidents to which one's friend's letter is a reply" (*Letters*, 1:189). As her life has been mirrored in his letters, so her letters likewise reflect his experiences back to him, bringing together the past and the present, events experienced separately but shared in the exchange of letters.

Johnson, for his part, imagines her rereading his letters; inquiring as to whether she keeps them, he writes on August 2, 1775, "They will, I hope, always be in some degree the records of a pure and blameless friendship, and in some hours of languor and sadness may revive the memory of more cheerful times" (*Letters*, 1:295). If one of the most powerful impressions produced by the experience of reading what I have called Johnson's "Apology" is the warm imaginative sympathy that inhabits Johnson's letters to Hester Thrale, another is the insufficiently celebrated editorial intelligence of Hester Lynch Piozzi. Alienated from family and friends, prevented by modesty and convention from waging open war with her critics, she used epistolary materials to construct a ventriloquized autobiography that is strategically effective, tactically efficient, emotionally compelling, readable, and persuasive.

Notes

1. Edward A. Bloom and Lillian D. Bloom, eds., *The Piozzi Letters: Correspondence of Hester Lynch Piozzi, 1784–1821*, vol. 1, *1784–1791* (Newark: University of Delaware Press, 1989), 156.
2. By April 1787, Piozzi had accumulated about four hundred Johnson letters (Bloom and Bloom, *Piozzi Letters*, 1:235n1).
3. Johnson's "Queeney letters" were first published in 1934.
4. Katherine C. Balderston, ed., *Thraliana: The Diary of Mrs. Hester Lynch Thrale (Later Mrs. Piozzi), 1776–1809*, vol. 2, *1784–1809* (Oxford: Clarendon, 1942), 680.
5. James L. Clifford, *Hester Lynch Piozzi (Mrs. Thrale)*, 2nd ed. (New York: Columbia University Press, 1987), 265.
6. Hester Lynch Piozzi, *Anecdotes of the Late Samuel Johnson LL.D. during the Last Twenty Years of His Life*, ed. Arthur Sherbo (1786; New York: Oxford University Press, 1974), 141; Hester Lynch Piozzi, *Letters to and from the Late Samuel Johnson, LL.D.* (London: Cadell, 1788), 1:ii.
7. Clare Brant, *Eighteenth-Century Letters and British Culture* (New York: Palgrave Macmillan, 2006), 17.
8. I call Johnson's correspondent "Mrs. Thrale" and the editor of *Letters* "Piozzi." Using the surname Thrale without the honorific "Mrs." could

lead to confusion in an essay that mentions other correspondents also named Thrale. And as I have argued elsewhere, in both her published works and her conversation Piozzi conceptualized "Mrs. Thrale" as a separate, historical character. See Lisa Berglund, "Why Should Hester Lynch Piozzi Be Doctor Johnson's Mrs. Thrale?," *Names: A Journal of Onomastics* 64, no. 4 (December 2016): 189–201.

9. Deirdre Le Faye, *Jane Austen's Letters*, 3rd ed. (New York: Oxford University Press, 1995), 156. The accuracy of Austen's quotation suggests that she either owned a copy of *Letters* or had read it with exceptional care. She is quoting a letter in which Mrs. Thrale responds to Johnson's comments on her lengthy description of a regatta, suggests a trip to Cairo, and then exclaims, "Well! now all this is nonsense, and fancy, and flight, you know, for my master has his great casks to mind, and I have my little children" (*Letters*, 1.270).
10. Clifford, *Hester Lynch Piozzi*, 315.
11. Bloom and Bloom, *Piozzi Letters*, 1:294.
12. Bruce Redford, *The Converse of the Pen: Acts of Intimacy in the Eighteenth-Century Familiar Letter* (Chicago: University of Chicago Press, 1986), 213.
13. Of the two important omitted letters and her other editorial changes, R. W. Chapman says, "She did right, I think, to suppress both. In editing Johnson's letters she allowed herself to make certain omissions . . . details of sickness, childbirth, or domestic finance; some of them might have given pain or offence. There is nothing here for complaint" (R. W. Chapman, ed., *The Letters of Samuel Johnson, with Mrs. Thrale's Genuine Letters to Him*, vol. 3, *1783–1784, Letters 821.2–1174* [Oxford: Clarendon, 1952], 301). Chapman does observe that Piozzi's edition did not indicate omissions except in the cases of dashed-out names, unlike Boswell's practice with letters included in the *Life of Johnson*.
14. [Arthur Murphy], review of *Letters to and from the Late Samuel Johnson, LL.D.*, by Hester Lynch Piozzi, *Monthly Review* 78 (March 1788): 331.
15. Chapman was the most persistently hostile modern critic of Piozzi's *Letters*, although his intolerant view of her editorial practice softened over the decades. In *Johnson, Boswell and Mrs. Piozzi: A Suppressed Passage Restored*, Chapman's "Prefatory Note" gloats over Piozzi's

"simplicity and guile" as it introduces a facsimile reproduction of a letter from which Piozzi's edition suppressed a paragraph praising Boswell's *Tour of the Hebrides* (London: Oxford University Press, 1929). (Piozzi had been encouraged to cut the paragraph by the two-faced Samuel Lysons, who after assisting her in preparing her edition, blabbed about the omission to Boswell.) Seventeen years later, Chapman's article "Mrs. Piozzi's Omissions from Johnson's Letters to the Thrales" lists all the silent omissions from Johnson's letters, many trivial or related to the writer's health. "She seems to have been, at the worst, indifferent honest," Chapman acknowledges (R. W. Chapman, "Mrs. Piozzi's Omissions from Johnson's Letters to the Thrales," *Review of English Studies* 22, no. 85 [January 1946]: 28). Ultimately, in his 1952 edition of Johnson's letters, Chapman offers a critical but not unbalanced assessment of her achievement.

16. [Murphy], *Monthly Review*, 328, 331.
17. Bloom and Bloom, *Piozzi Letters*, 1.257n2, letter of June 2, 1788.
18. The Marquis of Lansdowne, ed. *The Queeney Letters, Being Letters Addressed to Hester Maria Thrale by Doctor Johnson, Fanny Burney and Mrs. Thrale-Piozzi* (New York: Farrar & Rinehart, 1934), 109.
19. Clifford, *Hester Lynch Piozzi*, 316.
20. Piozzi, *Anecdotes*, 152.
21. Redford, *Converse*, 210–211.
22. For Johnson's insulting treatment of Mr. Cholmondeley, see Piozzi, *Anecdotes*, 145.
23. A similar exchange is recorded in one of Mrs. Thrale's letters; she asks him to "recollect complaining once to me of flatulence, when I could really with difficulty sit to hear you for very agony both of body and soul.—I'm sure I recollect your kind recantation, when you confessed that it is was like lamenting a scratched finger in his chamber, who, the day before, had broken both his legs" (*Letters*, 1.330).
24. Emphasizing his identification with the Thrale family is Johnson's use of the pronoun "we" in recommending retrenchments: "Supposing that our former mode of life kept us on the level, we shall, by the present contraction of expence, gain upon fortune a thousand a-year, even though no improvements can be made in the conduct of the trade" (*Letters*, 1:66).

25. Redford, *Converse*, 219.

26. William McCarthy, *Hester Thrale Piozzi: Portrait of a Literary Woman* (Chapel Hill: University of North Carolina Press, 1985), 139.

27. [Murphy], *Monthly Review*, 325.

28. The twelve-letter series runs as follows: CXXVI: Ralph, the Thrales' two-year-old son, continues ill, while Queeney is looking after ten chickens and studying; they are considering another autumn in Brighton. CXXVII: Ralph continues ill. CXXVIII: Hester is writing by every post, Henry is traveling to Derby, the girls are studying with Baretti, who is annoying Hester; Ralph continues ill, they are discussing how to settle the estate. CXXIX: Henry continues summer building. CXXX: Ralph has died. CXXXI: Henry did not visit Johnson when he came to Derby; Hester and Baretti have reconciled; they have named Johnson a trustee of the estate. CXXXII: Queeney has written, the peacock is hurt (possibly abused) and a cat has been killed; Hester is doing better; their summer plans still undetermined. CXXXIII: nothing. CXXXIV: nothing. CXXXV: Hester sent a present to Johnson's stepdaughter Lucy Porter. CXXXVI: Hester visited Johnson's friend Anna Williams; Henry has ceased digging a pool. CXXXVII: Johnson reflects on whether she keeps his letters, Sophy has had a headache, and Hester is worried (*Letters*, 1:273–301).

29. John Radner, *Johnson and Boswell: A Biography of Friendship* (New Haven, CT: Yale University Press, 2013), 146–147.

30. Clifford, *Hester Lynch Piozzi*, 266–267.

31. Bloom and Bloom, *Piozzi Letters*, 1:235, note 1.

32. McCarthy, *Hester Thrale Piozzi*, 140.

2

The Education of Alexander d'Arblay

The "Idol of the World"

PETER SABOR

If Alexander d'Arblay had died in April 1819 at the age of twenty-four, instead of living on for another seventeen years until January 1837, his obituary, or at least one approved by his mother and other members of the Burney family, might have read as follows. Alexander Charles Louis Piochard d'Arblay, the only child of the distinguished French artillery officer General Alexandre-Jean Baptiste Piochard, comte d'Arblay and his English wife, the novelist and dramatist Frances Burney d'Arblay, was born at Great Bookham, Surrey, in December 1794. His paternal grandfather, Lieutenant-Colonel Pierre Piochard d'Arblay, was also an artillery officer and a Chevalier de Saint-Louis. His maternal grandfather, Dr. Charles Burney, was the foremost music historian of his age; his maternal uncle, Dr. Charles Burney the younger, was an eminent classical scholar and book collector. Three months after Alexander's birth, his mother's first tragedy, *Edwy and Elgiva*, opened at the Theatre Royal, Drury Lane. Auspiciously, the play that followed it was James D'Egville's celebrated afterpiece *Alexander the Great*, in which the hero's carriage was drawn across the stage by two elephants.[1] No wonder, given his illustrious namesake and ancestry, that the infant was termed by his fond mother the "Idol of the World."[2]

Although Alexandre d'Arblay was a Catholic, Alexander was brought up as a Protestant at the behest of his father, who observed that "since he was an Englishman *born*, he should be an Englishman *bred*."[3] His first seven years were spent in England where he was taught at home, primarily by his mother, and given a series of pieces to recite, including a speech from Henry Fielding's comedy *Tom Thumb*. While English was his mother tongue, he soon acquired fluency in French after his parents moved from their Surrey home to live in Paris in 1802. His formal education began in September 1804, when, at the age of nine, he was enrolled for a year at a boarding school directed by Louis-Prince-Ferdinand Sencier in Passy, the village close to Paris where his parents were then residing. Here he achieved remarkable success, winning four first prizes. In September 1805, Alexander was enrolled at a boarding school in Paris, directed by Jacques-Antoine Hix. At the end of his first year there he won a second and five first prizes.

After his mother returned with him to England in 1812, Alexander was enrolled in the highest form at Charles Burney's school at Greenwich. Frances d'Arblay had originally intended to rejoin her husband in Paris, where Alexander had been accepted into the highly prestigious Ecole Polytechnique. Instead, however, after a year of fruitful studies at Greenwich, his first year of schooling in English, Alexander was admitted to Gonville and Caius College, Cambridge, with a Tancred Scholarship in medicine, which he took up in October 1813, at the age of eighteen. He also won a college scholarship in classics, awarded for his translation of Demosthenes. In July 1814, at the end of his first year at Caius, Alexander was given the opportunity to serve beside his father as a lieutenant in the company of Louis XVIII's household troops, led by the Duc de Luxembourg. Declining this offer in order to continue his studies at Cambridge, he remained at Caius until November 1816. In that month he resigned his Tancred Scholarship and migrated to Christ's College as a pensioner, so that he could take a bachelor of arts degree. News of his progress reached Jane Austen, a longtime admirer of his mother's novels, who wrote to her sister Cassandra in November 1816, "Perhaps I may marry young M^{r} D'arblay."[4] After intensive study in mathematics, he graduated as tenth wrangler in January 1818. His academic success was swiftly rewarded by his election, at the age of twenty-three, as a scholar of Christ's in February and as a fellow of the college in March. In September 1818 he was ordained as a deacon of the Church of England by the Bishop of Salisbury, and the following April as a priest by the Bishop of Chester.

Alexander d'Arblay showed great promise in three distinct disciplines: mathematics, chess, and poetry. Trained in France to study mathematical analysis from a Leibnizian, rather than a Newtonian, perspective, he was a founding member of the Analytic Society at Cambridge, together with his famous contemporaries John Herschel and Charles Babbage. He was among the strongest players of chess at Cambridge, devoting much time to the study and practice of the game. His extraordinary powers of memory were evidenced when, a month before his ordination as priest, he was said to have memorized in its entirety Thomas Moore's six-thousand-line oriental poem *Lalla Rookh*.[5] As well as reciting and writing poetry, he also turned his hand to translation from French to English and English to French: in 1815 he undertook a French version of Alexander Pope's "Elegy to the Memory of an Unfortunate Lady."[6]

Obituaries, of course, tend to present an anodyne version of their subjects, and the one I have fabricated here is no exception. My purpose is to examine Alexander d'Arblay's education more closely, in order to throw new light on his childhood and youth and on his difficult relationship with his mother. I am not concerned with his later life as a clergyman and versifier, which I have studied elsewhere in an essay devoted to Alexander as a case study in depression.[7] Instead, I focus on his education at home, at French schools, at his uncle's Greenwich school, and at his two Cambridge colleges, while considering how and why the idol of the world became, for his family and friends, a byword for idleness. In doing so, I demonstrate the truth of Samuel Johnson's remark, also cited by Marilyn Francus in her essay in this volume, that "there has rarely passed a life of which a judicious and faithful narrative would not be useful."[8] Frances d'Arblay, in her three-volume *Memoirs of Doctor Burney*, provided a lamentably wooden portrait of her father, who in her version of his life could do no wrong at all. Had she published a "Memoirs of the Reverend Alexander d'Arblay," it too would surely have whitewashed her son's numerous shortcomings—in the manner of the mock obituary I have furnished above. In the remarks that follow, I show Alexander as he appeared to the world at large, as well as to his notoriously protective and often self-deluded mother.

Schoolboy in France and England

During his first ten years, Frances d'Arblay had high hopes of a brilliant future for her son. At just three weeks he was already, she believed, showing signs of exceptional talents. The baby, she wrote to Dr. Burney, "is a very interesting little Creature, already, & has a thousand little promises of original intelligence."[9] At Camilla Cottage, while her soldier husband turned gardener was planting vegetables, Frances was teaching Alexander a variety of subjects; "[he] improves," she wrote to her father, "in all that I can teach."[10] As well as English and French, he studied Latin and the Bible with her, both the Old Testament and the New. He also learned recital pieces. Before his fourth birthday, he could already declaim Ariel's song in *The Tempest*, "Come unto these yellow Sands," and before long his repertoire also included the opening scene of Nathaniel Lee's tragedy *Theodosius*, a passage from Henry Fielding's *Tom Thumb* ("Ha! dogs! Arrest my friend before my face!"), Joseph Addison's hymn "The Spacious Firmament on High," and William Shenstone's *A Pastoral Ballad*: all recited to Princess Sophia at Buckingham House in April 1800, shortly after his fifth birthday.[11] Another set piece was a passage from a French translation of Butler's *Hudibras*, which he spoke while brandishing a toy sword in "the attitude of fencing."[12]

Alexander's homeschooling continued for over two years in Paris and then Passy, after his mother moved to France in April 1802 to rejoin M. d'Arblay. In a letter to Marianne Waddington, Frances refers to Alexander as "a Child whom I have no right to detain from school but by being myself his constant instructress."[13] She kept him at home out of concern for his delicate health, and at first this made him less than fully bilingual; as she remarked in a letter to Dr. Burney, "He is able to express every thing he wishes in french, but as we always talk English together, & he lives with me constantly, English is still the superior language."[14] He now received tuition from his father in mathematics, Latin, French, and geography, while Frances taught him history, English, orthography, and religion.[15]

When Alexander was eventually enrolled at a secondary school in Passy in 1804, it was as a day student. The school, located on the same street as his home, had eighty pupils, all but four of whom were boarders. He attended for just three or four hours each morning and was mocked as a mother's boy, as Frances herself remarked: "Poor Alex," she wrote, "has been called Bebe! with great contempt by one of these young gentlemen."[16] There are clear signs here that Frances was already the overly protective mother that she would never cease to be, even when Alexander was a mature adult. After his recovery from an illness, she sought and received permission from M. Sencier for her son to attend school only after breakfast. She would also "wrap him up very warm," as she recorded in a letter to her husband.[17]

Despite his attenuated participation in classes, Alexander's first and only year at the Passy school was crowned with academic glory. In a letter to her father, Frances describes the end-of-year ceremony at which her son won four first prizes, each one rewarded with a book and, in her words, "a crown of Laurel & Oak."[18] Dr. Burney's reply is surprisingly brisk. "I must own," he wrote, "that it astonished me. That such a wild, restless & spoiled little chap, with all his natural quickness of parts sh^{d} so soon submit to study & application in so many different branches of human knowledge, & succeed in them all beyond his fellows!" Somewhat ominously, he added, "There may perhaps, be a little danger that all this applause, & conviction of his superior powers over other children of the same age may render this dear boy a little *avantageux*, & provoke the world to be a little spiteful, & to wish to mortify him, by giving him less praise than he deserves."[19] At this stage of his life, however, Frances would acknowledge no shortcomings in her beloved son, other than what she repeatedly termed his "sauvagerie": signifying both wildness and awkwardness in company. In her next letter to her father she refers to his "most balmy words" about Alexander, ignoring entirely the warning about spoiling him.[20] His parents read numerous books aloud to him, in English and in French, and marveled at his development; "wonderful & beautiful is his progress," Frances confided to her diary, a few months before the end of his schooling at Passy.[21]

When the d'Arblays returned from Passy to Paris in September 1805, Alexander was enrolled in a much larger school in the quartier Champs Élysées. One of sixteen day pupils taught, together with 156 boarders, by twenty masters,[22] Alexander would remain here for seven years, from the ages of ten to seventeen. His first year was another academic triumph, as Frances recounts at great length in a letter to her father. At the prize-giving ceremonies in August 1806, he did still better than he had at Passy, winning one second and five first prizes, including the ones for French grammar and composition.[23] After only three years in France, he had clearly mastered the language. During Alexander's first school year in Paris, though, there were signs of trouble to come. One is the strange account that Frances gives of the resentment supposedly felt by Alexander's classmates of his success in class, and of his resolving, in response, to become a slacker instead of a swat. "This new character," she tells her father, "by degrees grew so agreeable to him, that he now suddenly dropt all application, & in a short time, became the idlest & most wanton Boy of the Class!"[24] Knowing how eager his parents were for him to succeed, the child seems to have found a ready way to justify his lack of application. Even at the prize-giving ceremonies, Frances is struck by her son's failure to conform, commenting that there is a "wanton *gaucherie* which pervades all he does," and "he has not the least idea how to present himself, nor the smallest care how he is arranged."[25] In a letter to Marianne Waddington, Frances drew attention to some more of Alexander's shortcomings. Her "riotous Boy," she wrote, was "the pride of our lives, but his spirits are so ungovernable that he fills us with alarm for his safety, nay his life, by his careless fearlessness of danger, & untameable vivacity & vehemence of temper."[26]

Although Alexander would spend another six years at his Paris school, there is a notable absence in his mother's voluminous journals, diaries, and letters for the period of any mention of further prize winning. Academically, he seems to have attained his greatest success at the age of eleven; he would have other moments of glory, but none to compare with that of 1806. On one occasion, in October 1808, Frances writes to M. d'Arblay that their son's theatrical style of orating has attracted both the mockery of his classmates and the criticism of his teacher, who tells him, "Laissez là, mon Enfant, ces Gestes et ces mouvemens, et cet emphase. Montrez du chaleur, c'est bien; quelque petit movement, aussi, est bien;—mais que cela vient du sujet; il faut être toûjours naturel; tout ce qui est extravagante manque son effet."[27] Extravagance of various kinds came naturally to the now adolescent Alexander. In a letter of September 1810, Frances writes, with obvious concern, "He is terribly singular, & more what they here call *sauvage* than any creature I ever beheld. He is untameably wild, & averse to all the forms of society. Where he can have got such a rebel humour we conceive not, but it costs him more to make a bow than to resolve 6 different problems of Algebra, or to repeat 12 pages from Euripides: and as to making a civil speech—he would sooner renounce the World."[28] The same strained attempt at humor in what is clearly not a humorous subject is found in a letter of about the same date that Frances wrote to her husband's uncle, Jean-Baptiste-Gabriel Bazille. Now fifteen, Alexander was proving a trial to his mother when she received visitors, acting in the sullen way that might be expected of a modern teenager: "Alex grandit beaucoup, il est toujours aussi sauvage . . . que jamais. Dieu sait quand il lui prendra la fantaisie de se civiliser! Je crois que je ferai fête ce jour là, et que j'inviterai toutes des dames, et surtout les demoiselles de ma connoissance, pour voir l'ourse dompté. Quel etonnement et joie lorsque Alex ne prendra pas leurs chaises! n'entrera pas avant elles dans la chambre! ne se servira pas le premier au depart; repondra lorsqu'on lui faite une question, et fera une reverence où du moins ôtera le chapeau lorsqu'il les rencontre!"[29] He was also acquiring the habit of chronic lateness that would cause him endless difficulties later in life. On one occasion, as Frances notes in her diary for January 1812, "My giddy Alex has had a fall in running with the furious haste required to repair his tardy negligence to his Lycée—& a broken knee keeps him now at my side. When will <he> be a little wiser, my poor etourdi?"[30]

Alexander's education in Paris came to an abrupt end. In July 1812, before the end of the summer term, he and his mother hurried away from the city to Dunkirk and then on to England, as Frances records at length in her well-known Dunkirk journal. Among her motives for leaving France, and her beloved husband, at this time was the impending threat for Alexander of conscription into the French army; he would turn eighteen in December 1812, at which age he would normally be required to register for military service. As his mother, though not his father, could see, he would surely have been a hopelessly incompetent soldier. For all his early promise, it was now becoming clear that the idol of the world had a number of character defects, including lethargy, lack of purpose, and vanity. A letter to his father from Dunkirk shows him striving for rhetorical effect, concluding portentously, "prions Dieu que la chere plume puisse incesssament vous donner des nouvelles."[31] Frances, who continued the letter on the same sheet, was merciless about Alexander's prose. "Pray," she urges her husband, "avoid all praise. It ruins him. Already he sits down to write to you with all the labour of vanity, his brow knit, Eye severe, not suffering a word to be said to him, & resting upon his Elbows a quarter of an hour thinking how to begin. This has only happened since you have called his Letters *charmantes*."[32]

A more favorable portrait of Alexander emerges in a letter by his cousin Charlotte Barrett (later editor of the seven-volume *Diary and Letters of Madame d'Arblay*), written shortly after his return to England in August 1812. Here Barrett reports on the plans of Frances and her son: "She is to stay in England *certainly* till the end of October, & all the winter if M. d'Arblay is well & can spare her. He, poor soul, could get no passport. Alec is promised admission into the Polytechnic school in Paris, in wch 300 young men are finished in Sciences &c. generally those who have distinguished themselves by previous attainments; & *those only*, in all France, are exempted from the conscription for life, that they may be literati & savans & so on. This is a delightful circumstance for my poor dear Aunt."[33] Barrett envisioned Alexander's being admitted into the Ecole for the 1813–1814 academic year, and thus being spared from military service. In the event, Frances would remain with him in England for the next two years. His "promised admission" into the Ecole Polytechnique was thus of no avail, although in a letter of November 1812, Frances writes optimistically that he has "returned rigourously to his preparatory studies" for the highly competitive French college.[34] Barrett was much impressed by Alexander's mathematical prowess. In the same letter she writes that her brother Clement Francis, then twenty and an undergraduate at Caius College, had turned to his younger cousin for help with a mathematics equation. "Clem," she remarks, "says that Alec is very forward in mathematics & w^{d} shine in any english university."[35]

Alexander's formal education, which had ceased on his leaving Paris in July 1812, would not resume until November. Frances planned to have him enrolled at her brother Charles's school in Greenwich, but Alexander was reluctant to become a pupil there. The problem was, as she wrote in a letter to her father, that the school was now being run not by Charles, the celebrated classical scholar, but by his son, Charles Parr Burney, who was only nine years older than Alexander. To have studied with Charles Burney, Alexander declared, would have been an honor, but "as to his Cousin, he was but his Cousin, however learned or clever he might be." Alexander, his mother reports, was neglecting his studies in

England and "had got into idle ways of vague occupations, without any fixed pursuit, or methodised plan." Happily, an offer by Charles Parr's young wife, Frances Bentley Burney, to play chess with Alexander won him over; chess was always his favorite pastime, and he never turned down an opportunity to play a game. To his mother's delight, he was admitted directly into the sixth form at Greenwich after he had, in her account, "acquitted himself amazingly well upon his examination."[36]

In general, Alexander's first and only year as an English schoolboy went smoothly. Writing at length, in May 1813, to Alexandre in Paris, he was obviously eager to impress his father with the extent of his studies, but he did seem to be enjoying the school's remarkably rigorous curriculum. The boys, he tells Alexandre, work diligently at Latin, Greek, mathematics, in particular, and, knowing how to please his father, assures him that he devotes much of his leisure time to reading French and English literature: "J'apprends par coeur à peu près 100 vers de Racine ou de Corneille ou de Voltaire tous les jour dans les vacances de Midsummer, et aussi de Milton, Shakespeare, Dryden, ou Pope, jusqu'à ce que je sache tous leurs plus beaux morceaux, dont je sais déjà un assez bon nombre; j'ai dans ma tête tout l'art Poëtique de Boileau, et j'espere dans peu en pouvoir dire autant de la Henriade et des Odes d'Horace dont j'apprends 2 ou 3 par jour."[37] Alexander was also well liked by his fellows, to the surprise of Frances, who was, as she wrote, "afraid his shyness would have made him quite unpopular";[38] and despite the plan favored by the absent M. d'Arblay to enter Alexander for the Ecole Polytechnique, Frances began to plan for him to continue his education in England. Her brother Charles, who in 1777 had been sent down from Caius College for stealing books from the University Library, was now, thirty-five years later, a close friend of the present master of Caius, Dr. Martin Davy. In 1808 he had received a belated master of arts from Cambridge and in 1812 a doctorate in divinity. With Charles in good standing at Caius, Frances quickly came to regard the college as Alexander's future home. An additional attraction, as she discovered, was the possibility of his winning a scholarship, the Tancred, that would pay a substantial amount toward the cost of his Cambridge education: over a hundred pounds per annum both during the period of study and for three years thereafter.[39] She and Charles together organized a campaign to sway the Tancred electors in Alexander's favor, and since one of the electors was the governor of Chelsea Hospital, where their father resided, he too was brought into the cabal, despite his advanced age. In a letter to Dr. Burney of January 1813, Frances wrote a script for him to use in an appeal to the governor, Sir David Dundas. Dr. Burney was to describe Alexander as "a youth who is just returned from France, to finish his education in the land of his birth, & who ardently desires that it should be at an English University, for which his studies abroad have prepared him; but for which, unaided, his fortune would be insufficient."[40] There were, of course, some white lies here: Alexander had returned from France not for an English education but rather to escape the possibility of military conscription; he had to be coaxed into attending Greenwich school, and the ardent desire for him to attend Cambridge was more his mother's than his own. In another letter to her father she wrote of her high hopes that Alexander would win the scholarship, adding, in an unconsciously revealing remark, "It will be so superb a finish for *our* education."[41]

Both Frances and her brother Charles were tireless in their pulling of strings. Queen Charlotte herself was drafted in by Frances, and she agreed to put pressure on two of the electors. The campaign was long and arduous, but ultimately fruitful. As Frances announced in a letter to the queen of March 1813, Alexander's rival for the scholarship eventually withdrew his candidacy,[42] and after he had proved that he was an Anglican, born in Great Britain—a requirement for the Tancred—Alexander was admitted into Caius in April, with a Tancred Studentship in Physic. For the remainder of the school year, Alexander was strongly encouraged to make progress in geometry and calculus. Mathematics would be his principal field of study at Cambridge, and as he had acknowledged in a letter to his father of September 1812, he was well behind his peers in his knowledge of geometry; his fellow pupils, he declared, "la faisait six fois mieux que moi."[43] The French system favored algebra, at which he excelled, but in Cambridge and at the Greenwich school, geometry was paramount. He was also deficient in his grasp of the classics, at least in the view of Charles Parr Burney, who analyzed his pupil's shortcomings at length in a letter to Frances of October 1813, where he describes his regret that he has been unable "to remedy the defects of [Alexander's] early Classical education.—Too often does he trip even in the Elements of Grammar,—in which most essential branch of knowledge he seems never to have been well-grounded. All his best exertions will be needed to overcome this disadvantage:—fancy & association are always at work,—but for sober nouns & verbs he has no relish."[44] The letter elicited a defensive reply, in which Frances attributes her son's shortcomings to his early success. She depicts him as a wunderkind, struggling to live up to his former achievements; his application has been "too forcible & ardent for his physical fabric, &, by overstretching his powers, has now slackened their elasticity." His first years in France, she writes, were "gilt with such triumphant fame, that it has rendered all quiet & rational reward of toil insipid, & scarcely worth attainment."[45]

Just a few weeks later, Frances was rejoicing in Alexander's prowess once again. He had, unexpectedly, won a Caius entrance prize in classics, in competition with ten or twelve other matriculating students; both his language exercises and his translation from Demosthenes had been judged the best. In a letter to Dr. Burney, Frances declares that "this revives all my hopes of restoring him to the Literary pursuits which so often have crowned him with Laurels in France. . . . How will his Greek professor in Paris, M. Hugot, who was warmly attached to him, & always pronounced that he might, if he would apply, be a second Dr. Charles Burney, as a *Helleniste*—how will he rejoice when this event may be told to him!"[46]

Student and Fellow at Cambridge

Alexander was nothing if not inconsistent. Having revived the hopes of his parents with the Tancred scholarship and the classics prize, he seemed set to become a distinguished scholar at Caius College, but this was not to be. The Michaelmas term of his first year was a disaster. His cousin and fellow collegian at Caius, Clement Francis, despite his admiration for Alexander's prowess in algebra, wrote a letter to Frances on Christmas Day of 1813, recommending that her son withdraw from the college because of his indolence and numerous shortcomings in comportment.[47] This was followed by a softer letter from Charlotte Barrett, explaining that Alexander's geometry was still much below par; he was also offending the authorities at Caius by failing to attend compulsory morning chapel, and hence receiving laborious impositions (literary tasks and exercises imposed as punishments).[48] Worse still, Charles Burney Jr. had received a stern letter from one of Alexander's tutors at Caius, Benedict Chapman. It contained a long list of charges against the feckless young man, including his frequent absences from chapel, lectures, and the dining hall, and threatened to have him sent down.[49] The despairing Frances asked her brother: "What step can I take to avert a blow so deplorably ruinous to all my hopes?—nay, almost to my powers of existence?—For where—& how can I finish his education for his future prosperity, if he is withdrawn from Cambridge? I am wholly without resource, for he is utterly unfit, nay, incapable for any mode of life that is not literary or scientific."[50] In the Lent term, Alexander made an effort to mend his ways. In a letter to his mother, he reported a conversation with his other college tutor, William Gimingham, who told him, "Your present conduct & regularity has perfectly satisfied me in every respect,—& that I now look upon the irregularities of the former term as completely done away!"[51] Dr. Davy also wrote to Charles Burney about Alexander's reformation, declaring, according to Frances, that "even the learned Dons are now satisfied with him."[52] Frances, meanwhile, was taking measures of her own, marshalling a host of Cambridge acquaintances and contacts to spy on her son for her and even, on the advice of her sister Charlotte, enlisting the services of his college servant to ensure that he rose on time; she was to "persecute at His door in a morning, to watch him for meals, & to attend to his fires."[53] In addition, she engaged a private tutor, John Alty. Alexander, she wrote to her brother Charles, thought that Alty "may remind him of his engagement to study mechanics, &c, & not abandon himself, as heretofore, to his eternal Algebra. If so, 'twill be £10 admirably employed."[54]

For all her watching over Alexander, Frances remained remarkably ignorant of the terms of his Tancred scholarship. His father, still absent in France, was equally ill-informed. Both parents believed that their son was destined for a clerical career. M. d'Arblay, in a letter to Frances of April 1814, writes of "le plan que nous avions toujours eu d'en faire un bon et honnête *clergyman*," while Frances writes to her husband, "In 3 years, if industrious, he may take his degree, & then we may seek him some Church benefice."[55] Yet Alexander's Tancred scholarship was specifically reserved for students graduating as bachelor of medicine; he was studying to become a physician, not a cleric. It is astonishing to find Frances, in a letter to Alexander, telling him that "some one has hinted to me that you *might* take your Degree as D.M.—let me hasten to inform you that your Padre would never consent to that; for reasons too long for detail, but that I am certain are insuperable."[56] As Edward and Lillian Bloom note tartly, "from the beginning of his University matriculation, [Alexander] and his parents presumed he had special dispensation as to the curriculum he studied, the degree he took, and the career he was to prepare himself for."[57] How wrong the d'Arblays were will appear shortly.

Further complicating matters was a new plan that Alexandre d'Arblay conceived for Alexander's future. In a letter of July 1814, he tells Frances that he has enlisted their son in the cavalry regiment of the duc de Montmorency-Luxembourg,[58] an egregiously ill-advised move, since he baulked even at the relatively liberal rules and regulations of his Cambridge college; it is hard to imagine him submitting to military discipline. Alexandre's startling announcement caused a rare dispute between husband and wife, who were usually in marital accord. In one of her letters, Frances pointed out some of the obvious objections: "Can you really think [Alexander] adapted to a military life? the *brusqueris* of his character, yet timidity of his Nature, joined to an unconquerable ignorance of the ways of the world, & an absence & thoughtlessness that make him never ready for any appointment; nor steady to any engagement—surely seem bars insuperable, without counting my own repugnance to a Son of the Two Nations entering that career. He has never, also, mounted a Horse, & daily he grows more near sighted."[59] M. d'Arblay, however, was reluctant to relinquish the scheme. A military career in France now seemed to him the best way for Alexander to achieve the renown that he and Frances had always thought to be their son's natural due.

At Cambridge, little renown was coming Alexander's way. In May 1814, he had, at his mother's suggestion, taken an examination in classics in the hope of winning a prize, but failed badly; Frances referred to this as a "disgrace," caused in part by his neglecting his studies in favor of chess.[60] She also blamed her son's early success at his school in Paris for his present failings: "Those fatal 6 prizes turned his understanding into presumption, & his application into caprice. He thought—& still thinks—he could, & can, do *what* he pleases *when* he pleases. This perverse secret vanity casts him upon indolence & whim."[61] Since she could no longer watch over her wayward son, at least while he was absent from her in Cambridge, Frances hired several local tutors to aid him in his studies. The first of these, recommended by the Reverend William Haggitt, chaplain at Chelsea Hospital, was James Bellamy, who had taken his bachelor of arts in 1812. In the summer of 1814, Alexander took tutorials with Bellamy thrice weekly; as he wrote to his father, "j'étudierai les parties seches et Geometriques qui je n'aurais guères le pouvoir, ou la Courage, d'étudier tout seul."[62] Other tutors followed: Richard Gwatkin, who took his bachelor's in 1814 and was made fellow of St. John's in the same year, and James Paterson, who received his bachelor of arts in 1809 and was engaged to give Alexander lessons daily for a month. Frances lamented the cost of all this private coaching, but told her brother, "I will gaily live in a Cell, rather than splendidly in a Palace, to save [Alexander] from another *disgrazia*."[63]

Even with these additional tutorials, Alexander continued to struggle at Caius. Dr. Chapman, whom Frances described as "the severest & most rigid of all the Tutors," warned her that her son "will certainly be *rusticated* if he does not entirely reform."[64] To her brother Charles she wrote, "My poor Alex frightens me to death! . . . he feels, at times, so utterly without energy, that a total indifference comes over him for his lot in life!—which he only rouses from by his sole positive joy & propensity, Algebra!"[65] Charles was now ready to write him off, sending Frances a letter, not extant, that she described as a "dagger" to her, and her friend Georgiana Waddington warned her that he "never . . . can succeed at Cambridge."[66] In the face of all this bad news, Frances even contemplated moving from Bath to Cambridge to be next to Alexander. Her son, not surprisingly, rejected the plan: "*He* cannot bear to have me stationed [there], & has made me, & even his Father, think such a measure would expose him to ridicule, & *uselessly*; for I could not be at his side before 7.—nor at the *preparatory* moments of other attendance," Frances wrote.[67]

For a few weeks in October 1814, the d'Arblays planned to withdraw their son from Cambridge, even at the cost of the Tancred scholarship. In a letter to Charles, Frances writes that they will spend the winter together in France and by May will be back in England;[68] Alexander's college bills would have to be paid in full and his furniture sold. After further deliberation, Frances decided to travel to France alone, while Alexander returned to Cambridge to begin his second year. In a letter to Hester Maria Thrale, Frances gives a studied account of what was obviously a tense and possibly acrimonious episode: "My Alexander finished . . . his long vacation. His indulgent Father gave him his choice, to continue at Cambridge, or to come over with us, & enter into the Garde du Corps, where M. le Duc de Luxembourg, his Father's *Capitaine*, had already had his name inserted as a supernumerary: but Alex, true to his Mathematical passion, decided to remain. I say nothing of the pang it cost me to leave the poor inexperienced, credulous, & most unworldly youth to himself."[69] Despite, or perhaps *because* of, his mother's absence, Alexander now began to achieve some success in his studies. In December 1814, he won second prize in a college mathematics examination. Frances, to her discredit, responded negatively, writing to Alexander, "I am unwilling to tell you my . . . surprise at hearing of a 2^d place only in the Mathematics."[70] When, much later, she edited her journals and letters for publication, she removed the wounding suggestion that the second prize was discreditable, replacing it with affectionate words of encouragement: "Don't lose courage dear dear Alex, the second place is the nearest to the first. I love you with all my heart!"[71] Alexander would never see this revised sentence, which came to light only when Charlotte Barrett's edition of his mother's journals and letters was first published in 1842, five years after his death.

With his parents now due to remain abroad until their return to England in October 1815, Alexander should have had room to develop as an adult. He had still, though, to contend with a stream of letters from France, many of which reproached him for his failures as a correspondent, and when he did write, his mother not infrequently found fault either with the length of his letter or with its style. On one occasion, he described a visit to Norbury Park and his thoughts on seeing their former family home, Camilla cottage. Rather than thanking him for the account, however, Frances replied, "Your expressions upon its view lose much of their effect by being over strained, re*cherchée*, & *designing* to be pathetic. We never touch others, my dear Alex, where we *study* to shew we are touched ourselves. I beg you, when you write to me, to let your pen paint your thoughts as they *rise*, not as you seek for, or labour to embellish them. I remember you once wrote me a Letter so very fine from Cambridge, that if it had not made me laugh, it would certainly have made me sick."[72] Surprisingly, Frances allowed this admonition to be included in the published edition of her journals and letters without any later revisions.

By the end of his second year at Caius, Alexander had given up any ambition to graduate with distinction. His thoughts on the subject were reported to Frances by Charlotte Barrett, in whom he was wont to confide, not realizing, apparently, that his cousin was among his mother's army of voluntary spies. "I really do not much think," she wrote, that "our dear Alexander will ever plod in the Cambridge way—he is disgusted, very reasonably, with the bad style of mathematics there, & he now tells me that it is too late for him to *read for a high degree*, for he has been so long idle while his opponents were working hard . . . for *distinction* he must look to his future achievements in the world, rather than to these college studies, which he half despises & entirely dislikes."[73] But while Alexander was content to settle for academic mediocrity, blaming the Cambridge system for his shortcomings, his mother remained as ambitious as ever. She was heartened by some good news in the Michaelmas term of Alexander's third year at Caius, when the usually censorious Dr. Chapman sent the d'Arblays a positive report on their son.[74] She was also cheered by a long letter from Alexander in which he wrote of his wish to continue studying with a private tutor. His first choice, George Peacock, who had been made fellow of Trinity in 1814, was unavailable, but he would study mathematics with John Herschel, son of the famous astronomer, who would teach him, as he assured his mother, "quite in the Cambridge manner."[75] Frances, though, knew that Alexander lacked the discipline to put such tuition to good use. As she wrote to her sister Charlotte, "He lives upon his *intentions*! And thus they never become *performances*, & he, ultimately, is as heavily disappointed as myself; & infinitely more surprised than any one at the result."[76]

Disappointments and surprises were frequent during the Lent and Easter terms of 1816, when the d'Arblays, both parents and son, eventually grasped the terms of Alexander's Tancred Studentship in medicine. Gradually it became clear that he could not, as he thought, graduate as a bachelor of arts; the special dispensation that they had always expected would not be forthcoming after all. In March 1816, M. d'Arblay wrote to Alexander that he should, if need be, forfeit the Tancred in order to graduate with a bachelor of arts: he had always been repelled by the idea of his son's holding a medical degree, let alone practicing medicine.[77] For several months more the d'Arblays continued to hope that Senate would pass a special Grace, enabling students such as Alexander to graduate as a bachelor of arts at the Tripos examination before proceeding to a medical degree; they were encouraged in this belief by Dr. Davy, Master of Caius, and the Reverend John Kaye, Master of Christ's and vice-chancellor of the university, both friends and former pupils of Charles Burney Jr. Alexander's college tutor Dr. Chapman had other ideas, however, and in July 1816 he expressed those views unequivocally in a letter to M. d'Arblay. Alexander, he wrote, had now "kept all the terms necessary for the degree of M.B.," and in consequence he could no longer keep his rooms in college. "If there was not," he continued, "that objection to his returning into residence, I should find another strong one in his total inattention to college discipline." The letter concludes with a stinging rebuke: "I have long thought . . . that it has never been his intention to follow the profession attached to his Studentship. If I am right in this opinion, he ought instantly to resign it, as he is sadly abusing a very liberal foundation intended solely to assist in the education of Medical Students. The only way for him now to get out of the difficulty he is placed in, will be for him to remove to some other College, where he may keep the remaining term, & take the B.A. degree next Christmas."[78] Almost three years after his Cambridge matriculation, Alexander would have to change colleges and relinquish his scholarship. Although he had friends at Trinity College and wished to move there, his father favored Christ's, where Dr. Kaye could be a useful ally. In the Michaelmas term of 1816, Alexander was still nominally a student of Caius, but without his rooms in college was now staying with his mother in Bath. This was perhaps the lowest point of a generally undistinguished undergraduate career. In a letter to her ailing husband, Frances paints a sobering portrait of the former idol of the world, now aged twenty-one: "At present, at every contrariety, & every contradiction, he fires into a violence, when he is unguarded, that is revolting; while upon every disappointment, he sinks into a dejection & despondence, without struggle, or resource, as if the World were at an end, & he had nothing left to do but to die. . . . He is, in truth, at this moment, an alternate compound of Apathy & of Enthusiasm—all vehement with energy, or half annihilated with disgust."[79] Dr. Kaye, however, was working on Alexander's behalf, and after protracted negotiations with various college and university authorities he could eventually tell Charles Burney that his nephew would be admitted to Christ's in January 1817.[80] Putting a brave face on the matter, Frances wrote to Dr. Davy at Caius, withdrawing Alexander from the college and justifying this action with a witty allusion to Molière: "So fixed he is, from his nearly exclusive turn to Mathematics, that we cannot take upon ourselves so heavy a responsability [*sic*] with the dead as well as the living, as to make him *le medecin malgré lui*."[81] Frances was evidently pleased with this turn of phrase, using it again in a letter to her old friend Princess Elizabeth, in which she also announced that "he is going to be transferred from Caius to Christ College."[82] Frances habitually referred to Christ's as "Christ Church," confusing it in her journals and letters with the Oxford college that she had visited during the royal tour of August 1786. In writing to the princess, and knowing that her letter would be shown to Queen Charlotte, she was at pains to avoid such errors but still repeatedly and erroneously referred to the college as "Christ" instead of "Christ's."

Alexander was formally admitted to his new college as a pensioner in December 1816. He left Bath for Cambridge a month later, characteristically late, since the Lent term had begun ten days previously.[83] He was not given rooms at the college, but Dr. Kaye found him lodgings in nearby Sidney Street. Kaye took a keen interest in Alexander's welfare, as Frances wrote in a letter to Hester Maria Thrale. Her son, she remarks, has returned to Cambridge: "What will follow, we know not yet—nor whether he will better accommodate himself to College Discipline in his New abode than in the former. Dr. Kaye, the Master, takes him most kindly by the hand with every sort of encouragement."[84]

Against all odds, Alexander actually flourished at Christ's. His tutor, the Reverend Joseph Shaw, was popular with the students and far better disposed toward him than the unbending Dr. Chapman.[85] In March Alexander wrote a letter to Frances, describing in detail his success in a major mathematical examination, an "Act" in Cambridge parlance. He asked his mother to spread word of his success among her friends and family—for which she needed no urging—and even told her how to explain his triumph in layman's terms: "The way to make people understand this is to say that my grand final Examination of the University that I am to be at (always talk big) is not till January—but that there has been a preliminary Exam^{n} in March that I went thro' with great éclat—That's the way, do you see?—Hourray! Hourray!"[86] On the same day he wrote an equally lengthy letter to his father, in which he relishes the thought of Dr. Chapman's astonishment at his success: "[il] sera tout stupéfait en apprenant que je me suis fais bien tiré d'un Examen où il s'attendait à me voir couvert de ridicule."[87] A few days later, Alexander had further good news for his delighted parents: he had achieved similar success in the Opponency examination that followed the Act. They responded jointly in a letter which Mme. d'Arblay began with an exultant couplet:

Hourra! Hourra! vive Hourra!
Vive Alex! vive Charles! vive Louis! vive d'Arblay![88]

Even his uncle Charles Burney, who had lost all faith in Alexander during his wasted years at Caius, was now optimistic, suggesting to Frances that he might graduate as senior wrangler: the name given to the student who was first in his graduating class.[89]

The Easter term at Cambridge, however, brought some setbacks. In April Alexander learned from Dr. Kaye that he could not hold a scholarship at Christ's; they were allocated by county, and there were no vacancies for someone from Surrey, where Alexander was born.[90] Frances, understandably, regretted the strain that this placed on the family's finances and feared that Alexander was resuming his idle ways, in particular wasting time at his beloved game of chess. In May he wrote his father a birthday letter, telling him of his hopes of becoming a fellow of the Royal Society, alongside his brilliant contemporary Charles Babbage. Frances dismissed this as a distraction from his main task, regretting "that New chimæras of *different* Honours—all in Air!—draw you away from the fair & probable success of a regular High Degree."[91]

In the event Frances's anxieties were unjustified, at least as regards Alexander's final examination. During the Long Vacation, he joined a study group led by Edward Jacob at Ilfracombe. Although Jacob was younger than Alexander, he had already graduated as senior wrangler in 1816 and had agreed to coach eight students over the summer at the Devonshire seaside resort. Frances, characteristically, accompanied her son, who unlike his fellows would receive his lessons from Jacob gratis in what she termed "such spare moments as his leisure & friendship can bestow."[92] Well known to readers of Frances d'Arblay's later journals as the site of her near drowning, as she was stranded by an incoming tide, Ilfracombe also played a crucial role in Alexander's education. He spent three full months there, from the beginning of July to early October 1817, and although Jacob had many concerns about his dilatory progress, the coaching eventually paid off. In the final examinations, held in January 1818, Alexander placed tenth out of twenty-eight Wranglers: the equivalent of a good first-class honors degree. In recognition of this accomplishment, he was elected as scholar of Christ's in February and then made fellow of the college in March, at the age of twenty-three. Congratulatory letters poured in, of which the wittiest was one by Alexander's aunt Esther Burney: "We always loved dear Alexander, & have *successively* thought him a pretty *fellow*,—a clever *fellow*,—& a charming *fellow* . . . some times an absent *fellow*—often have we thought it would be difficult to find his *fellow*; and now that he has gotten a *ship* in addition, he will sail before the wind."[93] Unknown to Frances, and to her modern biographers, during the first thirteen months of his fellowship at Christ's, from his election in March 1818 to his ordination as priest in April 1819, Alexander became a favorite victim in the college's Combination Room, where the fellows, then as now, retired to drink after dining in Hall. For social blunders of various kinds, as I have discussed elsewhere, he incurred a record number of fines, all recorded in the college's wonderfully informative Wine-Books.[94] These sums were charged in the form of bottles of wine; fellows were eager to fine hapless newcomers such as Alexander in order to reduce the common expenses. Among his numerous fines was one in October 1818, shortly after his ordination as deacon, "for offering to bet that he will not be fined for the next four days." This bet incurred a fine because the only bets permitted were those in which bottles of wine were wagered: Alexander, characteristically, had failed to specify this. Adding insult to injury, he was promptly fined on both the next day and the fourth day after the wager, ensuring that he had to pay another bottle for losing a bet that he had already been fined for making.

In addition to recording fines, the Wine-Books record the dates of all the bets made between fellows and, where possible, the date of the outcome. One of these, Alexander's only unsettled bet, made in February 1819, is perhaps the most interesting of the series: "that the next time Mr. d'Arblay goes to town he will beat the Automaton." The Automaton, also known as the Mechanical Turk, was a chess-playing device, dressed in Turkish costume; it purported to be a machine but in fact was manipulated by a concealed human operator. That Alexander should have wished to play this formidable contraption, and to bet on his success, is perfectly in character, but because of the exceptional strength of its operators, he would almost certainly have failed to win. In over three hundred games played in 1819–1820, despite always taking the black pieces and conceding a pawn, the Turk lost on only six occasions.[95]

Some of Alexander's other bets point to his reputation for unreliability and sloth. In October 1818 he lost, to two fellows, a bet that he "would rise every day for the next fortnight before seven." In March 1819, he lost a bet that he "will not be at Chapel tomorrow morng." Apparently fancying himself as an athlete, d'Arblay lost a bet, also in March 1819, that he could beat another fellow in a fifty-yard race. A month later, he lost a second bet to the same fellow, this time over a hundred-yard race, and with the odds against him raised to three to one. On both occasions, his adversary "won in a Canter."

Alexandre d'Arblay died in Bath in May 1818, a few months before his son's ordination as deacon. The ceremony took place at Winchester Cathedral, with John Fisher, Bishop of Salisbury, presiding; he was an old friend of Frances d'Arblay from her court years, when he was canon of Windsor. She was not present, but enjoyed recounting the story as told to her by Alexander. She did, however, attend her son's ordination as priest, at St. James's Church, Piccadilly on Easter Sunday 1819, writing a prayer in her diary on the occasion: "I fervently pray to God that my Son may meet this his decided Calling with a disposition & Conduct to Sanction its choice!"[96]

The pious phrase "his decided Calling" makes Alexander sound like a fervent young priest, about to embark on a life of service to the Anglican Church. The reality, however, as Frances d'Arblay well knew, was very different. In a strange, self-addressed memorandum dated June 5, 1818, titled "On the Subject of My Entering Orders," Alexander declares that once ordained as priest he will have no need to enter the church, since his fellowship at Christ's will provide a steady income. The fellowship, he writes, "will be a perfect sinecure, my time and residence being of my own disposal; till I either marry, or take a living, if I should think fit."[97] The document is signed and sealed by Alexander and witnessed by his mother, who thus gave his decision not to seek a clerical position her formal consent. Alexander did eventually become a curate, accepting a position at a new chapel in Camden Town in his thirtieth year, and had several of his sermons printed, but his cavalier disregard for his duties made him subject to repeated complaints by his parishioners.[98] Even the mock obituary that I fabricated for Alexander at the beginning of this essay could scarcely claim that he had succeeded in what was obviously not his calling in life.

In a letter to her brother James, sent a few weeks before Alexander's twenty-first birthday, Frances d'Arblay drew a portrait of the son whom she now termed "my too—too exentric Alex." "He seemed," she wrote, "an Exotic in France, from having been born in England; he seems so also in England, from having been bred in France!—Yet the Amalgamation, could he steady his pursuits, might cause him to figure to advantage, & with approbation, in either Country."[99] Sadly, Alexander was seldom able to steady his pursuits or figure to advantage in either England or France. Many theories about the nature of his malaise have been proposed, none of them altogether persuasive.[100] There was, as his mother lamented, "something *morbid* in his constitution that *paralyzes his character*."[101]

In his later life, Alexander clearly suffered from depression, but it is difficult to determine the source of his ills, and equally difficult to assess the extent of his parents' responsibility. During his childhood and youth in Paris, his mother had already decided that he was incorrigibly absent-minded and undisciplined: that, like the Laputans in Book III of Swift's *Gulliver's Travels*, he could never apply himself to anything without the help of a flapper. And to flap, she believed, was her maternal duty: without such flapping, in her view, Alexander would never have graduated from secondary school, let alone have become tenth wrangler at Cambridge and fellow of Christ's. It is also possible, however, that her flapping and fussing infantilized him. His father was absent in France for many of his formative years, yet he could be overbearing: most notably in enlisting his unwitting son as a French army officer, though Alexander never took up this role. Perhaps what Alexander lacked most was what we today would call tough love: a love, maternal and paternal, that would have helped him to acquire self-reliance, rather than one that seems to have frozen him in a state of perpetual adolescence. His mother's fame seems never to have been a problem for Alexander. What was a problem, and one that he could never overcome, was his parents' conviction that he would acquire fame himself. For one whose natural place was among the idle of the world, it must have been hard to be proclaimed the Idol of the World.

Notes

1. See *The Complete Plays of Frances Burney*, ed. Peter Sabor et al. (London: Pickering and Chatto, 1995), 1:xiii.
2. Frances d'Arblay to James Burney, June 18, 1795, and to Charles Burney, Jr., June 18, 1795, in *The Journals and Letters of Fanny Burney (Madame d'Arblay)*, ed. Joyce Hemlow et al. (Oxford: Clarendon, 1972–1984), 3:116, 121.
3. Frances d'Arblay to Susanna Phillips, February 21–23, 1798, *Journals and Letters*, 4:77.
4. Jane Austen to Cassandra Austen, November 3, 1813, in *Jane Austen's Letters*, ed. Deirdre Le Faye, 4th ed. (Oxford: Oxford University Press, 2011), 260.
5. *Journals and Letters*, 10:482n5.
6. Charlotte Barrett to Frances d'Arblay, November 1815, quoted in Joyce Hemlow, *The History of Fanny Burney* (Oxford: Clarendon, 1958), 387–388.
7. See Peter Sabor, "Creative and Uncreative Gloom: Frances Burney and Alexander d'Arblay," *European Spectator* 11 (2010): 19–41.
8. Samuel Johnson, "*The Rambler* 60," in *The Yale Edition of the Works of Samuel Johnson III*, ed. W. J. Bate and Albrecht B. Strauss (New Haven, CT: Yale University Press, 1969), 320.
9. Frances d'Arblay to Dr. Charles Burney, January 9, 1795, *Journals and Letters*, 3:93.
10. Frances d'Arblay to Dr. Charles Burney, April 27, 1800, *Journals and Letters*, 4:415.
11. Frances d'Arblay to Susanna Phillips, December 1798; Frances d'Arblay to Dr. Charles Burney, March 22, 1800; Frances d'Arblay to Frederica Lock, [late] November 1824, *Journals and Letters*, 4:233, 407n2, 11:569–570n10.
12. Frances d'Arblay to Alexandre d'Arblay, October 27, 1801, *Journals and Letters*, 5:16.

13. Frances d'Arblay to Marianne Waddington, ca. July 27, 1802, *Journals and Letters*, 5:377.
14. Frances d'Arblay to Dr. Charles Burney, March 23, 1803, *Journals and Letters*, 5:433. Kate Chisholm is mistaken in stating that Alexander "arrived in Paris with only a few words of French" (*Fanny Burney: Her Life, 1752–1840* [London: Chatto and Windus, 1998], 208).
15. Frances d'Arblay to Dr. Charles Burney, January 20, 1806, *Journals and Letters*, 6:528.
16. Frances d'Arblay to Alexandre d'Arblay, October 3–4, 1804, *Journals and Letters*, 6:484n2, 485.
17. Frances d'Arblay to Alexandre d'Arblay, October 20, 1804, *Journals and Letters*, 6:509, 510.
18. Frances d'Arblay to Dr. Charles Burney, January 20, 1806, *Journals and Letters*, 6:529.
19. Dr. Charles Burney to Frances d'Arblay, July 30, 1806, Osborn Collection, Beinecke Library, Yale University.
20. Frances d'Arblay to Dr. Charles Burney, October 22, 1806, *Journals and Letters*, 6:547.
21. Frances d'Arblay, Diary for April 23, 1805, *Journals and Letters*, 6:753.
22. Frances d'Arblay to Dr. Charles Burney, 1806, *Journals and Letters*, 6:548–549n8.
23. Ibid., 6:556–557.
24. Ibid., 6:551.
25. Ibid., 6:556.
26. Frances d'Arblay to Marianne Waddington, November 11, 1806, *Journals and Letters*, 6:566.
27. Frances d'Arblay to Alexandre d'Arblay, October 24, 1808, *Journals and Letters*, 6:578.
28. Frances d'Arblay to Frederica Locke, September 16, 1810, *Journals and Letters*, 6:591.
29. Frances d'Arblay to Jean-Baptiste-Gabriel Bazille, July 1810, in *The Additional Journals and Letters of Frances Burney*, ed. Peter Sabor, vol. 2, *1791–1840* (Oxford: Oxford University Press, 2018), 148.
30. Frances d'Arblay, Diary for January 23, 1812, *Journals and Letters*, 6:808–809.

31. Alexander d'Arblay to Alexandre d'Arblay, July 15, 1812, *Journals and Letters*, 6:652.

32. Frances d'Arblay to Alexandre d'Arblay, July 15, 1812, *Journals and Letters*, 6:652.

33. Charlotte Barrett to Marianne Francis, August 24, 1812, Barrett Collection, British Library.

34. Frances d'Arblay to Marianne Waddington, November 19, 1812, *Journals and Letters*, 7:53.

35. Charlotte Barrett to Marianne Francis, August 24, 1812, *Journals and Letters*, 7:21n12.

36. Frances d'Arblay to Dr. Charles Burney, November 2–3, 1812, *Journals and Letters*, 7:40, 41.

37. Alexander d'Arblay to Alexandre d'Arblay, May 19, 1813, Archives Nationales, Paris; see *Additional Journals and Letters*, 2:xxv.

38. Frances d'Arblay to Dr. Charles Burney, November 5, 1812, *Journals and Letters*, 7:47.

39. Frances d'Arblay to Dr. Charles Burney, February 22, 1813, *Journals and Letters*, 7:87n9.

40. Frances d'Arblay to Dr. Charles Burney, January 26, 1813, *Journals and Letters*, 7:76.

41. Frances d'Arblay to Dr. Charles Burney, February 22, 1813, *Journals and Letters*, 7:87, emphasis added.

42. Frances d'Arblay to Queen Charlotte, March 16, 1813, *Journals and Letters*, 7:97–98.

43. Alexander d'Arblay to Alexandre d'Arblay, September 27, 1812, *Journals and Letters*, 7:32.

44. Charles Parr Burney to Frances d'Arblay, October 1813, *Journals and Letters*, 7:40n4, 187n1.

45. Frances d'Arblay to Charles Parr Burney, October 11, 1813, *Additional Journals and Letters*, 2:236–237.

46. Frances d'Arblay to Dr. Charles Burney, October 13, 1813, *Journals and Letters*, 7:198–199.

47. Clement Francis to Frances d'Arblay, December 25, 1813, *Journals and Letters*, 7:225n2.

48. Charlotte Barrett to Frances d'Arblay, January 1, 1814, *Journals and Letters*, 7:221n5.

49. Frances d'Arblay to Charles Burney, *post* January 5, 1814, *Journals and Letters*, 7:226n4.
50. Ibid., 7:225.
51. Alexander d'Arblay to Frances d'Arblay, March 29, 1814, *Journals and Letters*, 7:244–245n2.
52. Frances d'Arblay to Charlotte Broome, April 2, 1814, *Journals and Letters*, 7:264.
53. Frances d'Arblay to Charlotte Broome and Charlotte Barrett, February 16, 1814, *Journals and Letters*, 7:249.
54. Frances d'Arblay to Charles Burney, February 15, 1814, *Journals and Letters*, 7:246.
55. Alexandre d'Arblay to Frances d'Arblay, April 8, 1814; Frances d'Arblay to Alexandre d'Arblay, April 29, 1814, *Journals and Letters*, 7:277, 329.
56. Frances d'Arblay to Alexander d'Arblay, August 28–September 30, 1815, *Journals and Letters*, 8:472.
57. *Journals and Letters*, 7:277n3.
58. Alexandre d'Arblay to Frances d'Arblay, July 3, 1814, *Journals and Letters*, 7:388.
59. Frances d'Arblay to Alexandre d'Arblay, July 8, 1814, *Journals and Letters*, 7:393.
60. Frances d'Arblay to Alexandre d'Arblay, June 9, 1814, *Journals and Letters*, 7:363.
61. Frances d'Arblay to Alexandre d'Arblay, July 13, 1814, *Journals and Letters*, 7:401.
62. Alexander d'Arblay to Alexandre d'Arblay, July 13, 1814, *Journals and Letters*, 7:401n7.
63. Frances d'Arblay to Charles Burney, September 6, 1814, *Journals and Letters*, 7:464.
64. Ibid., 7:465, 464.
65. Frances d'Arblay to Charles Burney, September 19, 1814, *Journals and Letters*, 7:468.
66. Frances d'Arblay to Charles Burney, October 4, 1814; Frances d'Arblay to Marianne Waddington, October 13, 1814, *Journals and Letters*, 7:472, 477.
67. Frances d'Arblay to Charles Burney, October 4, 1814, *Journals and Letters*, 7:472.

68. Frances d'Arblay to Charles Burney, October 14, 1814, *Journals and Letters*, 7:480.

69. Frances d'Arblay to Hester Maria Thrale, February 11, 1815, *Additional Journals and Letters*, 2:249–250.

70. Frances d'Arblay to Alexander d'Arblay, April 26–May 6, 1815, *Journals and Letters*, 8:116.

71. Ibid., 8:116n9.

72. Ibid., 8:114.

73. Charlotte Barrett to Frances d'Arblay, July 8–10, 1815, *Journals and Letters*, 8:542n2.

74. Frances d'Arblay to Charles Burney, Jr., November 22, 1815, *Journals and Letters*, 9:10.

75. Alexander d'Arblay to Frances d'Arblay, November 1–6, 1815, *Journals and Letters*, 9:20n9.

76. Frances Burney to Charlotte Broome, October 23, 1815, *Journals and Letters*, 9:20.

77. Alexandre d'Arblay to Alexander d'Arblay, ca. March 8, 1816, *Journals and Letters*, 9:78–79.

78. Frances d'Arblay to Charles Burney, Jr., July 26, 1816, *Journals and Letters*, 9:171–172.

79. Frances d'Arblay to Alexandre d'Arblay, October 29–November 2, 1816, *Journals and Letters*, 9:267.

80. Frances d'Arblay to Charles Burney, Jr., November 30, 1816, *Journals and Letters*, 9:287n1.

81. Frances d'Arblay to Martin Davy, November 30, 1816, *Journals and Letters*, 9:289–290.

82. Frances d'Arblay to Princess Elizabeth, January 6, 1817, *Journals and Letters*, 9:300.

83. Frances d'Arblay to Charles Burney, Jr., January 20, 1817, *Journals and Letters*, 9:306n6.

84. Frances d'Arblay to Hester Maria Thrale, March 3, 1817, *Additional Journals and Letters*, 2:291.

85. Frances d'Arblay to Alexander d'Arblay, February 21, 1817, *Journals and Letters*, 9:320n4.

86. Alexander d'Arblay to Frances d'Arblay, March 7, 1817, *Journals and Letters*, 9:340–341n14.

87. Alexander d'Arblay to Alexandre d'Arblay, March 7, 1817, Berg Collection, New York Public Library.
88. Frances d'Arblay to Alexander d'Arblay, March 14, 1817, *Journals and Letters*, 9:348.
89. Frances d'Arblay to Charles Burney, Jr., March 16, 1817, *Journals and Letters*, 9:357n6.
90. Alexander d'Arblay to Frances d'Arblay, April 23, 1817, *Journals and Letters*, 9:372n2.
91. Frances d'Arblay to Alexander d'Arblay, May 23, 1817, *Journals and Letters*, 9:408.
92. Frances d'Arblay to Charlotte Broome, May 17, 1817, *Journals and Letters*, 9:403.
93. Esther Burney to Frances d'Arblay, March 16, 1818, *Journals and Letters*, 10:863n56.
94. See Sabor, "Creative and Uncreative Gloom," 28–30, and Anthony Steel, *The Custom of the Room: Early Wine-Books of Christ's College, Cambridge* (Cambridge: Heffer, 1949). The Wine-Books are still housed in the college's Combination Room. I am grateful to the Master and Fellows of Christ's for permitting me to examine them.
95. See Tom Standage, *The Turk: The Life and Times of the Famous Eighteenth-Century Chess-Playing Machine* (New York: Walker, 2002).
96. Frances d'Arblay, Diary for April 11, 1819, *Journals and Letters*, 11:90n2.
97. Alexander d'Arblay, "On the Subject of My Entering Orders," Berg Collection, New York Public Library.
98. Sabor, "Creative and Uncreative Gloom," 38–39.
99. Frances d'Arblay to James Burney, November 22, 1815, *Journals and Letters*, 9:26.
100. Margaret Anne Doody suggests that Alexander "may have been homosexual without quite knowing it"; Claire Harman contends that his "symptoms have similarities to those of a drug or alcohol addiction, specifically opium addiction." See Doody, *Frances Burney: The Life in the Works* (New Brunswick, NJ: Rutgers University Press, 1988), 380, and Harman, *Fanny Burney: A Biography* (London: HarperCollins, 2000), 352.
101. Sabor, "Creative and Uncreative Gloom," 41; Frances Burney to Charles Burney, September 19, 1814, *Journals and Letters*, 7:468.

3
Trying to Set the Record Straight
Alicia LeFanu, Frances Burney D'Arblay, and the Limits of Family Biography

MARILYN FRANCUS

A biography written by a family member lures the reader with the prospect of unknown, private information. More than a standard biography, the family biography entices readers with inside information that will surprise or, at minimum, lead readers to reconsider their notions of the biographical subject. The greater the fame of the biographical subject, the stronger the lure of the family biographer. Both Alicia LeFanu and Frances Burney D'Arblay relied on the attractions of family biography to draw in the reader for a larger purpose: to fix a family legacy—to "fix" in the senses of "to repair" and "to set." By analyzing LeFanu's *Memoirs of the Life and Writings of Mrs. Frances Sheridan* (1824), a biography of her grandmother, and Burney's *Memoirs of Doctor Burney* (1832), a biography of her father, this essay demonstrates the strengths and limitations of family biography as a genre.[1] Burney and LeFanu's respective memoirs shed light on the expectations of authors and readers of biography, and as nineteenth-century works about eighteenth-century figures, they illuminate the complicated intersection between biography and historiography.

Burney and LeFanu faced the challenges that all biographers face: in acquiring and assessing evidence, deciding how to craft a life narrative, and determining which narrative(s) of that life to tell. But their tasks were further complicated in that they were engaged in literary biography and family biography as well. The biographical subject's accomplishments are part of the justification for writing memoirs, and the primary claim to fame for both Charles Burney and Frances Sheridan was their publications. Burney and LeFanu needed to represent those publications (for the reader who may never have heard of them), integrate them into the life narrative, and comment on the value and importance of those publications in compelling ways—all of which is easier said than done. In addition, as family biographers seeking to promote particular family narratives, Burney and LeFanu confronted the delicate task of convincing readers that their vision of family history (which they were clearly implicated in) was the one to be believed. As the works of Burney and LeFanu bring into focus the challenges of writing biography, literary biography, and family biography, it is worth clarifying these issues of genre before analyzing their *Memoirs* in greater detail.

Biography tends to attract questions of form and methodology, as do associated forms of life writing such as autobiography, diaries, memoirs, and, more recently, blogs and tweets. These questions emanate from the hybrid nature of biography, which has characteristics of both history and the novel, and manifests tensions between fact and fiction, documentation and narrative art. As Dee Garrison observes, "The biographer must operate in accordance with strict rules of evidence—measuring the validity of documents, weighing contradictory findings, adding scrupulous footnoting. Yet the techniques of the novelist are also essential. One must shape and order the evidence, deal with flashbacks, develop believable characters, dramatize crucial moments, and analyze human relations—all this without conscious distortion of fact."[2] Given these characteristics, it is not surprising that biographers and scholars of biography—including Burney and LeFanu in their respective *Memoirs*—express concerns about evidence: the lack of evidence, and how to respond to gaps of information; grappling with overwhelming amounts of evidence; assessing the veracity and usefulness of evidence and choosing which evidence to present.

Nor is it surprising that biographers and scholars of biography also muse about narrative: how to capture a life in words, and whether it is possible to do so; whether to follow a chronological sequence or not; how to locate the biographical subject in a variety of contexts (including social, familial, professional); how to balance competing narrative interests; what it means to interpret a life. Although neither Burney nor LeFanu was a professional biographer, they both could draw upon their experience as published novelists in crafting extended narrative. These concerns about evidence and narrative combine, as Garrison suggests, as biographers and scholars of biography wonder about the truth, and whether it can ever be determined, and if so, whether it should revealed. These ethical, literary, and epistemological questions are magnified when the reader and the surviving relatives of the biographical subject are taken into consideration. Perhaps it is appropriate then that there seems to be little scholarly consensus about life writing, other than it is a popular, evolving genre that is product of multiple, difficult variables that can serve a variety of personal and ideological functions.[3]

The *Memoirs* by LeFanu and Burney wrestle with these issues of life writing, along with the more specific concerns of literary biography and family biography. Michael Benton argues that literary biography triangulates the biographer with the biographical subject (the biographee) and the literary output of the biographee—and that knowledge of the biographee's writings is a primary motive for the reader to read the literary biography, and for the biographer to write it.[4] In a sense, the writings of the biographical subject haunt the literary biographer, the reader, and the literary biography itself. For the reader, literary biography often encourages biographical criticism of those writings, even in a postmodern age that has declared the death of the author. For the literary biographer, the biographical subject is embedded in a network of texts that must be represented and analyzed, so among its many other imperatives, the literary biography needs to proffer literary scholarship, if not criticism. If Benton's template of literary biography is correct, a fourth element comes into play when the biographer is also a writer of fiction—for then the literary biography is haunted not only by the literary works of the biographical subject, but by those of the biographer as well. In the case of Burney, her *Memoirs* suggest that the haunting by the biographer's fiction, rather than the biographee's, may have been among her goals.

Both *Memoirs* show Burney and LeFanu struggling with the publications of their subjects. LeFanu provides an extended summary of Frances Sheridan's most famous work, her novel *Memoirs of Miss Sidney Biddulph*, and some information about its reception, but little commentary. LeFanu mentions Sheridan's other publications—and Burney mentions her father's works—but neither provides a substantive discussion of them. (I recognize that I am stretching the category of literary biography here, since Charles Burney primarily wrote music history, not fiction or literary nonfiction. But musical texts and music history are embedded in culture much in the same way that literature is, and require contextualization and analysis similar to that of literary biography.) Burney and LeFanu were established authors before publishing their respective *Memoirs*, and admittedly, that does not necessarily mean that they were critics. Still, one would think that LeFanu, as a novelist and a poet, would have some thoughts about her grandmother's novels and plays. Burney, who was raised in a home frequented by composers, musicians, and singers, had acquired musical taste and knowledge in her youth; moreover, as Charles Burney's amanuensis for *A General History of Music*, she was well positioned to comment on her father's works. So the lack of commentary seems striking given the knowledge of Burney and LeFanu, the expectations of literary biography, and that readers are interested in such biographical subjects because of their writings.

The prerogatives of family biography also define Burney's and LeFanu's *Memoirs*. For the purposes of this essay, I am defining "family biography" as a text written by a family member about another family member (or members), as opposed to a biographer who writes a biography about a family. Paul Reitter describes the many difficulties in crafting the latter sort of family biography in his analysis of Alexander Waugh's *The House of Wittgenstein* (2009), noting that Waugh was criticized for emphasizing the lives of some family members more than others, mischaracterizing family members, and misinterpreting family dynamics within and across generations. Family member biographers are more likely to be criticized on these counts because they are implicated in the biography in ways that a biographer writing about someone else's family is not. The family member biographer's preferences and biases are more evident, and often expected by the reader; there is less of a pretense toward objectivity, and/or less of an ability to maintain a pretense of objectivity.

As Jeremy Popkin, a historian who archived his family's papers, observes,

> Engagement with one's own family and particularly with life writing documents about them—letters, oral interviews, diaries, and autobiographical writings—can never be objective and disinterested. It is always bound to stir up strong reactions and to raise questions about one's own relationship to both the relatives concerned and the materials with which one is confronted. Consciousness of the emotional stakes involved in reading first-person accounts from one's own relatives should also make us aware of the presence of the same issues when we deal with the life writing of authors with whom we have no genealogical connection.[5]

Popkin argues that reading a relative's life writing makes a reader aware of the issues of the genre, and that awareness should be applied to life writing by nonrelatives. I would like to turn Popkin's argument slightly, by suggesting that the status of the family member biographer inevitably inflects the reader's analysis of the biography, whether the reader is a relative or not, and that a reader is more likely to recognize (and question) the family member biographer's choices regarding evidence, analysis, and narrative as self-interested. It is difficult—and perhaps impossible—to read Burney's *Memoirs* without constantly being reminded that she is Charles Burney's daughter. While LeFanu's status as Frances Sheridan's granddaughter is less emphasized in her *Memoirs*, LeFanu's status as a Sheridan comes through loud and clear. As a result, the reader's awareness of the family member biographer draws the reader's attention toward the mechanisms of biography—and to the choices that every biographer, family member or not, makes in the construction of the narrative. Thus family biography makes the methodology of biography apparent.

These formal and methodological concerns about biography, literary biography, and familial biography frame the analysis of Burney's and LeFanu's *Memoirs*, as do the cultural circumstances in which they were writing. Both wrote in the wake of Samuel Johnson's famous biographies and his comments on the genre, which were foundational to the analysis of biography in the eighteenth century and continue to resonate in biography studies today. (Of the contemporary scholars of biography cited in this essay, Johnson is referred to by Michael Benton, Amy Culley, Richard Holmes, Elizabeth Podnieks, Miranda Seymour, and James Walters.) Among Johnson's important contributions to the field is the argument that every life has didactic value, making humanist claims for biography that move beyond the notion that exemplary lives are the only ones worth writing or reading:

> I have often thought that there has rarely passed a life of which a judicious and faithful narrative would not be useful. For, not only every man has, in the mighty mass of the world, great numbers in the same condition with himself, to whom his mistakes and miscarriages, escapes and expedients, would be of immediate and apparent use; but there is such an uniformity in the state of man, considered apart from adventitious and separable decorations and disguises, that there is scarce any possibility of good or ill, but is common to human kind. . . . We

> are all prompted by the same motives, all deceived by the same fallacies, all animated by hope, obstructed by danger, entangled by desire, and seduced by pleasure.[6]

It is consistent, then, that Johnson's biographical method focuses on revealing the character of the subject, rather than providing a list of accomplishments: "[Biographers] imagine themselves writing a life when they exhibit a chronological series of actions or preferments; and so little regard the manners or behaviour of their heroes, that more knowledge may be gained of a man's real character, by a short conversation with one of his servants, than from a formal and studied narrative, begun with his pedigree, and ended with his funeral" (*Rambler* 60, p. 322). As a practitioner of biography, however, Johnson recognized that this was easier said than done. Excavating character is difficult, and Johnson's concerns about biography anticipate those noted above:

> If a life be delayed till interest and envy are at an end, we may hope for impartiality, but must expect little intelligence; for the incidents which give excellence to biography are of a volatile and evanescent kind, such as soon escape the memory, and are rarely transmitted by tradition. . . . If the biographer writes from personal knowledge, and makes haste to gratify the publick curiosity, there is danger lest his interest, his fear, his gratitude, or his tenderness, overpower his fidelity, and tempt him to conceal, if not to invent. There are many who think it an act of piety to hide the faults or failings of their friends, even when they can no longer suffer by their detection; we therefore see whole ranks of characters adorned with uniform panegyrick, and not to be known from one another, but by extrinsick and casual circumstances. . . . If we owe regard to the memory of the dead, there is yet more respect to be paid to knowledge, to virtue, and to truth. (*Rambler* 60, pp. 322–323)

It is not easy to capture a character, even if the biographer knows the biographical subject well; the biographer may have biases regarding the biographical subject that will lead the biographer to conceal the truth or offer panegyric; and information about the subject's character may be lost if a biography is written too long after the subject's death. While James Boswell's wildly successful *Life of Johnson* (1791) fulfilled much of Johnson's agenda for biography, most writers who attempted to follow the Johnsonian prescription for the genre had difficulties doing so, including novelists like Burney and LeFanu.

At the end of the eighteenth century and beginning of the nineteenth, a number of women ventured into biography, as Hester Thrale Piozzi did with her *Anecdotes of the Late Samuel Johnson* (1786). Anna Seward's *Memoirs of the Life of Dr. Darwin* appeared in 1804, followed by works like Elizabeth Benger's *Memoirs of the Late Mrs. Elizabeth Hamilton* (1818) and her *Memoirs of Mr. John Tobin* (1820). Women wrote collective biographies, like Mary Pilkington's *Biography for Girls* (1799) and *Biography for Boys* (1799), Mary Hays's *Female Biography* (1803), and Mary Roberts's *Select Female Biography* (1829). There were personal memoirs, by Mary Robinson (1801) and Mary Ann Radcliffe (1810), and some publications of female correspondence, such as Elizabeth Carter's letters to Catherine Talbot and Mrs. Vesey (1809).[7] But family biography seemed to be a male preserve: the most famous instances include William Godwin's biography of his wife, Mary Wollstonecraft, *Memoirs of the Author of a Vindication of the Rights of Woman* (1798); Montagu Pennington's biography of his aunt, *Memoirs of the Life of Mrs. Elizabeth Carter* (1808); and Henry Austen's 1818 biographical notice of his sister, as a preface to Jane Austen's posthumously published *Northanger Abbey* and *Persuasion*. As men were relied upon to authorize family narrative and sort out family history, Burney and LeFanu were unusual, and unusually positioned, as they entered the field.

LeFanu's *Memoirs of the Life and Writings of Mrs. Frances Sheridan*, published in 1824, attempts to recuperate the literary reputation of her grandmother, the novelist and playwright Frances Sheridan. Burney's three-volume *Memoirs of Doctor Burney*, published in 1832, looks to burnish the status of her father, Charles Burney, the musician, composer, and music historian. In some ways, these works and their context are similar: LeFanu and Burney were both established authors, and members of culturally prominent families. The Sheridans could claim four generations of cultural distinction starting with Thomas Sheridan (1684–1746), the educator and poet who befriended Jonathan Swift, while the Burneys had two generations of musicians and authors.[8] Neither LeFanu nor Burney was a biographer by profession; both were writers of fiction, and as novelists, both had useful experience with extended narrative. Both chose to title their works as "memoirs," with the resonances of memory and recollection—arguably the memoir allows for more digression and analysis than the chronologically bound biographical "Life" that Johnson disliked. Both had access to information that was not available to the public: LeFanu had some family correspondence and the recollections of her mother, Elizabeth Sheridan LeFanu, while Burney had family correspondence, Charles Burney's papers, and his draft of his memoirs. Both were writing as a generation was passing: of Charles Burney's eight children, only Frances, Charlotte, and Sarah Harriet were alive when the *Memoirs* were published in November 1832 (his eldest daughter Esther having died the previous February), and of Frances Sheridan's four children, only Elizabeth was alive in 1824.

But there are significant differences here as well. LeFanu was responding to external forces shaping family history, in the wake of a critical, unauthorized biography and less-than-flattering death notices for her uncle, Richard Brinsley Sheridan, who had died in 1816.[9] Burney had no unsympathetic biographies or notices, nor any scholarly or public criticism of Charles Burney to contend with. These contrasting contexts led to differences in authorial tone and stance in these works: LeFanu was a bit defensive as she set the record straight, overtly taking on the public perception of her family, whereas Burney appeared to be nostalgic as she set the family record. Yet as Janice Farrar Thaddeus argues, Burney was also trying "to set the record straight" (202, 211) by editing family history for public consumption. Burney's concealed corrections of family narrative would not have been discerned by most readers, unlike LeFanu's publicly admitted agenda of amending family history. These variations in authorial stance were reinforced by the status of Burney and LeFanu as professional writers. Burney had been a respected author since the publication of her first novel, *Evelina*, in 1778; while her literary reputation had been on the wane since the publication of *The Wanderer* in 1814, she was still respected despite (or perhaps because) of publishing little since then.[10] Burney was eighty years old when the *Memoirs* were published in 1832. Although she was in the final phases of her career, Burney was confident in her abilities and reputation, with a legacy to protect but with little left to prove. LeFanu, on the other hand, was thirty-three years old and in the midst of her career when she published her *Memoirs* in 1824. She had published poems in 1809 and 1812, and five novels between 1816 and 1823, but in the wake of being dropped by her publisher, LeFanu was still looking to achieve cultural cachet. But the most significant difference was that Burney had had direct access to her subject: she had lived with her father, served as his copyist, and socialized with his friends for years, while LeFanu never met her grandmother, who had died decades before she was born.

Both LeFanu and Burney marketed their *Memoirs* based on the cultural power of their family legacies. The title page of LeFanu's *Memoirs* (figure 3.1) cites her relationship with her grandmother, and LeFanu emphasizes the status of her famous uncle, Richard Brinsley Sheridan, who is named twice on the title page. It is telling that Frances Sheridan is first defined by her status as Richard Brinsley Sheridan's mother, and then as an author—and that both times Richard Brinsley Sheridan's name appears in a larger font than the titles of Frances Sheridan's works. So while the title of the volume is *Memoirs of the Life and Writings of Mrs. Frances Sheridan*, Alicia LeFanu's intention to address Richard Brinsley Sheridan's reputation and the challenge of reviving Frances Sheridan's forgotten literary output seem to be evident right from the beginning. The invocation of familial cultural capital was not unusual for LeFanu: the title page of her first novel, *Strathallan*, states, "by

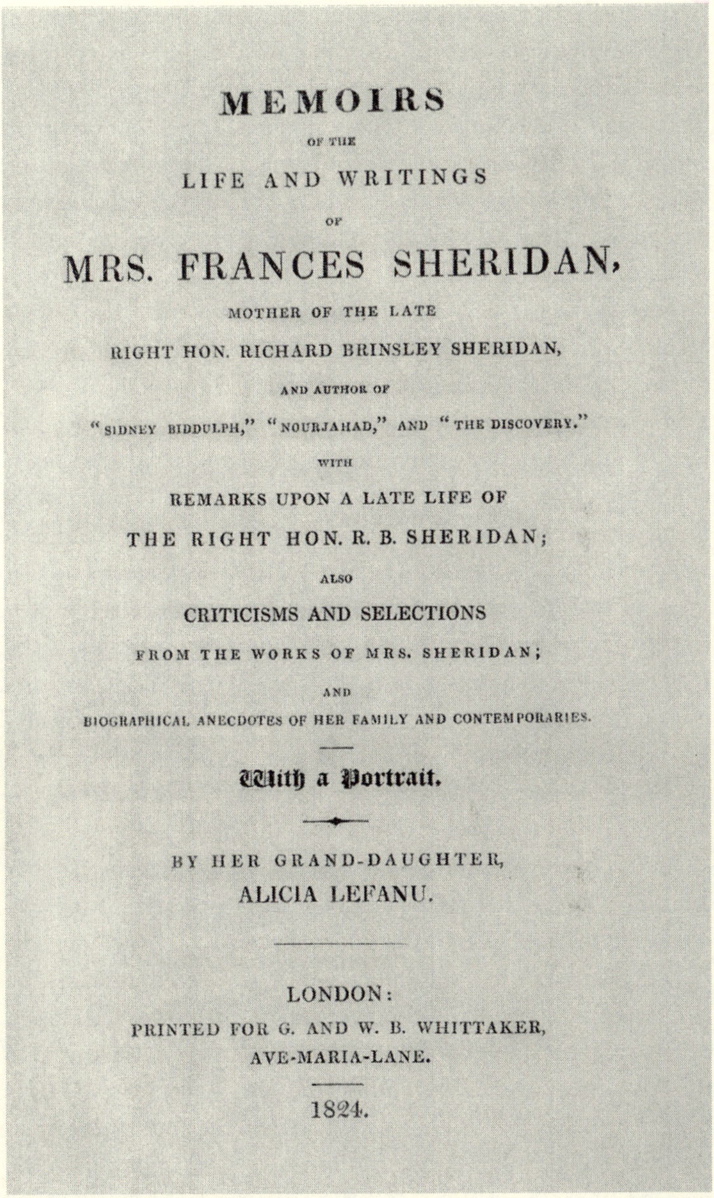

MEMOIRS

OF THE

LIFE AND WRITINGS

OF

MRS. FRANCES SHERIDAN,

MOTHER OF THE LATE

RIGHT HON. RICHARD BRINSLEY SHERIDAN,

AND AUTHOR OF

"SIDNEY BIDDULPH," "NOURJAHAD," AND "THE DISCOVERY."

WITH

REMARKS UPON A LATE LIFE OF

THE RIGHT HON. R. B. SHERIDAN;

ALSO

CRITICISMS AND SELECTIONS

FROM THE WORKS OF MRS. SHERIDAN;

AND

BIOGRAPHICAL ANECDOTES OF HER FAMILY AND CONTEMPORARIES.

With a Portrait.

BY HER GRAND-DAUGHTER,

ALICIA LEFANU.

LONDON:

PRINTED FOR G. AND W. B. WHITTAKER,

AVE-MARIA-LANE.

1824.

FIGURE 3.1. Title page of Alicia LeFanu's *Memoirs of the Life and Writings of Mrs. Frances Sheridan* (1824).

Alicia LeFanu, Grand-daughter to the Late Thomas Sheridan, M.A." Similarly, her poem "Rosara's Chain" was presented as the work of "The Niece to the Right Honourable Richard Brinsley Sheridan."[11] But if, as Anna Fitzer suggests, LeFanu's purpose in composing the *Memoirs* was to identify with her grandmother and write herself into a tradition of female writing, that purpose was overcome by the need to defend the familial accomplishments and honor of the Sheridan men.[12]

Burney did not feel compelled to remind readers of her father's accomplishments on the title page of *Memoirs of Doctor Burney* (figure 3.2)—perhaps because they were still reasonably known, since Charles Burney died eighteen years before the publication of her *Memoirs*, as opposed to the fifty-eight-year span between Frances Sheridan's death and the publication of LeFanu's *Memoirs*. Yet Burney too locates herself in terms of her subject, as Dr. Burney's daughter: "By his daughter, Madame D'Arblay," in a font size that is second only to that of the title. The text of the title page signals the centrality of Burney in this project: it is her arrangement of manuscripts and family papers, her personal recollections, and most importantly, through the epigraph from *Evelina*, her literary legacy that are featured here. LeFanu is advertising her uncle, who jostles against her grandmother for attention. Burney, however, is arguably advertising herself.

Both LeFanu and Burney construct authorial personae as they address the impetus for writing memoirs and their authority regarding their subjects in their opening remarks. LeFanu claims in her preface that she "was encouraged to the undertaking, by the advice and assistance of several intelligent friends; and, principally, by the approbation of the Rev. Dr. SAMUEL PARR:[13] whose regard for the virtues, and admiration of the talents of Mrs. Frances Sheridan, induced him kindly to extend to the Author the great advantage of his valuable observations and corrections, during the progress of the work" (v). LeFanu makes a point of emphasizing the authority of her sources: her mother (vi, 313) and "documents of the most undoubted authenticity" (313). But LeFanu admits that much of the family correspondence is missing, and she resists

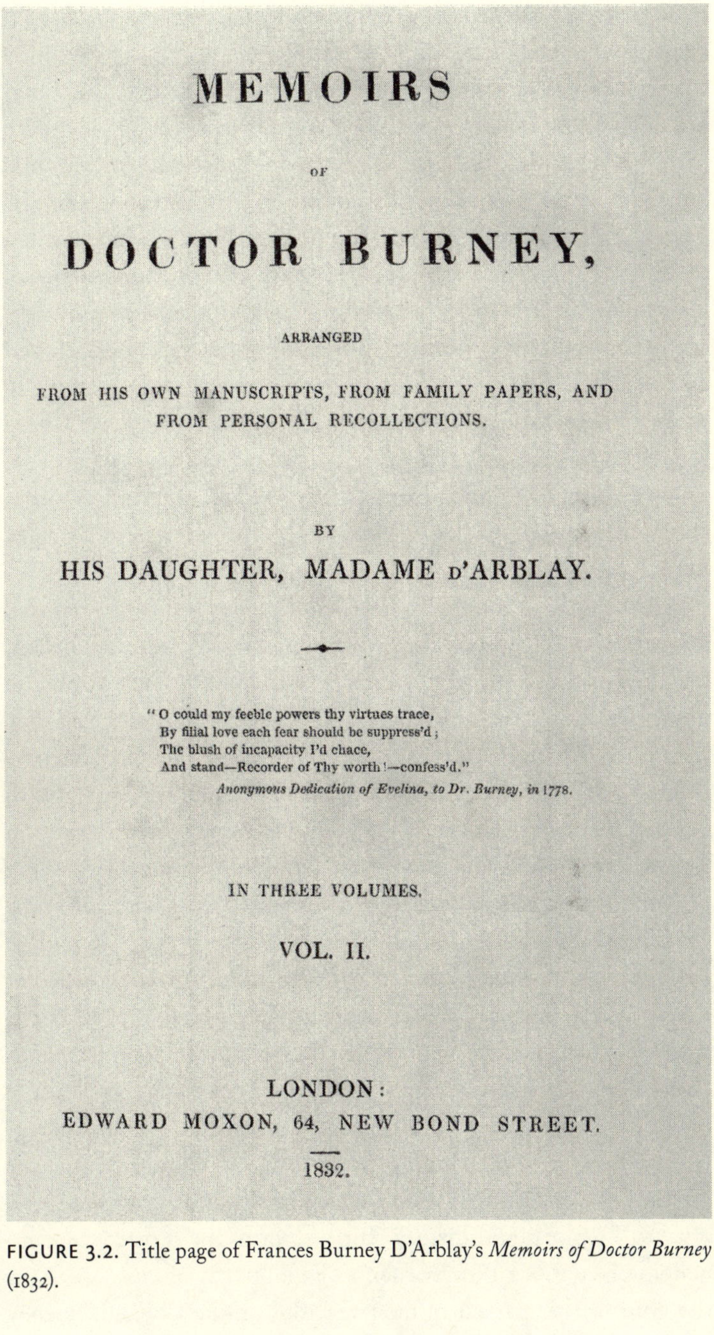

MEMOIRS

OF

DOCTOR BURNEY,

ARRANGED

FROM HIS OWN MANUSCRIPTS, FROM FAMILY PAPERS, AND FROM PERSONAL RECOLLECTIONS.

BY

HIS DAUGHTER, MADAME D'ARBLAY.

"O could my feeble powers thy virtues trace,
By filial love each fear should be suppress'd;
The blush of incapacity I'd chace,
And stand—Recorder of Thy worth!—confess'd."
Anonymous Dedication of Evelina, to Dr. Burney, in 1778.

IN THREE VOLUMES.

VOL. II.

LONDON:
EDWARD MOXON, 64, NEW BOND STREET.

1832.

FIGURE 3.2. Title page of Frances Burney D'Arblay's *Memoirs of Doctor Burney* (1832).

including published family correspondence, because she cannot insure its accuracy (206–207).[14] LeFanu also suggests that family sensibilities—romantic, filial, sentimental—hindered the transmission of information, which complicates her task: "Many more particulars relating to Mrs. Sheridan might have been collected, but that the mention of her name caused with it recollections so painful to her husband, that his children, from a sense of duty, abstained from recalling, by imprudent questions, the memory of his irreparable loss" (377).[15] LeFanu is self-conscious about working from a deficit of information regarding Frances Sheridan and takes care to be honest and forthright about her sources. In doing so, LeFanu reveals some of the processes of biography and the concerns that biographers face (as noted above), in order to cultivate a position of credibility from which she can respond to other texts and sources, particularly those regarding Richard Brinsley Sheridan.

In her preface (titled "Preface, or Apology," with its classical resonances of self-justification), Burney states, "The intentions, or, rather, the directions of Dr. Burney that his Memoirs should be published; and the expectation of his family and friends that they should pass through the hands of his present Editor and Memorialist, have made the task of arranging the ensuing collations with her own personal recollections, appear to her a sacred duty from the year 1814" (1:v). For Burney, this project is authorized by her father (unlike LeFanu, who is encouraged by Dr. Parr, not Frances Sheridan)—and her family expects her to perform it (unlike LeFanu, who seemingly is not laboring under any such expectation).[16] Thus Burney's status as a family member biographer is underscored from the beginning. Burney constructs herself as "Editor" and, tellingly, "Memorialist." As "editor" suggests that the reader will be reading a crafted (and perhaps incomplete) narrative, as Burney selects among documents, "memorialist" invokes monuments, with implications of panegyric, as well as commemoration, memory, and history. The weight of the project seems to lie more heavily on Burney than LeFanu, partly because she is, as she notes in her preface, a mourner. But unlike LeFanu, Burney claims her authority is natural (and seemingly inevitable) because of her familial access: "And the circumstances which render her its recorder, grow out of *the very nature of things*: she possesses all his papers and documents; and, from her earliest youth to his latest decline, not a human being was more confidentially entrusted than herself with the occurrences, the sentiments, and the feelings of his past and passing days" (1:vii, emphasis added). And unlike LeFanu, Burney reveals the challenges of writing biography in her private papers, not publicly: sorting through Charles Burney's voluminous papers was exhausting, and as she wrote to her sister Esther, the materials were not what she had hoped and expected them to be, which complicated the composition of the *Memoirs* considerably.[17]

It is from these positions that LeFanu and Burney try to set the record straight and fix their respective family legacies. For LeFanu, this involved reminding the public of the career of Frances Sheridan—mostly through an extended synopsis of her most famous novel, *Memoirs of Miss Sidney Biddulph*—and taking to task John Watkins, the author of *Memoirs of the Public and Private Life of the Right Honorable Richard Brinsley Sheridan, with a Particular Account of His Family and Connexions* (1817). If readers of literary biography are haunted by the writings of the subject, as Benton suggests, then LeFanu seemed concerned that that was not likely to happen in her grandmother's biography. The eighty-four-page synopsis of *Sidney Biddulph*, which composes nearly a quarter of *The Memoirs*, suggests the extent to which LeFanu thought Frances Sheridan's work had been forgotten. (It may also signal a means to fill the volume when faced with a dearth of biographical material.) Sheridan's other less famous works garner brief mentions, and as noted above, LeFanu does not provide much commentary on any of Sheridan's writings. Instead, LeFanu turns censor, first correcting Watkins about Garrick's liberality in producing Frances Sheridan's play *The Discovery* (111–112), his claims that Sheridan wrote *Nourjahad* during her stay in Windsor (297), and that her comedy, *A Trip to Bath*, was approved by Garrick and Johnson after her death (301). But these corrections are minor compared to

Watkins's errors regarding her grandfather and her uncle, which LeFanu finds everywhere. LeFanu claims that Watkins misrepresents Thomas Sheridan's career by labeling him "an itinerant lecturer and actor" (352), and that Watkins proffers incorrect information about Thomas Sheridan's pupils, lectures, theatrical performances, publications, and his relationship with his sons (318–319, 319–320, 350–351, 359–361). LeFanu also takes Watkins to task for distorting the state of Richard Brinsley Sheridan's finances (339ff., 399–403), misconstruing Richard Brinsley Sheridan's marriage to Elizabeth Linley (397–402; see also 414–419) and misattributing *The School for Scandal* to Frances Sheridan (or a daughter of a Thames Street merchant) rather than Richard Brinsley (404–412). If there is an opportunity to correct Watkins, even on a small detail, LeFanu pursues it, in an effort to amend the public record of her family history.

For Burney, setting the record straight meant characterizing her father as a hardworking, self-made man—sought after by people of talent and rank, and socializing with the best and brightest of his age.[18] Unlike LeFanu, Burney has an excess of information, so Burney does not provide synopses of, or commentaries on, her father's writings; Burney faces different authorial challenges because she has more information than she needs to present Dr. Burney's career in light of his character and cultural milieu. Dr. Burney's professional successes—his writings on his musical tours of France, Italy, and Germany; his doctorate from Oxford (1:213); his *General History of Music*; his work on the Handel commemoration; his election to the Royal Society (1:254) and the Literary Club (2:377); his royal pension (3:368) and nomination to the Institute of France (3:389–392)—all get their due. Burney acknowledges her father's disappointments as well: his failure to be appointed as the master of the king's band twice (1:185–188, 3:71, 75–78), his social gaffes (2:10–13, 2:182–187), and his stymied efforts to build an English conservatory (1:233–244) among them. The list of Dr. Burney's associates is a who's who of the period, featuring Garrick, Goldsmith, Smart, Johnson, Thrale, Reynolds, and Burke, with cameo appearances by Hume, Gibbon, and

Rousseau. She records that members of the royal family enjoyed discussing music with Dr. Burney, particularly the king and the prince of Wales. Dr. Burney's closest friends—like Samuel Crisp, William Bewley, Thomas Twining—were not quite so eminent, but Burney notes whenever possible that the luminaries of the age were interested in them too, as a way to elevate and justify the quality of her father's social circle. Burney's Dr. Burney is a man of feeling, sensitive to his friends' joys and sorrows and, as time goes on, a sincere mourner at their deaths. He's a loving husband and a proud father, particularly of the accomplishments of his second daughter, Frances.

This last point influences the *Memoirs of Doctor Burney* most strongly—Burney's representation of herself and her relationship with her father.[19] Burney witnessed her family history, which distinguishes her *Memoirs* from Alicia LeFanu's; Burney is a character in the narrative, and LeFanu is not. As a result, it is difficult for a reader to avoid subjecting Burney to judgment or questioning Burney's authorial judgment, since she is clearly implicated by the text. The use of Burney's letters in the *Memoirs* heightens this readerly response, for Burney's letters document her career in conjunction with her father's (since they traveled in the same circles), along with her father's responses to her career. Burney starts relying on her letters to fill in the family narrative toward the end of volume 1—to describe the visit of James "Abyssinian" Bruce to their home (1:297–298)—and turns to them frequently thereafter. Burney includes some occasional poems by Dr. Burney and a few excerpts of his correspondence in the first two volumes of the *Memoirs*. But it is not until nearly the middle of volume 3, documenting his years after 1795, that Burney includes significant samples of Dr. Burney's correspondence and journals (3:240ff.). Even at this point in the text, Burney emphasizes her editorial hand, claiming that it was justified by her father: she comments that many of her father's memoranda were filled with "monotonous prolixity of detail" (3:383), and that Dr. Burney sanctioned the destruction of records that he thought would have been boring for a reader (3:420).

The subjectivity of the family member biographer is evident in the imbalanced treatment of accomplishments of Burney's talented siblings as well. James Burney's writings about Captain Cook, Charles Jr.'s status as an eminent classicist, and Sarah Harriet Burney's novels are summarized in three pages (3:409–411), a passing mention in comparison to the narratives of the publication and reception history of *Evelina* (nearly fifty pages of the text), *Cecilia*, and *Camilla*, and Burney's position at court.[20] Burney documents her introduction to the Streatham circle by her father in the *Memoirs*, and frequently notes the people who want to meet Dr. Burney and Frances Burney together—or people who approach Dr. Burney in order to meet his famous daughter.[21]

The reviews of LeFanu's *Memoirs* reflect her efforts to fix the family legacy, but the critical response was perhaps not quite as she expected. LeFanu was looking to reinforce a Sheridan family narrative of talent and cultural capital across generations: LeFanu wanted to elevate the reputation of her grandmother as an important novelist, safeguard the political and literary reputation of her uncle, and achieve some reflected glory for herself. But while reviewers recognized LeFanu's intentions in the *Memoirs*, the hoped-for Frances Sheridan revival did not occur. Reviewers found much to respect in Frances Sheridan's literary career, but generally they were not interested in it. The *Gentleman's Magazine* declared that Sheridan was a "superior authoress" (533), and the *New Annual Register* stated that she was "an able Novelist" "possessed of more than ordinary talent" (10). But LeFanu's eighty-four-page description of *Sidney Biddulph* in the *Memoirs* did not change its reputation. The *Monthly Review* observed, "Altogether, Sidney Biddulph, though not likely to regain her former popularity, or to resist the setting in of so many new tides of taste and new modes of composition as have prevailed since her days, is justly intitled a place in our libraries" (258). The comments in the *Gentleman's Magazine* on Sheridan's blockbuster novel from 1761 were brusque and impatient: "Her Sidney Biddulph is a well-written novel, but of very vexatious operation upon the nerves of readers. . . . The hero is a dupe, the heroine a victim: . . . Both the sufferers are, however, honourable and conscientious people; and it is a real mortification when the unworthy thrive by means of such virtues. Sidney Biddulph is not, therefore, to us a pleasant novel; and though the unpleasant ones may be good medicines, yet who likes taking physic?" (533–534).

The reviewers either briefly mentioned Frances Sheridan's other writings or ignored them, as they turned their attention to the Sheridan men. The *Monthly Review* proclaimed that Frances was primarily remembered as the mother of Richard Brinsley—and that the *Memoirs* failed to provide new information about him: "The name and the promise emphatically given in the title-page awakened some agreeable hopes of new and curious anecdote relative to that highly-gifted genius. We were disappointed" (259). Although the *Monthly Review* expressed frustration that there was not more information on Richard Brinsley Sheridan—"the little in her Memoir that pertains to Mr. Sheridan is its most interesting part" (259)—the last two chapters of the *Memoirs* are devoted to defending the Sheridan men, and this "little" is more than a quarter of the text, from page 311 to page 435.

The *Literary Chronicle*, which commented on all of Frances Sheridan's works, argued that LeFanu was obligated to write the *Memoirs* for the sake of Richard Brinsley Sheridan, articulating the implicit justification for this family biography: "This work as an imperative duty which Miss LeFanu owed, if not to her grandmother, at least to her uncle, to vindicate his character from the misstatements and insinuations of his biographers" (177). The *Gentleman's Magazine* review briefly discussed Frances Sheridan's youth and *Sidney Biddulph*, then focused on Thomas Sheridan's career while noting in passing, "we should have liked to have seen far more of Richard Brinsley Sheridan" (534). The *New Annual Register* summarized the response from the critics: "Wife and mother of two celebrated men, herself possessed of more than ordinary talent, Mrs. Sheridan certainly deserved some record of her memory; though her life, like that of most other women, passed in the same round of domestic duties and with little or nothing of adventure, *is most interesting from its relation with the lives of others*" (10, emphasis added).[22]

If the *Memoirs of the Life and Writings of Mrs. Frances Sheridan* intended to recuperate and elevate her grandmother's literary reputation, LeFanu's text was largely a failure. There was little evidence of Frances Sheridan on the cultural landscape while LeFanu was composing the *Memoirs*—just a few theatrical and juvenile versions of her oriental tale, *Nourjahad*, at the beginning of the nineteenth century—and the *Memoirs* did not generate a Frances Sheridan renaissance.[23] Although the life of Frances Sheridan was, as LeFanu put it, "more interesting than that of most literary women" (1), Frances Sheridan was generally ignored by the literary and scholarly communities until the rise of women's studies in the last quarter of the twentieth century. Even now, LeFanu's 1824 *Memoirs* is still the standard biography for Frances Sheridan, which speaks less to the quality of LeFanu's work than it does to the degree of interest in Frances Sheridan.

At its best, the *Memoirs* reveals some particulars of Frances Sheridan's life and career, and provides a case study of the challenges that women writers faced during the middle of the eighteenth century. Yet the frequent displacement of Frances Sheridan from her biography—as the description of Thomas Sheridan's career takes up swathes of the early part of the text, the extended synopsis of *Sidney Biddulph* much of the middle, and the ongoing defense of Richard Brinsley Sheridan much of the end—suggests that LeFanu had other goals in mind. LeFanu's portrait of Frances Sheridan as domestic, talented, and loyal presents a "proper" Sheridan—one who could mediate the criticisms that accrued so easily around the Sheridan men. In essence, Frances Sheridan's biography provided a platform for LeFanu's defenses of the Sheridan men—defenses that garnered attention but did not settle the debates about the contentious careers and behaviors of her grandfather and uncle. Despite LeFanu's efforts, the Sheridan family record was not fixed in any sense, as the competing biographies of Richard Brinsley Sheridan throughout the nineteenth and twentieth centuries make evident.[24]

Burney's *Memoirs* did not fix her family history either, and Burney's modern biographers have documented the scathing contemporary reaction to her work. The one-paragraph notice in the *Examiner*, while not as (in)famous as the *Quarterly Review*'s twenty-nine-page commentary,[25] sums up the response:

> Three bulky volumes of great names, large words, and small anecdotes. If any one wishes to be carried back to the inanities and pomposities of the Johnsonian epoch, almost bodily, he will do well to peruse the solemn formalities of the once sprightly authoress of Evelina and Cecilia. The literature and the loyalty of the faithful subjects of George III seem to have been equally worthy of a great people. The absurd devotion of the Burneys to the old Court is certainly more disgusting, and only less rational, than their profound and trembling veneration for Dr. Johnson, Barker, and the literary Club in general. The character of old Dr. Burney, the musical Tourist, the amiable busy-body, all vanity, loyalty, and nobility, is most unconsciously depicted by his admiring daughter: but the subject of a parent's likeness, by the hand of devout, though perhaps blundering affection, is something too good to be laughed at. Mad. D'Arblay herself, however, must not expect to escape ridicule for her illustrious obscure [in] style, for her affected overvaluing of all persons that have praised her, and for perpetual egotism, marked as it is by her pretended rejection of the first person. "This memorialist" may talk just as offensively of herself as Counsellor Ego himself, and this is a point which she in him assuredly spares not. (774)[26]

Too long, too mannered, too much Frances, and too out of date. Burney failed to burnish her father's reputation. Her *Memoirs* provided no particular insights into the works of Charles Burney, and proffered an idealized vision of his character that was not particularly compelling.[27] The Literary Club stories of Johnson, Burke, and Thrale, while the subject of Burney's nostalgia, and part of the justification of her father's eminence, were not enough to retain the audience. As one of Burney's biographers, Margaret

Anne Doody, writes, "She [Burney] labored in her biography to produce a father cheerful, generous, and sophisticated—the man she believed he had really always wanted to be" (377). Burney would have been in a better position if she had had a faulty biographer to respond to, like LeFanu, to justify her authorship as a defense of her father. Instead of capturing her father's life and times, and justifying a three-volume memorial to Dr. Burney, Burney seemingly captured herself—and worse, she did not appear as the reviewers wished, as the "sprightly authoress" of *Evelina* and *Cecilia*.

Based on LeFanu and Burney's memoirs, I would like to suggest some of the strengths and limits of family biography as a genre—and in doing so, hopefully illuminate the expectations of readers of biography, and the intersection between biography and historiography. First, consider the relationship of the biographer to his or her subject. Biographers often write, publicly or privately, about their task: the difficulty of recreating an individual, the challenges of locating and assessing evidence, the risks of identifying too much with a subject, the concern that the description of a life shades into justification or celebration. As Popkin suggests, readers do not necessarily read the biographer in the biography, but they should—and Burney's and LeFanu's respective *Memoirs* show that the status of the family biographer shapes the reader's response (as the reviewers' remarks suggest) and highlights the issues regarding an author and his or her biographical subject. The family biographer's bias is anticipated—and seemingly can be forgiven, as in the case of LeFanu—as long as the biographer is not projected into the biography. Readers respected Burney's love and veneration of her father, but they did not want her to overwhelm her father's biography. It is significant that Croker, whose distaste for Burney's works was all too evident in the *Quarterly Review*, made the case that it would have been better if Burney had published her own memoirs, separate from her father's (107, 125).

Readers can read through biases, and they expect to do so in a family biography: that is the trade-off for the inside information that the family biographer is assumed to provide. But the reviewers show that when family biographers do not provide new, confidential information (as LeFanu seemingly did not) or proffer new, less-than-fascinating information (as Burney did), readers become irate and question the family biographer's judgment. It is not enough for LeFanu to correct Watkins's mistakes about Thomas Sheridan and Richard Brinsley Sheridan—and it is not enough for LeFanu to present her grandmother's biography if literary styles have changed, and no one cares about women's history or Frances Sheridan's works any longer. It is not enough for Burney to provide biographical sketches of Charles Burney's famous friends, or descriptions of his social engagements, if readers feel sufficiently informed about Johnson and his circle (which they probably did after Boswell's *Life of Johnson*)—or if no one cares about the singers, composers, or musicians of the late eighteenth century. That Burney's three-volume *Memoirs* were filled with new information that her readers deemed to be less than important—those "small anecdotes"—was a significant deterrent to its critical reception. Every biographer grapples with deciding what to include and exclude in a biography, and every reader of biography has expectations of the contents. But the tension between what a biographer provides and what the reader expects is heightened in the case of the family biographer.

This tension is exacerbated further when the family biographer wants to set the record straight, which involves shaping information to fit into a desired family narrative rather than revealing family narrative. Standards of propriety, social codes, concerns about ego, reputation, and embarrassment, and ongoing familial politics all lead to discretion, obfuscation, and evasion, which shape the family biography to this day, even in light of the current "tell all" sensibility. In the postmodern period, claiming the constructed nature of biography is not surprising, and given Johnson's comments, I doubt that it was particularly surprising in the long eighteenth century either. But the constructed nature of biography may be closer to the surface and more accessible in family biography than in other forms of life writing—especially when the family biographer's agenda of promoting a particular family narrative runs counter to the audience's agenda of discovering family secrets. Biographers pick and choose evidence and develop narratives as much as family biographers do, but the motives for (and signs of) those choices are not always as evident as in the family biography.

Or differently, where the biographer may lack access to information, which can change the narration of a biography, it seems more likely that the family biographer chooses not relay information, stymying the reader's desire. As a result, the agenda of the family biographer becomes evident as some parts of family history are emphasized, others ignored, and some interpreted disingenuously. Both Burney and LeFanu desired to align their family narratives with social expectations of class and gender, and both works reveal the pressures in doing so, particularly in Burney's class-conscious, name-dropping text. Both Burney and LeFanu buried family scandals: Richard Brinsley Sheridan's affairs, Charles Burney Jr.'s thefts from Cambridge Library, and the liaison between James and Sarah Harriet Burney among them. And Burney and LeFanu attempted to conceal or reinterpret less-than-flattering information about family members, including Thomas Sheridan's temper and Charles Burney's obsequiousness. They did so to develop family narratives that focused on multitalented, multigenerational excellence—narratives that generally were not challenged, and that had implications for their careers. For Anna Fitzer, LeFanu's *Memoirs* allow LeFanu to locate herself professionally through the precedent of a female writer in her family; for Janice Farrar Thaddeus, Burney's *Memoirs* reveal her desperate need to explain her career.

It may be possible to understand Burney's authorial choices in the *Memoirs of Doctor Burney* only in light of Burney's journals, letters, and fiction, which can be done now that all three sources are available. Only Burney's fiction was available when the *Memoirs* were published in 1832, and her fiction provided an incomplete frame of reference, as Burney's authorial persona as a writer of fiction ("the sprightly authoress of Evelina and Cecilia") varied widely from her persona as biographer. It is not surprising that the conflation of those authorial personae—admittedly encouraged by

Burney's presence in the *Memoirs*—generated disappointment and frustration. But recognizing those authorial personae as distinct enables a more nuanced understanding of the position of the family biographer vis-à-vis their subject, their craft, and their career. Similarly, to excavate LeFanu's *Memoirs*, a stronger understanding of LeFanu's life, career, and writings is needed to clarify the stakes and ideology of her authorship, and the content of the biography she produced. The family biographer highlights that biographers are not relaying unvarnished truths, but telling a constructed narrative. Biography—and historiography for that matter—is more literary and less factual than perhaps either the audience or authors want to admit.

The critics' responses to Burney and LeFanu's family biographies demonstrate another important point: timeliness. As Johnson noted, writing a biography involves temporal risk. The family biographer runs a risk of writing the biography too soon, and being seen as exploiting the fame of a dead relative. And the family biographer runs a risk of writing a family biography too late, and losing the audience, and the possibility of fixing the family narrative, altogether. Both Burney and LeFanu seem to have written their family biographies too late, as the Georgian period was deemed to be quaint and no longer of interest in the 1820s and 1830s. Neither author could have predicted the circumstances and the timing of composing their family biographies. Nor is there a clear calculus for assessing cultural relevance of a biographical subject at any moment in time, which affects the way that the information in the biography will be perceived and assessed. Given that biographies take years to write (as Burney particularly acknowledges), there is no guarantee that a biography will be relevant years after its inception.

Family biographies highlight the concerns about biography as a genre—concerns about knowledge, truth, accuracy, and authorial agenda—and raise questions about the value of biography for historiography. Neither LeFanu nor Burney was challenged as an authority regarding their biographical subjects, and neither achieved their goals to set the family record straight. Yet as the works of LeFanu and Burney demonstrate, the family biography may be more illuminating than its nonfamilial counterpart because it exposes its methodology, in what it emphasizes and what it ignores, and thereby reveals the frameworks of biography that might otherwise be obscured.

Notes

1. Frances Burney D'Arblay published the *Memoirs* as "Madame D'Arblay," but to avoid the awkward locution of "Burney D'Arblay" I refer to her as "Burney," which follows the scholarly convention when referring to her publications.
2. Qtd. in Jenny Coleman, "Vested Interests: The Con Artist, the Historian, and the Feminist Biographer," *a/b: Autobiographical Studies* 25, no. 1 (2010): 19. Cf. Leon Edel, "Biography: A Manifesto," *Biography* 1, no. 1 (1978), 1–3.
3. See Peter France and William St. Clair, eds., *Mapping Lives: The Uses of Biography* (Oxford: Oxford University Press, 2002), especially Miranda Seymour's essay, "Shaping the Truth," William St. Clair's "The Biographer as Archeologist," and James Walter's "'The Solace of Doubt'? Biographical Methodology after the Short Twentieth Century." See also in the bibliography the studies on biography of David D. Anderson, Michael Benton, Meg Jensen, and Frederick R. Karl. For the status of biography as an academic subject, see Richard Holmes, "The Proper Study?," in France and St. Clair, *Mapping Lives*, 7–18. On life writing in new technology and media, see Elizabeth Podnieks, "Introduction: 'New Biography' for a New Millennium," *a/b: Auto/Biography Studies* 24, no. 1 (Summer 2009): 1–14. For the history of Western biography, see Catherine N. Parke, *Biography: Writing Lives* (New York: Twayne, 1996), chap. 1.
4. Michael Benton, "Literary Biography: The Cinderella Story of Literary Studies," *Journal of Aesthetic Education* 39, no. 3 (2005): 44–57, 51.
5. Jeremy Popkin, "Life Writing in the Family," *a/b: Auto/Biography Studies* 25, no. 2 (2010): 174. See also his comments regarding his interventions with his family archive, and the power of the family biographer: "As I sorted their papers, deciding what to discard, what to

include in the collection of my father's professional papers that he had agreed to donate to UCLA, what to offer to other people—the letters their parents had written to my parents, for example—and what to keep myself, *I significantly transformed these materials.* I can now open a file drawer and pull out dossiers relating to various family members, organized in ways that suit my particular purposes. *In my archive, documents have acquired new relationships to each other that their creators could not have imagined*" (174, emphasis added).

6. Samuel Johnson, *The Rambler*, ed. W. J. Bate and Albrecht Strauss (New Haven, CT: Yale University Press, 1969), 320. The Johnsonian corpus on biography is extensive, and it is beyond the scope of this essay to include all of Johnson's significant remarks on the genre; accordingly, I am using *Rambler* 60 as an archetypal instance of Johnson's opinions on biography.
7. For a survey of scholarship on eighteenth-century women's life writing, see Amy Culley, "Women's Life Writing in the Long 18th Century: A Critical Survey," *Literature Compass* 12, no. 1 (2015): 1–11. Female autobiography was comparatively rare in this period; see Janice Farrar Thaddeus, *Frances Burney: A Literary Life* (New York: St. Martin's, 2000), 189.
8. After Thomas Sheridan (1684–1746), the Sheridan family's cultural eminence continued with his son, Thomas Sheridan (1719?–1788), the actor, stage manager, and elocutionist, and his daughter-in-law, Frances Sheridan (1724–1766), a novelist and playwright—and through their children: Richard Brinsley Sheridan (1751–1816), playwright, stage manager, and British politician; Charles Francis Sheridan (1750–1806), an author of historical and political tracts, and Irish politician; Alicia Sheridan LeFanu (1753–1817), a playwright and Dublin literary hostess; and Elizabeth Sheridan LeFanu, a novelist. Alicia LeFanu (1791–~1844), Elizabeth Sheridan LeFanu's daughter, led the next generation as a poet, novelist, and biographer. The Burneys' cultural capital originated with Charles Burney (1726–1814), a famous musician, composer, and music historian, and continued among his children: Esther Burney (1749–1832) a famed harpsichordist; James Burney (1750–1821), a naval officer and author; Charles Burney Jr. (1757–1817), a classicist and educator; Sarah Harriet Burney (1772–1844), a novelist;

and Frances Burney D'Arblay (1752–1840), a novelist, playwright, diarist, and biographer.

9. The unauthorized biography was John Watkins's *Memoirs of the Public and Private Life of the Right Honorable Richard Brinsley Sheridan, with a Particular Account of His Family and Connexions* (London, 1817). See Jack D. Durant, "*Truth* for Sheridan: A Biographical Dilemma," in *A Fair Day for the Affections*, ed. Jack D. Durant and M. Thomas Hester (Raleigh, NC: Winston Press, 1980) for the mixed notices of Sheridan's death (120–121).
10. Burney's diminished reputation seems to be consistent with cultural stereotypes of aging women in the period. See Devoney Looser, *Women Writers and Old Age in Great Britain, 1750–1850* (Baltimore: Johns Hopkins University Press, 2008) for an analysis of Burney's late career, especially in contrast to Maria Edgeworth's (31–34; 34–41; 49–50). See also Looser's discussion of age, aging, and cognition in the *Memoirs* in her essay, "'Her Later Works Happily Forgotten': Rewriting Frances Burney and Old Age," *Eighteenth-Century Life* 37, no. 3 (2013): 1–28.
11. For evidence of Alicia LeFanu's use of family connections to market her work, see the title page of *Strathallan*; for "Rosara's Chain," see Anna Fitzer, "Relating a Life: Alicia LeFanu's *Memoirs of the Life of Frances Sheridan*," *Women's Writing* 15, no. 1 (2008): 32–54.
12. See Fitzer, "Relating a Life," 32–33.
13. According to the *Oxford Dictionary of National Biography*, Samuel Parr (1747–1825) was a schoolmaster and minister who taught at Harrow. Parr was appointed in November 1766; he knew Richard Brinsley Sheridan, who was enrolled at Harrow in 1762 and left in either 1767 or 1768. See Thomas Moore, *Memoirs of the Life of the Right Honourable Richard Brinsley Sheridan* (London: Longman, 1825), 8–9; W. Fraser Rae, *Sheridan: A Biography* (New York: Henry Holt, 1896), 67–70.
14. LeFanu may be referring to the letters of Frances and Thomas Sheridan that Samuel Whyte published in his *Miscellanea Nova* (Dublin: Robert Marchbank, 1800).
15. Burney makes a similar comment about her father's response to the death of her mother. See *Memoirs*, 1:150. Burney devoted considerable time to her parents' marital narrative in the *Memoirs*—one of the many

instances of authorial preference shaping familial narrative. Burney hated her stepmother, who gets short shrift in *The Memoirs* despite the fact that Elizabeth Allen and Charles Burney were married contently for twenty-nine years. See Marilyn Francus, *Monstrous Motherhood: 18th-Century Culture and the Ideology of Domesticity* (Baltimore: Johns Hopkins University Press, 2012), 162–166.

16. See Burney's letter to her sister Esther (November 25, 1820) in Frances Burney, *Journals and Letters*, ed. and introd. Peter Sabor and Lars Troide (New York: Penguin, 2001), 546–547. Cf. Kate Chisholm, *Fanny Burney: Her Life* (London: Chatto and Windus, 1998), 272.
17. See letter to Esther Burney (November 25, 1820), *Journals and Letters*, 548–549.
18. This characterization of Dr. Burney is emphasized to the end, in his epitaph cited on the last page: "The pride of his family; the delight of society; the unrivalled and chief and scientific historian of his tuneful art, beloved, revered, regretted, in his 87th year, April 12th, 1814, breathed, in Chelsea College, his last sigh: leaving to posterity a fame unblemished, built on the noble fabric of self-acquired accomplishments, high principles, and pure benevolence; goodness with talents; gaiety with taste, were of his gifted mind the blended attributes: while the genial hilarity of his airy spirits, flowing from a conscience without reproach, prepared, through the whole tenor of his earthly life, with the mediation of our blessed Saviour, his soul for Heaven" (*Memoirs of Doctor Burney*, 3:436).
19. As Ulph writes, "[The] *Memoirs of Doctor Burney* is nevertheless a significant articulation of Burney's fraught relationship not merely with her father, but also with the cultural and professional implications of being Dr. Burney's daughter. *Memoirs* should thus be understood as a careful staging of that inheritance" (152–153). See also 162, 165. See Cassandra Ulph, "Authoring the 'Author of My Being' in *Memoirs of Doctor Burney*," *Eighteenth-Century Life* 42, no. 2 (2018): 152–169.
20. James's assignment to work with Captain Cook is mentioned earlier in *Memoirs* (1:269–271), but his writings are not commented upon. For the publication and reception history of *Evelina*, see *Memoirs*, 2:121–171; for *Cecilia*, see 2:216–218, 240–241; for *Camilla*, 3:205–207, 210–211, 214–219;

and for her position at court, 3:80–84, 89, 93–96, 102, 107–108, 110–113, 126, 128. Cf. Thaddeus, *Frances Burney*, 195.

21. See Burney's comments on Dr. Burney's friendship with Burke, *Memoirs*, 2:219, which shift to Burke's desire to meet Frances, 2:220–238, and Burke's lovely note to Burney once he reads *Cecilia* (2:240). Burney suggests that Burke arranges the Chelsea College organist position for Dr. Burney partly out of respect to Frances (2:373–376). Cf. Duc of Liancourt, and somewhat differently, Brissot de Warville, approaching Dr. Burney because they want to meet Frances (2:333, 334–335). See also Burney's comments on mutual invitations for herself and her father to socialize with the bluestockings (2:263, 278), Soames Jenyns (2:288), and Madame de Genlis (3:41, 61).
22. See Marilyn Francus, "Shaping a Legacy: Alicia LeFanu's *Memoirs of the Life and Writings of Mrs. Frances Sheridan*," *Female Spectator* 17, no. 1 (2013): 6–7.
23. Frances Sheridan had a niche in literary and cultural history by the end of the eighteenth century, as her name appeared in a number of biographical dictionaries, including *A New and General Biographical Dictionary* (1798) and Mary Hays's *Female Biography* (1803). (In *A New and General Biographical Dictionary* [1795], the biographical information about Frances Sheridan was nested in the entry for Thomas Sheridan.) Sheridan's play, *The Discovery*, was printed in some theatrical anthologies at the end of the eighteenth century, and James Harrison included *Sidney Biddulph* and *Nourjahad* in his anthology, *The Novelist's Magazine* (1789), but her works generally did not appear in the canon-forming anthologies of the early nineteenth century.
24. For biographies of Richard Brinsley Sheridan, see in the bibliography those by Thomas Moore, Margaret Oliphant, W. Fraser Rae, Walter Sichel, and Fintan O'Toole. Some see Sheridan as a much-maligned politician, others as a conniver and profligate. For a different reading of Sheridan family history, see Conrad Brunström, *Thomas Sheridan's Career and Influence: An Actor in Earnest* (Lewisburg, PA: Bucknell University Press, 2011).
25. John Wilson Croker, who savagely attacked Burney's fourth novel *The Wanderer*, wrote a vicious review of *The Memoirs* in the *Quarterly Review* in April 1833. For a summary of Croker's review, and the

responses to *The Memoirs*, see Looser, "'Her Later Works Happily Forgotten.'" The narrative of Croker's reviews of *The Wanderer* and *Memoirs* appears in all the major biographies of Burney.

26. "Counsellor Ego" refers to Thomas Erskine, first Baron Erskine (1750–1823). According to the *Oxford Dictionary of National Biography*, after Erskine "chaired a second meeting of the society [the Friends to the Liberty of the Press], on 19 January [1793], he was parodied in print as 'Counsellor Ego,' who admitted he was 'nervously diffident,' and wished 'for every man's approbation.'"

27. Charles Burney's modern biographer, Roger Lonsdale, declared that Burney's text was so fantastic and problematic that "the *Memoirs of Dr. Burney* can indeed be taken as Fanny's last novel" (447). For a discussion of Burney's errors and misrepresentations in the *Memoirs*, see Roger Lonsdale, *Dr. Charles Burney: A Literary Biography* (Oxford: Clarendon, 1965), 438–455. Cf. Miriam Benkovitz, "Dr. Burney's Memoirs," *Review of English Studies* 10, no. 39 (1959): 257–268, and Ulph, "Authoring the 'Author of My Being,'" 153. The problems of Lonsdale's account of Charles Burney are the subject of Todd Gilman's essay in this collection.

4
The Life of Isabelle de Charrière
"Written by Herself"

VICTORIA WARREN

In 2001, the coauthors of a book about autobiography noted, "Life narrative is indeed a moving target of ever-changing practices without absolute rules"; the authors defined "life narrative" as a subset of "life writing," both of which were differentiated from formalized autobiography and biography.[1] Today we see life writing as the umbrella term for all of the above. My work here argues that life writing includes spontaneously written letters, originally private, as well as other pieces of writing. Furthermore, the English-speaking world needs to study more fully the life written in another language. Isabelle de Charrière or Belle de Zuylen (1740–1805) was an international writer. Born Isabella Agneta van Tuyll van Serooskerken to Dutch parents, she moved from their home (ancestral castle Zuylen and city-house in nearby Utrecht) to Switzerland in 1771. She traveled in England in 1767; she lived in France for almost two years in the 1780s. Her written work—nearly all originally in French[2]—includes a self-portrait, novels, essays, plays, and music. She was also a prolific letter writer. Over twenty-five hundred of her letters are extant. Charrière did not leave behind a full-length autobiographical text, but she wrote her life in letters and other works. They provide a record of life events and ideas; her interaction with major Enlightenment thinkers; her thoughts regarding international politics, the law, and the French Revolution; and her progressive ideas on education, gender, and cultural mores. Her life writing is valuable, then, as a record of her remarkable individual life and as a cultural, political, and intellectual history of the period in which she lived.

The earliest evidence of Charrière's life writing is contained in two recently discovered letters that she wrote in 1756 at age sixteen. In these letters to the Comte de Dönhoff, she tells him that she had fallen in love with him when she first met him at her aunt's two years earlier, but that she had fought against it. Unusually aware for a nobly born teenage Dutch Protestant girl of the era, she knew of his sexual affairs; her good sense told her that she would be merely one of his many conquests. She says she was ashamed of herself "for loving a man . . . unworthy to be loved, and who made it almost his sole study, his only occupation to make love to all women."[3] Despite her eighteen-month absence from Utrecht, she was unable to dispel her attraction to him; but upon returning she rejected his advances. In a remarkable letter, she writes,

> My choice could flatter the most proud man, my tenderness would have satisfied the most . . . tender person; but all of it falls on a man who is insensible to the prize, who is unworthy of it because of his inconstancy, and his libertinage. . . . If it is true that you love me at present as you say, it is a love that scarcely merits the name. . . . You are too accustomed to change the object to fix on me. Also, don't think that I am flattered by your attentions. I, whom Nature and education have made above most of my sex, I who believe I merit the homage of the most indomitable soul, . . . would I be content with the leftovers of your heart? If reason and pride have little empire over my sentiments, they will have absolute control over my actions. . . . Adieu D[önhoff], may my love soon be nothing more than a thought after waking. (Letters to Dönhoff, my translation)

These two letters are important records of Charrière's early life as Belle de Zuylen, and they also provide insight into the kind of frankness and practical reasoning that would characterize Charrière throughout her life. They also look forward to the self-portrait's image of herself. There she attempts an honest assessment of herself, without false modesty.

Her writing is an assertion of self; her defiance of convention is practical. These early life writings establish her voice. In 1762, when she was twenty-two, Belle de Zuylen published her first fictional piece, *The Nobleman* (*Le Noble*), which tells the story of Julie, who, like the author, is a baron's daughter. Julie exhibits little respect for her noble heritage. When she climbs out of her window to elope, she throws down her family's ancestral portraits to provide a solid landing place in the mud.[4] The van Tuyll family, embarrassed by their daughter's satire of the nobility, suppressed the work. In 1763, she wrote a self-description, "Portrait of Mlle de Z[uylen] under the name of Zélide, written by herself."[5] The concise and insightful piece was not printed during her lifetime, but it circulated widely in manuscripts and caused considerable comment. It fascinated contemporary readers but was criticized as egotistical and improper for a woman to have written. One journalist sneered that she aimed to "pass for a *savante*," and another critic accused her of attempting to "soar above her sex."[6] At a young age, the well-educated and witty Belle de Zuylen sought to carve a place for herself in the public world of ideas.

Calling herself Zélide, she wrote this self-portrait (character analysis) in the third person. She begins, "Zélide is good only on principle"; it is an "effort," she says, to be "sweet and amenable, and causes her the agony of a martyr." Her vanity, she tells us, is "unbounded." She sees herself as "too sensitive to be happy and has almost stopped seeking happiness; she seeks goodness, but flees regret and looks for amusement. Pleasures for her are rare, but they are intense." She concludes the portrait's main section, "With less sensitivity, Zélide would have had the soul of a great man; with less intellect and reason, she would have been only a weak woman" (*OC*, 10:36–39). Akin to the long-eighteenth-century genre of brief written "characters," her *Portrait* was unusual in its author's incisive analysis and choice of subject—herself.

The self-portrait marks an early step in the process of self-definition in Charrière's life—both as she lived it and in her life writing. Experience may have modulated some of her sharp categorizations, but it would never change her assertion of her own voice. In 1760 she began a fifteen-year correspondence with David-Louis Constant d'Hermenches, a Swiss (and French Protestant) married military officer serving the Dutch when they initially met. Eighteen years her senior, he had a womanizing reputation, but their relationship was not physical. In fact, they seldom saw each other. Her letters give us a record of her thoughts and life events over a significant period. It is as if she kept a journal, but instead she addresses d'Hermenches; we get his responses to her observations, as well as her comments and replies to his questions. It is a remarkable correspondence, reflecting what its editors call "two minds of extraordinary vigor and scope" and engaging with life, philosophical ideas, feelings, relationships, history, literature.[7] She had read widely in classic French literature, in addition to Dutch and English publications. In an August 7, 1762, letter, d'Hermenches said she wrote better than anyone he knew, "not excepting Voltaire" (7). A month later, she wrote to him in a vein similar to that in her self-portrait: "When I am amused I say almost at random whatever comes into my head. . . . People say that I disdain all ordinary conversation, and that I think my intellect is superior" (*d'Hermenches*, 12). She added, people think it wrong that "I want to know more than most women," but, she said, "[I have no] life except by continual occupation of my mind." In September 1764, she wrote that what she found most rewarding was always "to be learning"; she voiced "an ardent desire for growth, for knowledge" (*d'Hermenches*, 183–184). Earlier that year, in July, she sketches this portrait of herself: "[You likely saw] that I knew how to reason soundly, but you don't know whether I act reasonably." She says she admires virtue and reason, but admits she does not always manage to act accordingly. Here she makes a striking statement: "If I had neither a father nor a mother I would be a Ninon, perhaps."[8]

But, she says, she does not want to make her parents miserable, so she will not be a Ninon. She characterizes her personality's facets: "Sometimes a musician, sometimes a geometer [she chose to study mathematics], sometimes a self-styled poet, now a frivolous woman, now a passionate woman, then a cool and tranquil philosopher" (*d'Hermenches*, 88–90).

On January 10, 1764, she wrote to d'Hermenches, "I have no system—all that systems do, I think, is lead one methodically astray" (48). This declaration would be in keeping with her later disillusionment with the French Revolution and her critique of Immanuel Kant's categorical imperative and other rigid moral systems. In this same letter, she noted, "my parents love me, and they are used to seeing me sometimes slip the shackles of custom" (49); and later that year she wrote, "Here one is vivacious all alone" (November 3–6; *d'Hermenches*, 210). But she was also practical. As she wrote to d'Hermenches on July 28, 1764, "What makes me and my mind such great friends is its excellence for everyday use" (97). Twenty-eight years later, she advised Benjamin Constant, who was floundering in gloomy abstractions, to follow Candide's advice at the end of Voltaire's novel, "*il faut cultiver notre jardin*" (May 13, 1792; *OC*, 3:362). On July 3, 1797, she wrote to her longtime friend Caroline de Sandoz-Rollin that philosophy should not remain an abstraction; it has to be applied to individuals: "If I go astray . . . at least I am walking with my feet on the ground rather than high up in the clouds" (*OC*, 5:331).

Along with Charrière's rich life of the mind, then, the life writing also shows the seamless interplay between her deeper philosophical thinking and the way philosophy for her was inseparable from daily living, including the ordinary fare of human existence. Her letters reveal her intellectual reading and analyzing; she also describes her life's events and the people she meets—sometimes they happen to be famous male figures. This April 22–26 letter from London in 1767 contains a delightful description of a dinner with David Hume: "What do you think we talked about? Roast beef and plum pudding! But we talked much less than we ate. . . . The roast chicken came before we had taken our leave of the pudding; it was set next to the fire to await us. A little dog came along, went straight to the chicken, and would undoubtedly have carried it off if David Hume had not gently held it back. . . . I very much liked Mr. Hume's attentiveness, and his honest and straightforward manners" (*d'Hermenches*, 361). She depicts philosopher Hume as down to earth; we also see her own ease in his presence.

The letters to d'Hermenches constitute the largest collection of Charrière's letters to a single correspondent, and her early letters reveal much about her as a young woman struggling with convention and the restrictions of gender. D'Hermenches urged her to visit his friend Voltaire, writing to her March 23, 1772: "You absolutely must come see him [at Voltaire's home in Ferney, France]; he is worthy of listening to you, and you are infinitely worthy of talking to him, for I always return to the fact that I know no one who has more wit than you—no one whose wit is more agreeable, more natural, nor of a sounder judgment" (*d'Hermenches*, 499). She replied on April 23, 1772, declining a visit and giving her opinion of Voltaire: "He's a malicious man with a great deal of wit. I will read him, but I will not go to worship him" (501–502). On November 17, she wrote to her husband's cousin's wife, Catherine de Charrière de Sévery, providing a fuller description of her impression of Voltaire's writing. She had been reading his *Questions sur l'encyclopédie*, she notes, and although she reads some articles "with pleasure," others, she says, "make me throw the book with impatience" (*OC*, 2:289).

Charrière's opinion of Rousseau was more favorable. She referred to his works often in her letters to d'Hermenches and seems to have read most of them at a young age. Later, although she acknowledged Rousseau's faults, she wrote several essays defending him against his critics, including a defense of his illiterate mistress Thérèse Levasseur, and in 1790 she wrote her *Éloge de [In Praise of] Jean-Jacques Rousseau* (*OC*, 10:199–211). Despite Charrière's gender as a woman in a largely male intellectual world, she writes a place for herself there (both publicly and privately) through her life writing and in her life itself.

The correspondence with d'Hermenches continued until 1776 and is a rich source of Charrière's life writing. As he told her in his July 29, 1764, letter, "It's a delight for me to follow all that your vivid and subtle imagination prompts in you about our conversations [letters], and I am more amazed each day to see that even in trifles, as well as in the most serious things, you are always guided by an exquisite good sense" (98). During the years that they corresponded, particularly before her marriage, she wrote to him without restraint, without self-consciousness, and without a concern for the conventionally proper.[9]

Letters to other correspondents also illuminate her life as she wrote it. In August 1763 James Boswell arrived in Utrecht to study law. He would become known as the great biographer of Samuel Johnson in England, but Charrière's letters reveal another side of Boswell—and underscore her assertion of self in life writing and in living a life "written by herself." Although he was shocked at what he called her "unlimited vivacity" (*Boswell*, 295), he found Belle de Zuylen intriguing. She mentions Boswell in a letter, February 25–March 5, 1764: "When I go out to some gathering, I chat and play with a young Scot who is sensible, intelligent, and ingenuous. The others don't suit me at all" (*d'Hermenches*, 61). Before Boswell's departure in June 1764, they began a four-year correspondence. But unlike d'Hermenches, who enjoyed the intellectual aspects of his correspondent and her refreshing comments on society's mores, Boswell was afraid of her unconventional writing. He was also troubled by her intellect, even as he was attracted to it. He wrote to his friend William Johnson Temple, "She is much my superior. One does not like that" (April 17, 1764; *Boswell*, 227).

Boswell was prudent and preachy in his letters to her. Belle de Zuylen was spirited and defiant, with a quicksilver wit. She was frank with him, but he apparently was too afraid of impropriety in a woman to appreciate her frankness. He accused her of licentiousness, but what she had said was outspoken—not "licentious." She explained to him on June 14–15, 1764, that a cold husband did not induce faithfulness in a wife, and yet he had advised her to select a cold husband. She said she would tell her husband, "If you wish me to love you always, the only way is to be always lovable" (*Boswell*, 299–300). Most unnerving for Boswell was her comment that if she did not have parents, she would never marry but would raise her children well and use her money beneficently. However, she added that she would not follow this course because she did not want to make her parents "miserable" (*Boswell*, 299–300). This was similar to her Ninon comment to d'Hermenches a month later. Boswell was also distressed by her theory of a good husband-wife relationship: "I should be well pleased with a husband who would take me as his mistress," she wrote, because then she would provide everything for him, and he would not be faithful only as "duty" (*Boswell*, 300). Boswell's agitated response to what he calls her "libertine sentiments" is contained in his letter of July 9, 1764, where he urges prudence and "reason": "Whatever men may do, a woman without virtue is terrible" (313). Either he misunderstood her meaning, or he was shocked that she would think of a wife in the same role as a mistress—sexual partner—and that she would articulate that thought.

Boswell was alarmed when Belle de Zuylen indicated her religious doubts. On June 18–19, 1764, she told him of her doubts regarding Revelation: "I am incapable of forcing my mind to believe what it does not understand" (*Boswell*, 307). Although she said in this letter that she kept her thoughts to herself because she felt it would be a "crime to destroy the belief of others when I can replace it only by an anxious doubt," Boswell was shocked. He wrote her a letter expressing his horror at her doubts: "Let Prudence be thy counsellor," he said pompously. "Pray make a firm resolution never to think of metaphysics. Speculations of that kind are absurd in a man, but in a woman are more absurd than I choose to express" (July 9, 1764; *Boswell*, 310–311). Clearly, he was wedded to the gendered double standard, even in thought. Perhaps Boswell was particularly distressed at her comments because he struggled with his own religious doubts and his penchant for sexual liaisons. At Utrecht and his further Continental trip, he wrote himself personal memos to be "retenue"—to improve his own behavioral self-control (e.g., avoid laughing inordinately) and retain his dignity (*Boswell* e.g., 40, 49, 147, 197).[10] Charrière was frank with Boswell, she said, because he was prudent and discreet—a Cato, she called him (*Boswell*, 298–300). In her June 18, 1764, letter she says that her previous letter, which had so alarmed him, was "an act of frankness, . . . the diary of the heart of a live and feeling woman" (*Boswell*, 303). It must have been difficult for spirited Belle de Zuylen, dealing with sober yet vacillating Boswell. She wrote to him on February 16, 1768, that "a strictly sensible person who read our letters would perhaps not find you too rational" (*Boswell*, 368).

Despite his fears, Boswell wrote to Belle's father on January 16, 1766, stating that he would like to marry her, but "her faults filled me with alarm." He would marry her, he said, only if she signed an oath in the presence of her father and two brothers, making four important concessions: (1) that she would be faithful, (2) that she would never see or correspond with anyone of whom he or her male relatives disapproved, (3) that she would never publish any works they disapproved of, and (4) that she would never speak against the religion or customs in whatever country she lived (*Boswell*, 346). He wanted her to sign away her independence in every area. In 1768 Boswell wrote to her proposing that he visit her and make plans to marry. He wrote to Temple on March 24, 1768, "I must have her. She is so sensible, so accomplished, . . . that I do not see how I can be unhappy with her" (*Boswell*, 373). To protect himself, Boswell included in his 1768 letter to her a criticism of her behavior, laying down the law concerning what he regarded as proper conduct. On April 26, he told Temple that he had "put in the plainest light what conduct I absolutely require of her" (*Boswell*, 373). Responding to his arrogance, she wrote—in what Boswell called an "acid epistle" (May 14, 1768; *Boswell*, 374)—that she would *never* marry him, and the matter ended, as did the correspondence and friendship.

Given Belle de Zuylen's portrait of herself as independent in mind and spirit, one can see why she would be outraged at Boswell's attempts to restrict her freedom. She had many suitors, but seemed to be in no hurry to marry. She wrote to Boswell on February 16, 1768: "I have fortune enough so that I do not need a husband's; I have a sufficiently happy cast of mind and enough mental resources to be able to dispense with a husband, with a family, and what is called an establishment. I therefore make no vows, I take no resolutions; I let the days come and go, deciding always for the better among the things which Fate presents to me with some power of choice" (*Boswell*, 369). Four years earlier when he expressed doubts, she replied, "You are very right to say that I should be worth nothing as your wife. We are entirely in agreement on that head. I have no subaltern talents" (June 18–19, 1764; *Boswell*, 305). Such words of hers, in addition to their message to Boswell, perhaps best define her rejection of the conventional role of women. She writes her life with the self-definition of herself as a woman among male equals.

On February 17, 1771, when she was thirty, she surprised her friends by marrying her brothers' tutor, Charles-Emmanuel de Charrière, a member of the minor Swiss nobility. Some of her friends were appalled that the "dazzling" Belle would marry an unassuming scholar, and later critics have considered various possible reasons.[11] If we look at her own words, however, we find the most reasonable explanation. She was in love with Charles de Charrière. In his unassuming way, he may have been a lot more "lovable" than Boswell or the many men of the world who were her usual suitors ("épouseurs," she called them sardonically). And she knew him well, his intelligence and his integrity: they had been friends for seven years, courting for two of those years before they married. She wrote to d'Hermenches of Charles de Charrière on January 11, 1771, "He loves me without illusion, without infatuation; he is sincere and just; . . . I love him, and I cannot resolve to live without him. When I judge him without illusion or infatuation or ardor or rapture, I still find there is no one superior to him in character or intelligence or temperament. How could one give up such a man!" (485). A few days later, when she was officially engaged, she wrote, "I will live in a pleasant country [Switzerland], I will live with a man I love and who deserves my love; I will be as free as an honest woman can be. I will retain my friends, my correspondences, the freedom to speak and to write" (*d'Hermenches*, 486). Charles de Charrière did not restrict her freedom. Most of her published works were written after their marriage, and she was free to travel and to continue correspondence with her many friends.

After marrying, Charrière wrote to her brother Ditie on May 13, 1771, describing her life: "[My husband is] the gentlest, the most reasonable, and the most tenderly loved in all the world"; "I am hindered neither in thoughts nor words nor actions: I have changed my name, and I do not always sleep alone—that's the only difference" (*OC*, 2:239). After summer 1771's two-month Paris honeymoon, the Charrières went to live with his two unmarried sisters and father in his family's home, Le Pontet, in Colombier, a village in Switzerland. Early twentieth-century biographers characterized her marriage as unhappy;[12] but more recently, critics have countered the earlier notion with evidence. Various letters show us Charles de Charrière's devotion to his wife and his respect for her works. Reading his letters reveals that he was a generous and insightful man who loved his wife "tenderly and durably," as Janet Whatley shows.[13] Isabelle Vissière asserts that her marriage to him "favored the maturation of her talent."[14] In 1774 when her beloved brother Ditie died, Charrière wrote to her brother Vincent in June, "If I loved my husband less, if I were less beloved by him, I don't know what would become of me, nor how I could endure what I am suffering" (*OC*, 2:308–309). Twenty years later, she wrote in a letter to a friend that she finished writing one of her works and "thanks to M. de Charrière, who wanted very much to copy it, all was done and my packet sealed"—ready for the printer (*OC*, 3:503).[15]

A major factor interfering with Charrière's happiness was her inability to have children. After marriage, when they did not occur, she consulted doctors and traveled to spas seeking a cure for infertility.[16] This is one area where even as an independent-minded author, Charrière's ability to "write" her life was sorely shaken. Yet the letters reveal her quiet strength of mind; they also offer us glimpses into eighteenth-century European medicine. Her consulted doctors, from local Dr. Tissot to famous Dr. Daniel Langhans of Berne, all recommended the baths as the cure. On April 3, 1773, she wrote to Catherine de Charrière de Sévery, "If a doctor tells me that the bath at Aix would be good for my nerves and for becoming pregnant, my husband will willingly take me there" (*OC*, 2:300). On May 19, 1773, she wrote again: "[Doctors] claim that these waters [of Valais, 'to drink and bathe'] are fortifying and calming" (*OC*, 2:304). Yet she concludes, "[I am] tempted to believe that . . . [spas], doctors, and consultations are so many follies and that nothing would be as healthy as staying in one's garden with a work, a book . . . and a husband that one loves very much" (*OC*, 2:305). The devastating effect of these futile pregnancy attempts is suggested in Dr. Tissot's letter in 1775: "Mme de Charrière is changed to the point of being unrecognizable, she is sad, does not talk . . . ; people say she is pregnant; if she is not, she is very ill."[17] Perhaps she had also suffered a miscarriage.

For July–August 1776 Charrière and her husband were at Loëches-les-Bains at Valais. In September she learned to her sorrow that her father had died, and she wrote Catherine, "I returned home so content, so full of hope with agreeable projects! What a change! What a cruel surprise" (*OC*, 2:325). In 1777 the Charrières spent spring in Geneva, a city she remembered fondly from her childhood. In a letter to Catherine in April, she wrote, "There are many active people, well-informed people" (*OC*, 2:335). The Charrières would spend the first half of the year in Geneva for several years: Charrière's letters show her enjoyment in seeing her friends and taking part in the city's intellectual life. Yet in Geneva in 1781 she became ill and was confined to bed for a month. She later described her illness to Vincent's wife, Dorothea: "I will not tell you the same marvels of my stomach, with its frequent swellings" (February 21, 1785; *OC*, 2:457–458). After the Charrières left Geneva that year, M. de Charrière wrote to Vincent on July 29, "The Plombières baths are perfect for my wife: her stomach has diminished and softened; her strength has come back."[18] Charrière was not yet ready to give up on bearing children. In spring 1783 she went to

Strasbourg to consult the famous "Count de Cagliostro" (real name Guisseppe Balsamo) for his miracle cures. He did not cure her. She recalled in a February 1790 letter to friend Chambrier d'Oleyres, "Charlatan or prince, it doesn't matter: he was sensitive and often amiable; he had pity for me at a time when I was to be pitied" (*OC*, 3:187).

Yet even when pitiable, her life—and her writing—embodied self-directed development. During summer 1783 Charrière rented a house in Chexbres, a small village not far from Lausanne, known for its vineyards, farmland, and spectacular view of Lake Geneva. She remained there alone for part of the summer. At this time she turned again to her creative writing. The rustic scene and beautiful landscape would have provided an ideal writers' retreat. In January/February 1784, she published in Lausanne *Letters from Neuchâtel* (*Lettres neuchâteloises*), the first novel she had published since *The Nobleman* twenty years earlier. She would describe the 1784 novel's inspiration in a January 1804 letter to Taets van Amerongen: "A long time after [writing *Le Noble*], another fit of boredom, or rather sorrow, and the desire to distract myself, inspired me to write *Lettres neuchâteloises*. I had just seen in *Sara Burgerhart* (a Dutch novel) that in painting places and manners that one knows well, one gives to fictional people a precise reality" (*OC*, 6:558).[19] This letter is important for two reasons. It tells us where she got the inspiration to write a realistic novel based on local customs and people, an idea that she pursued in succeeding novels, and it also gives us an inkling into her state of mind when she secluded herself in the countryside retreat and began to write. It seems that after her Cagliostro consultation, she needed to sort her thoughts and seek respite, while assuaging her grief. She returned to her creative work.

The Charrières went to Geneva for several months at 1784's start. She published a second edition of *Letters from Neuchâtel* there and also wrote and published a second novel, *Letters of Mistress Henley Published by Her Friend* (*Lettres de Mistriss Henley, publiée par son amie*). This was the last time Charrière went to Geneva. As she wrote to a friend the next year, "Geneva has changed, and

I have changed" (*OC*, 2:470). When she left Geneva in May 1784, she went back to Chexbres without her husband, making clear that she wanted to be alone. She wrote few letters from this retreat. The only letter we have is to her brother Vincent on June 21, 1784, describing her Chexbres venue "in the middle of a beautiful summer": "This place is superb; I do not think there is anything more beautiful in the universe. At one's feet, the [Geneva] lake, surrounded by Savoy's mountains . . . Vevey and its laughing hill . . . [and in] the tableau, the valley, the Rhône which flows out of it, and the high Alps covered with snow. All of that is of a unique beauty, ravishing! For several years I have wanted to see this at my leisure, to admire it well, to really enjoy it" (*OC*, 2:413–414).

Critics have pondered the question of why Charrière chose to separate from her husband during this time. Various reasons have been posited for her self-imposed isolation. C. P. Courtney in his comprehensive biography suggests that perhaps she was distressed at Geneva's political situation or at Genevans' strong reaction to her novel *Mistress Henley* published in Geneva in 1784.[20] Regarding the former, Charrière wrote to her sister-in-law Dorothea on April 28, 1781, "[There are] two parties very agitated the one against the other, some particular insults, exaggerated wrongs from one party and the other, terror panics, sadness very well founded, etc."; "I doubt that Geneva will be a better place to stay next winter than this" (*OC*, 2:373). But the suggestion that biographers unduly seize is Benjamin Constant's claim in his *Le Cahier Rouge* that Charrière had had an affair with or an unrequited passion for a younger man. However, although various "young men" have been suggested, there is no real evidence to support the doubtful story.[21] Weighing more heavily than any of these suggestions is the effect of the yearslong struggle to become pregnant. Even with today's medical advances, repeatedly unsuccessful attempts to have a child can wreak havoc on a marriage. A solution for her was to withdraw into a kind of writers' retreat: beautiful, peaceful surroundings would calm her emotions—and could provide the perfect environment for a renewal of her creative writing.

Although we do not have letters by Charrière during this period, we have letters from her husband: they evoke for us her state of mind. Writing to her regularly at Chexbres, he visited twice. In August 1784, he wrote before his arrival. After he visited her, on August 30, he wrote, "I have rarely been as sad as I was in leaving Chexbres; the friendly air that you had with me during luncheon, several kind words that you said to me during my visit, the conflicting attitudes that you have shown me; the pity that you inspired in me; the desire to see you again at Colombier soon, and the fear that it would not be for our mutual happiness; all of that was churning in my heart and was choking me up, creating a need to cry that I could scarcely overcome. . . . I embrace you with all my heart" (*OC*, 2:436). Charrière came back to Colombier in September. Her third novel, *Letters Written from Lausanne* (*Lettres écrites de Lausanne*), was published early in 1785.

During this period when she wrote few letters, Charrière was productive in her creative work. In addition to the three novels, she had also written a play and was working on an opera, all within one year. Most of her novels are epistolary. The numerous personal letters that she had written over the years—creative works in themselves—provided an apprenticeship for her novels. The epistolary form can prevent closure and leave the story without resolution. Elizabeth MacArthur, in a study of epistolary novels by women, indicates that the insistence on closure in a literary work might be interpreted as "an attempt to preserve the moral and social order" where "'closures' [are] generally imposed on women."[22] Monique Moser-Verrey describes Charrière's use of the epistolary form as a way of articulating a female viewpoint: "These fictions . . . made known to men a point of view that very few women were able to articulate."[23] Madame de Staël objected to the lack of closure in Charrière's novels, telling her in an August 27, 1793, letter, "I know nothing more painful than your manner of beginning without finishing" (*OC*, 4:162). But as Joan Stewart observes, "Charrière understood that real lives do not necessarily have conclusions; they are but a train of consequences."[24] Charrière wrote life.

By July 1785, Charrière was ready to move on. She wrote from Colombier to her friend Chambrier d'Oleyres on July 2, "Between us, I am a little bored here; I do not know how to play [cards] and I have almost no liaisons. One of these days I am going—I am not sure where—maybe to the baths, maybe elsewhere. . . . I would like to spend the fall and winter in Paris perhaps, or Marseille, or Italy. I do not know if M. de Charrière would go with me, but since he only went to Geneva for me, it won't disturb him much not to go there. It would probably disturb him less if I stayed here, but . . . he leaves me mistress in that regard" (*OC*, 2:470). Two months later, Charrière set out on her own. Arriving in Payerne, she fell ill. On September 2 she wrote d'Oleyres from the inn where she was under a doctor's care, describing herself as a "poor sick person, who is half an idiot and does not know what she can or wants to do" (*OC*, 2:490).

At this point, the reader might ask why there has been so much speculation on why Charrière decided to be alone at Chexbres where she could write and enjoy the beauteous scene. Why is it so odd that the following year she wanted to get away and go to Paris? If she had been a male writer, commentators would not be perplexed. The writer's locales would be understood as wanderlust or the desire to be wherever he needed to be to keep the creative juices flowing. Why should it be different for Charrière? She did not have children to keep her at home, and she had sufficient money of her own to be independent. She had found her métier in her writing. As she said to Chambrier d'Oleyres on September 2, 1785, she needed "a change of place and to look upon new things" (*OC*, 2:490). Why can't we let it rest at that? The peace and beauty of Chexbres produced *Neuchâtel*; Geneva produced *Mistress Henley*; Chexbres and home Le Pontet produced *Letters Written from Lausanne*. Her subsequent stay in Paris was to produce her masterpiece, *Caliste*.

Charrière went to Paris in January 1786 and remained until September 1787. Her husband joined her in December 1786. She went to Paris not to enjoy the society life, but rather to work seriously on her music. Her letters reveal her musical engagement throughout her life; she wrote to her nephew Willem René van Tuyll, "To tell the truth, I have never studied anything as seriously as music" (March 3–5, 1800; *OC*, 6:30). She wrote piano sonatas, songs for keyboard, and operas. Letzter and Adelson contend that her Paris sojourn "was one of the most significant aspects of her career."[25] Writing opera was not new for her. She had written her first libretto in 1784, *L'incognito*, and had collaborated on the music with Italian composer Domenico Cimarosa. Only two of her letters from this period in Paris are extant, but the one to Vincent gives us a sense of this portion of her life writing: "Every day I spend six or eight or ten hours at my clavecin [harpsicord]; this is not a taste, it is a passion. . . . I don't do anything else [but music]" (*OC*, 2:500). Charrière worked on her music with Italian composer Florido Tomeoni and studied opera with Niccolò Zingarelli, a foremost composer of *opera seria*. Zingarelli later became one of Napoleon's favorite composers. While in Paris, Charrière made valuable contacts in the music world; when she came home to Colombier, she continued to work on opera as both a librettist and a collaborative composer.

While music was an important facet of the life Charrière wrote for herself, her published fiction is that too. Her novels from the 1780s, primarily epistolary, evoke a natural picture of a particular milieu and the people there. The satirical novel *Letters from Neuchâtel* published in 1784 apparently offended some residents of Neuchâtel, although elsewhere her novel was praised for its realism. In response to local criticism, Charrière wrote a poem for the second edition, addressing the "Good people of Neuchâtel": "do you claim / Not to have faults like everyone else? / Or do you want light shed only on the faults of others, / While general blindness covers your own?"[26] Today we appreciate this novel's astute realism depicting everyday events, and the detailed voices of a seamstress and a warehouse clerk and the lively heroine. As a piece of Charrière's life writing, although it is not autobiographical, it gives us a sense of her impressions and opinions of local people and popular mores. In writing this novel—after many years of attempting to play the role of "une femme à l'ordinaire" (*OC*, 2:321–322), a role both expected by society and recommended by her doctors for promoting pregnancy—Charrière had reverted to the feisty defiance of convention that had characterized her earlier life.

Also published in 1784, *Letters of Mistress Henley* portrays a woman caught in a marriage that destroys her selfhood.[27] Charrière wrote the novel in response to Samuel de Constant's 1783 Swiss novel (in French) *The Sentimental Husband, or Marriage as It Is Sometimes*, which chronicles an unhappy marriage from the perspective of a husband who is driven to suicide.[28] Charrière's novel depicts a different marriage from a wife's point of view. The protagonist marries by choice Mr. Henley, a gentleman, and becomes mistress of his home in an isolated area of rural England; her story is a potent delineation of a woman's loss of self. Her husband seems more formidable because his power (by law and tradition) is supported by a societal belief in his natural right to rule. By virtue of his position, he is in the right when it comes to their differences. It is important to note that in French, the word for "right" and for "reason" is the same. Hence, while Mr. Henley is the embodiment of *raison* in both its meanings, his wife is (supposedly) both wrong and unreasonable. Yet the text undermines this verdict, implying that some "reasonable" people are deemed so only because they have the power to command it. Mistress Henley refers to "people who are seen as reasonable" (15). Charrière believed that men did not have a monopoly on reason. As she wrote to her friend Henriette L'Hardy on October 22, 1792, it was primarily a matter of education: "Although I maintain that the faculties are by their origins the same, I cannot deny the reasoning faculty is more perfected in men, and that happens through study, solely through study" (*OC*, 3:428).

Immediately after Mistress Henley's arrival at Hollow Park, she begins to discover her position's "hollowness" or emptiness. The novel culminates in the inevitable consequence of her own silenced voice in the government of their life together. She writes, "I could not speak" (42), and she ceases to write the letters. The text suggests that the most likely prospect is either her literal death or a living death. Already, Mistress Henley can pronounce the epitaph for her selfhood, and her letters conclude with these words: "I am no more" (42).

Charrière's influential biographer Geoffrey Scott in 1925, after Philippe Godet in 1906, wrote that the novel portrayed her own marriage.[29] However, her husband was not a Mr. Henley. He did not try to destroy her selfhood. Moreover, unlike Mr. Henley, who did not listen to or consult his wife or seem to care about her wishes, Charles de Charrière was understanding of and saddened by any unhappiness. He was proud of his wife's accomplishments, encouraged her writing, and even gave himself writer's cramp from copying out her manuscripts for her. He was intelligent and erudite, although apparently he was no match for her wit. Charrière herself testified to his characteristically "doux" manner, writing to Dorothea in an April 1796 letter of "this man [who has always been] so easygoing" (*OC*, 5:238).

More reasonable is that *Mistress Henley* portrays what might have happened to Charrière had she married a man who attempted to curb her freedom. The character Mistress Henley is an act of imagination, not an autobiographical self. Charrière's authoring of this tale gives voice to a woman whose position as a married woman is made voiceless—the voicelessness that might have been Charrière's if she had signed an oath (in effect) like the one that Boswell had required for marriage. In a February 16, 1768, letter to Boswell, she says of Scotland and marriage, "I do not know your Scotland. On the map it appears to me a little out of the world. You call it 'a sober country.' I have seen it produce decidedly despotic husbands and humble, simple wives who blushed and looked at their lords before opening their mouths" (*Boswell*, 368). Charrière did not want to become that voiceless wife.

Mistress Henley could not find a way to assert her identity, but Isabelle de Charrière could—and did. Charrière's assertion of self was her writing: her correspondence, her essays,[30] her plays, her librettos, and her fiction. In a letter to Henriette L'Hardy on April 11, 1793, she advises her to write: "Write, write. You will make a most intimate acquaintance with yourself, when you write down what you have done and thought" (*OC*, 4:27). Interestingly her words were echoed two hundred years later by twentieth-century French feminist Hélène Cixous, who advised women that writing was a way of preventing their "annihilation."[31]

Also published in the 1780s were *Letters Written from Lausanne* (1785) and its sequel *Caliste* (1787). The former depicts the people of Lausanne and a mother's advice to her daughter, Cécile, on how to navigate the dangerous waters of social hypocrisy and gender, while retaining as much as possible her own freedom of spirit. It provides a realistic picture of their milieu, and gives us her ideas on gender, marriage, and the local mores.[32] One of Charrière's longtime friends, Claude de Salgas, wrote to her on February 20, 1785, that he recognized Charrière herself in the character of Cécile's mother: "I know that it is you, my dear Madame. I have always regretted that you did not have a daughter to raise; no one in the world would have been more qualified for it" (*OC*, 2:456).

The tragic story of Englishwoman Caliste is narrated in letters by William, a character introduced in the previous novel as an Englishman visiting Lausanne. In *Caliste*, we see Charrière's own life's questioning of rigid standards of morality. Caliste is a woman of strong feeling and superior intellect, whose mother had sold her to an English lord. She became the lord's mistress. When he died, she had a yearslong mutual love with William (the narrator), whose passivity and indecisiveness—and fear of social custom—led to her death.[33] This powerful novel is a vivid example of Charrière's social critique.

Charrière's various personal letters also convey her societal analysis in many areas, including her encounters with other authors. In 1777 when she was in Geneva, she finally agreed to visit Voltaire, but the visit was unsatisfactory. She wrote to her brother Vincent on June 7, "I only saw Monsieur de Voltaire for a moment; I found him less ugly, less old, less thin, less gaunt than he had been described to me. He made remarks on humility, on his age and honesty for me, after which he withdrew into his chamber, assuring me that he could not do otherwise and that he had been closeted in there when I arrived. . . . We were told that . . . he planned to come back to us but . . . Voltaire remained fixed to his chair; I was very annoyed. I would have liked to see him alone, at my ease" (*OC*, 2:339). Charrière's writing asserts her sense of self, which wouldn't succumb to worshipping Voltaire.

Her meetings with Denis Diderot were apparently more interesting, and he treated her as an intellectual equal. In a note to her pamphlet *Éclaircissements relatifs à la publication des Confessions de Rousseau* (1790), Charrière writes of a meeting with Diderot when he told her of his past conversation with Rousseau about the inspiration for Rousseau's *Discours sur* [the moral effects of] *les sciences et les arts*, which in 1750 won first prize at the Academy of Dijon. Rousseau had said he was on his way to visit his friend Diderot, who was in prison for writing against the idea of a providential God, when he spotted an advertisement for an essay contest on the question "Has the restoration of the sciences and arts contributed to the purification of morals?" Charrière recounts Diderot's telling her of his Rousseau conversation, the same as Rousseau had reported it, except that his response, she noted, "was more salient": Rousseau asked him which side the essay should take, and Diderot replied, "Good question! The one that no one will take" (*OC*, 10:194). Rousseau did ultimately take the unpopular position that art and science were destructive to morality. After his break with Rousseau in 1758, Diderot was angry at Rousseau's slanderous treatment of him. Charrière writes of meeting Diderot several times at The Hague in 1774. She said when she questioned him about Rousseau after their falling out, he "took on an air of Tartuffe, spoke of a bad heart, ingratitude, traitorous unworthy friends, and then he was silent, from discretion, from humanity" (*OC*, 10:194). In January 1802, Charrière wrote to Isabelle Morel of another conversation with Diderot, where they had spoken of plays with unsuccessful debuts and he said to her, "[You and I know] that *Le Misanthrope* [Molière, 1666] failed at its first performance" but became popular: "When our plays fail, we will be sure to speak of the *Misanthrope*; it is always a *Misanthrope* we have written" (*OC*, 6:477).

The 1790s were a busy time for Charrière's life writing. She wrote books, essays, letters, and music. The French Revolution figures prominently in her letters and published works in this decade.

After 1789 many refugees, primarily French aristocrats, flooded the area in which the Charrières lived in Switzerland. Her letters during the next several years indicate her keen interest in France's events. At first she sympathized with French Republicans' ideals and did not particularly like the French émigrés, some of whom she found boring, while others irritated her with their arrogance and pretensions. She wrote to Constant on June 17, 1790, "There is here a prodigious movement of French who are not amusing to me and grieve me" (*OC*, 3:219). After the massacre of the Swiss Guards in the Tuileries on August 10, 1792, Charrière became disgusted with the revolutionaries, but she still did not like the aristocrats. She wrote to Chambrier d'Oleyres on August 17, 1792, "I wish there had been a civil war to sweep the earth of many of those people on both sides" (*OC*, 3:404–406). On November 20–22, 1794, after France's Reign of Terror, she summarized her perspective to Henriette L'Hardy: "Equality and liberty were made to please me"; "and up to August 10, 1792, I still approved of the French more often than I blamed them. Since [then], I have had very different impressions, but the aristocrat émigrés did not become better or more interesting to my eyes; only their enemies were more hateful." She adds that she means the émigrés in general, not individually: "I have made among them [the émigrés] some exceptions, some distinctions, which I would have also made among the revolutionaries" (*OC*, 4:641). That she would indeed make distinctions among both groups is clear in her 1793 novel *Lettres trouvées dans des portefeuilles d'émigrés* (published in English as *Émigré Letters*), where she portrays Alphonse as a good aristocrat and Laurent, his friend, as a revolutionary who opposes the violence.[34]

This novel also depicts the kind of pretentious French refugees that she disliked. Set in England, it portrays the impressions the arrogant émigrés made on their hosts. An Englishwoman says sarcastically to a rude French aristocrat, "Sir, are you paid by the French patriots to bring the aristocracy into disrepute?" (188). In the same work, the abbé comments to Alphonse on these aristocrats "whose misfortune does not give them pause for thought, whose nobility . . . shows itself to be without dignity or generosity, without anything that might make it worthy of respect" (204). Charrière's acuity speaks further when Alphonse summarizes the situation, addressing the French people: "Too long oppressed, do you not now blush to outdo your oppressors in savage despotism? . . . Your tortures are a thousand times more barbarous than their barbaric lack of concern; they let you suffer while they indulged in their pleasures, but you make them suffer and insult them, and take pleasure in their sufferings. But this power which they did not use well, and which you in your turn are abusing, are you sure that you will be able to keep it forever?" (210). As Charrière foretold, they did not retain power. The novel was written in August 1793, and within a year Robespierre himself had been guillotined. Laurent, Alphonse's friend the revolutionary, becomes disillusioned as the killings escalate. He writes on July 2, 1793, that after he recovers from his wounds, he does not want to return to fight for "the indivisible republic, the invisible liberty, and the impossible equality" (232). He says he asks himself if it is right to inflict suffering for the sake of an ideal, and decides that "the holocaust is too great. . . . I can only see individual suffering" (241).

Between 1787 and 1794 at the Charrière home (Le Pontet in Colombier), she held what Courtney calls a "court" (or salon): friends came for conversation and sometimes heard readings of her work. Benjamin Constant visited, as did numerous other men and women.[35] In person and in letters, Charrière engaged in lively dialogue with her younger friends. As mentor/teacher to some, she even provided practical assistance—locating jobs for those in need. She also helped her servant. When her unmarried maid became pregnant (twice), and the straitlaced community wanted to force her out of town, Charrière protected her. The same maid Henriette Monachon was friendly with Charrière (e.g., together reading Locke). On January 16–19, 1792, Charrière wrote to Vincent, "My poor femme de chambre is pregnant. . . . You would not believe how much people inveigh against her, and I think also against me, against my indulgence. . . . She is universally detested" (*OC*, 3:331). Charrière was godmother to Henriette's son.

In *Three Women*, Charrière uses the Henriette incident to portray moralistic protagonist Émilie's realization that one cannot live by rigid moral systems; Émilie sees that a lived reality is more complex than any abstract system. The novel has been compared to *contes philosophiques* like Voltaire's *Candide* and Johnson's *Rasselas* (both 1759), with the difference that Charrière's characters function in the real world without any hint of fantasy.[36] *Three Women* is not autobiographically chronicling Charrière's life, but it depicts her philosophical thinking, which is based on her life experiences. In the novel, the Abbé de la Tour tells the story of three women, refugees from the French Revolution who have sought sanctuary in Altendorf, a German village. In these women we see three approaches to morality: innocent Émilie believes in the moral system inherited from her aristocratic family; Joséphine, her servant, who has been sexually exploited because of her class, recognizes the hypocrisy behind aristocratic pretenses to morality; and Constance, a worldly wise widow who has seen private and governmental corruption, can be associated with utilitarianism. Her story is told more fully in "Constance's Story" (unpublished during Charrière's lifetime). It portrays the exploitation of slaves and of women and the protagonist's realization of the corruption that surrounds her, even in her own family.[37] The Abbé in *Three Women* frames his narrative to his listeners in a social salon by saying to them, "Our conversations about Kant and his doctrine of duty have reminded me of three women I once met" (6). The attitude of Théobald, the novel's male protagonist, represents Kant's concept of the categorical imperative.[38] As the characters learn more about the world and each other, their ideas change and they adapt to circumstances.

Another theme in the novel is education, an important concern of Charrière's life. Many of her letters deal with education (e.g., *OC*, 2:458–459). The second part of *Three Women* consists of letters to the Abbé de la Tour, primarily from Constance. In her letters she tells that they have begun a school for the village children and records the schoolmaster's approach. Particularly striking is the question of the social construction of class and gender identities. The characters perform two experiments, one inadvertent and the other deliberate. In the first, two baby boys are born concurrently, one to a visiting countess and one to Émilie's servant Joséphine. The midwife wraps the babies in identical cloths and lays them on a daybed in the countess's room, taking care to place them apart. While she is out of the room, the count comes in, sees the two babies, and, believing that his wife delivered twins, picks them both up. Afterward, no one can tell the difference. Some people say, "blood will tell," but Charrière tells us that so far "blood has not said a word"! (151). Lady Altendorf adopts both babies and plans to raise them equally. In the second experiment, after a village mother's death, Constance gives the destitute twin babies to a couple, who agree to raise them equally, dressed alike and with reverse names: the girl is to be raised as Charles, the boy as Charlotte. Constance believes that "being born male or female does not determine a person's intellectual capacities"; she is certain that "given the same upbringing," the twins will "undermine received opinion on the differences between the sexes" (154, 157). Charrière's opinion on this question is suggested by her 1792 letter to Henriette L'Hardy, where she asserts that the faculties of men and women are the same; it is only education that gives men the advantage (*OC*, 3:428).

The novel *Three Women* reflects Charrière's questioning of preconceived notions of intellectual ability and her belief that one cannot live according to a rigid moral system. She affirms that one needs to take life as it comes, that experience is more important than any abstract system. This was a belief that Charrière had expressed early in her career and that her life confirmed. On March 16, 1802, three years before her death, she wrote to Constant, "I have never had a plan, never sought anything. I desired something briefly and then something else, and as I was deprived of what I had enjoyed for a few moments or what I had hoped for, I regretted and grieved. . . . I had no overall designs. . . . What astonishes me is that I am still alive, and I am also surprised to discover in myself, here and there, some vivacity, some movement in the soul" (*OC*, 6:493). Life writing transports us into the vivacity of this individual life and her era.

Putting together Charrière's letters (the twenty-five hundred extant), her fictional works, her essays, and her self-portrait, then, we recognize that Isabelle de Charrière was a woman who believed that one must live bravely, without regrets or false hopes, that rigid systems were misleading and would not stand up to experience, and that the most sustained happiness, for her at least, was in the use of her mind—in conjunction with the here and now, the realities of life. Charrière's works are treasures in which we see the vivid interplay of important concerns in life writing, such as "identity, subjectivity, memory, agency, history, and representation."[39] Her life writings are not confined to works that are specifically autobiographical, but together form a collection of writings that, when looked at in relation to one another, not only constitute a record of her ideas and everyday life events, but also provide a valuable window into the cultural, political, and intellectual life of her European milieus. In her writings, we see a woman who managed her own life with wisdom and aplomb despite the personal, legal, and cultural obstacles of her time and place. Her letters, in juxtaposition with her other works, delineate a remarkable eighteenth-century writer and thinker, who truly wrote her life.

Notes

1. Sidonie Smith and Julia Watson, *Reading Autobiography: A Guide for Interpreting Life Narratives* (Minneapolis: University of Minnesota Press, 2001), 7, 1–14.
2. Charrière's known work has been collected in *Oeuvres complètes d'Isabelle de Charrière/Belle de Zuylen*, ed. Jean-Daniel Candaux et al. (Amsterdam: G.A. van Oorschot; Geneva: Slatkine, 1979–1984), 10 vols. (henceforth cited *OC*, by volume and page). I have translated into English all the *OC*'s many letters/works that exist only in the original French, the separate Dönhoff letters, and secondary sources in French.
3. The letters to Dönhoff, in the archive of Gijsbert Jan van Hardenbroek in Utrecht (Utrechts Archief, 347–1: archives van Hardenbroek), are printed in the original French only in Kees van Strien and Madeleine van Strien-Chardonneau, "Belle de Zuylen/Isabelle de Charrière et le

Comte de Dönhoff," *Revue d'histoire littéraire de la France* 104, no. 2 (2004): 475–483. Charrière's distant cousin Hardenbroek copied the letters and preserved them along with other material, including unpublished original work of hers and copies of his own letters to her: e.g., his rejected marriage proposal to her. Dönhoff's name appears only once in her letters, in a 1764 letter to a friend commenting briefly that Dönhoff is dead; circumstances are not discussed. He had eloped with and married an English teenager without her parents' permission; he was engaged to another Englishwoman, who confronted him at his chateau. Nimègue's burgermeister reported that Dönhoff, caught as a near-bigamist, committed suicide. See van Strien and van Strien-Chardonneau, "Belle," 475. Belle's father's December 11, 1764, letter to Boswell refers to Dönhoff's death but says simply it "is not to be wondered at," implying his libertinage led to his death: see James Boswell, *Boswell in Holland, 1763–1764, Including His Correspondence with Belle de Zuylen (Zélide)*, ed. Frederick A. Pottle (New York: McGraw-Hill, 1952), 324–25 (henceforth cited *Boswell*).

4. Isabelle de Charrière, *The Nobleman* [*Le Noble*, 1762], in *The Nobleman and Other Romances*, trans. and ed. Caroline Warman (New York: Penguin, 2012), 19–20.
5. This work was not published but circulated in manuscript form; there are variations in the extant versions. I have used the *OC* French-language version of "Portrait of Zélide" (10:37–39).
6. For further discussion of *Portrait*'s contemporary reception, see Kees van Strien, *Isabelle de Charrière (Belle de Zuylen) Early Writings: New Material from Dutch Archives* (Leuven: Peeters, 2005); and Heidi Bostic, *The Fiction of Enlightenment: Women of Reason in the French Eighteenth Century* (Newark: University of Delaware Press, 2010), 165–168.
7. Isabelle de Charrière, *There Are No Letters Like Yours: The Correspondence of Isabelle de Charrière and Constant d'Hermenches*, trans. and ed. Janet Whatley and Malcolm Whatley (Lincoln: University of Nebraska Press, 2000), ix (henceforth cited *d'Hermenches*).
8. Anne (Ninon) de l'Enclos (1620–1705) was a French courtesan, freethinker, and patron of the arts. Known for her wit and beauty, she was self-supporting and maintained an independent lifestyle, entering into and ending monogamous liaisons as she chose.

9. After her marriage, Charrière wrote to d'Hermenches several times asking him to return her letters, but he never did. At his plan to remarry, she sent her brother Ditie to deliver her letter in person asking for her letters. On December 2, 1772, d'Hermenches wrote to her saying he had burned her letters, but he had not (507). They were part of his estate when he died in 1785 (523).
10. See also Gordon Turnbull, "Boswell and Belle de Zuylen: Language and Legislation," in *Isabelle de Charrière: Proceedings of the International Conference Held at Yale University in April 2002*, ed. Vincent Giroud and Janet Whatley (New Haven, CT: Beinecke Rare Book and Manuscript Library, 2004), 87–100.
11. Critics have speculated about what they call an unlikely choice. See Rolf Winiker, *Madame de Charrière: Essai d'un Itineraire spiritual* (Lausanne: Editions l'Age d'Homme, 1971), 22; Dorothy Farnum, *The Dutch Divinity: A Biography of Madame de Charrière, 1740–1805* (London: Jarrolds, 1959), 105. Anthony West, in *Mortal Wounds* (New York: McGraw-Hill, 1973), also claims personal events spurred Belle de Zuylen to marry Charles de Charrière: e.g., her mother died at forty-three (coincidentally after being inoculated against smallpox by an English doctor); d'Hermenches sought to divorce his wife, and Belle did not think he should do so.
12. Geoffrey Scott, *Portrait of Zélide* (1925; New York: Scribner's, 1959). Scott's assertion, reflecting that of Philippe Godet, *Madame de Charrière et ses amis, d'après de nombreux documents inédits*, 2 vols. (Geneva: Jullien, 1906), was widely accepted. Simone de Beauvoir wrote in *The Second Sex*, "It is marriage that slowly assassinated the brilliant Belle de Zuylen" (Paris: Gallimard, 1949), 2:319. On Beauvoir, see Janet Whatley, "Reading the Life of Isabelle de Charrière," in Giroud and Whatley, *Proceedings*, 131–148.
13. Janet Whatley, "The Engaged Life of a Quiet Man: Charles-Emmanuel de Charrière," *Cahiers Isabelle de Charrière / Belle de Zuylen Papers* 3 (2008): 23.
14. Isabelle Vissière, "Une intellectuelle face au mariage: Belle de Zuylen (Madame de Charrière)," in *Femmes savantes et femmes d'esprit: Women Intellectuals of the French Eighteenth Century*, ed. Roland Bonnel and Catherine Rubinger (New York: Peter Lang, 1994), 294.

15. One of Charrière's works on the French Revolution, *Lettres trouvées dans la neige* [Letters Found in the Snow, 1793], in *OC*, 10:223–254.
16. See the Whatleys' introduction to *There Are No Letters*, xxvi; and C. P. Courtney, *Isabelle de Charrière (Belle de Zuylen): A Biography* (Oxford: Voltaire Foundation, 1993), 302–304.
17. William and Clara de Charrière de Sévery, *La Vie de society dans le pays de Vaud à la fin du dix-huitième siècle*, 2 vols. (Lausanne: Bridel; Paris: Fischbucher, 1911–1912), 2:188.
18. Godet, *Madame de Charrière*, 1:237n2.
19. Elisabeth Wolff and Agatha Deken, *Sara Burgerhart* (orig. Dutch 1782; French trans. 1787).
20. Courtney, *Charrière*, 330–331.
21. Benjamin Constant wrote in *Le Cahier Rouge* (in 1807 but not published until 1907, after his death) that Charrière had a disappointing love affair with an unnamed younger man, but no evidence supports Constant's allegation. Scholars have attempted to identify the man, but Constant's biographer Dennis Wood, *Benjamin Constant: A Biography* (London: Routledge, 1993), 85–88, contends that Constant, who often manufactured incidents, may have made up the story.
22. Elizabeth MacArthur, "Devious Narratives: Refusal of Closure in Two Eighteenth-Century Epistolary Novels," *Eighteenth-Century Studies* 21 (Fall 1989): 5–6.
23. Monique Moser-Verrey, "Isabelle de Charrière en quète d'une meilleure entente," *Stanford French Review* 11 (Spring 1987): 76.
24. Joan Hinde Stewart, *The Enlightenment of Age: Women, Letters and Growing Old in Eighteenth-Century France* (Oxford: Voltaire Foundation, 2010), 222.
25. Jacqueline Letzter and Robert Adelson, "Isabelle de Charrière's Parisian Sojourn of 1786–87: A Turning Point in Her Operatic Career," in Giroud and Whatley, *Proceedings*, 119.
26. Isabelle de Charrière, *Letters from Neuchâtel* [*Lettres neuchâteloises*, 1784], in *Nobleman and Other Romances*, 74.
27. References are to this edition: Isabelle de Charrière, *Letters of Mistress Henley Published by Her Friend* [*Lettres de Mistriss Henley publiées par son amie*, 1784], trans. Philip Stewart and Jean Vache (New York: MLA, 1993).

28. Samuel de Constant's *Le Mari sentimental, ou le marriage comme il y en a quelques-uns* (1783) was reprinted soon after the 1784 debut of Charrière's *Henley*. See C. P. Courtney, *A Preliminary Bibliography of Isabelle de Charrière. Studies on Voltaire and the Eighteenth Century* (Oxford: Voltaire Foundation, 1980), 41–42.
29. Scott, *Portrait*, 76. See also Godet, *Madame de Charrière*, vol. 1, chap. 9.
30. She wrote and published essays and political pamphlets, e.g. 1788's *Observations et conjectures politiques* (Political Observations and Conjectures); mostly this collection's essays dealt with France or recent Dutch history. Fighting in the Dutch Republic (United Provinces) between the Orangists and the Patriots had ended with the latter's defeat: Charrière did not support either side but hoped to see the people living with individual freedoms. She suggested England's system as a solution (*OC*, 10:65). The collection also included her story *Bien-Né* (Well-Born); the title character is based on France's Louis XVI. Another character, La Sagesse (wisdom)—Charrière's voice—advises the king to exercise more self-control; pay more attention to his subjects; and give them more freedom. The king enacts Sagesse's advice and eventually "the economy reestablished itself [and] the nation flourished more than ever" (*OC*, 10:89). In 1789's essay *Lettres d'un évêque français à la nation* (Letters from a French Bishop to the Nation), Charrière's bishop advocates for income equality, prison reform, and religious toleration. Yet he also worries that in their eagerness to make changes, "people with the best intentions do not foresee the dangers in the remedies" (*OC*, 10:132).
31. Hélène Cixous, "The Laugh of the Medusa" (1975), in *Feminisms*, ed. Robyn R. Warhol and Diane Price Herndl (New Brunswick, NJ: Rutgers University Press, 1991), 334–335.
32. Isabelle de Charrière, *Letters Written from Lausanne* [*Lettres écrites de Lausanne*, 1785], in *Nobleman and Other Romances*, 103–172.
33. Isabelle de Charrière, *Caliste* [*Caliste, ou suite des Lettres écrites de Lausanne*, 1787], in *Four Tales*, trans. S[ybil] M. S[cott] (1926; Freeport, NY: Books for Libraries Press, 1970), 165–263.
34. Isabelle de Charrière, *Émigré Letters* [*Lettres trouvées dans des porte-feuilles d'émigrés*, 1793], in *Nobleman and Other Romances*, 183–255. Further citations are in text.

35. On friends with whom Charrière conversed/corresponded, see Courtney, *Charrière*, 443–471.
36. Isabelle de Charrière, *Three Women, a Novel by the Abbé de la Tour*, trans. Emma Rooksby (New York: MLA, 2007). References are to this edition. See Rooksby, introduction, xvi–xvii.
37. Isabelle de Charrière, "Constance's Story" ["L'Histoire de Constance"], in *Nobleman and Other Romances*, 283–315.
38. Also see Rooksby, introduction, ix–xxxiii; Bostic, *Fiction*, 156–157; and Judith Still, "Isabelle de Charrière's *Three Women*—Adopting and Adapting Hospitality after Kant," *German Life and Letters* 64 (2011): 19–30.
39. Miriam Fuchs and Craig Howes, "Introduction," in *Teaching Life Writing Texts*, ed. Fuchs and Howes (New York: MLA, 2008), 1–19.

5

Clashes of Conversations in James Boswell's *Hebrides* and *Life of Johnson* and "My Firm Regard to Authenticity"

JAMES J. CAUDLE

> Had his other friends been as diligent and ardent as I was, he might have been almost entirely preserved. As it is, I will venture to say that he will be seen in this work more completely than any man who has ever yet lived. And he will be seen as he really was . . .
>
> —James Boswell, *The Life of Johnson* (1791)

> Where, then, is the wonder, that . . . they, who see different and dissimilar parts, should judge differently from each other?
>
> —Samuel Johnson, *Adventurer* no. 107

In this essay, I look at how authenticity or accuracy in reporting particular keywords and potent phrases in conversations as close to their original form as possible came to be a primary value for James Boswell in his development as an author during the course of the years 1761 to 1791. He began his literary career in the early 1760s as indifferent to, or at times even mocking of, textual authenticity and accuracy. Subsequently, over the course of the later 1760s, the 1770s, and the 1780s, he became increasingly a stickler for accuracy, to the point of stirring up obnoxious controversies in the public newspapers with certain other authors who he felt to be inaccurate. That transition was especially prominent in his efforts from 1785 to 1793 to make his two full-scale Johnsonian biographical books stand out from the works of competitors such as John Hawkins and Hester Piozzi. After discussing this decades-long transition in Boswell's vision of the relative value of inventions and facts, I then proceed to look at the contemporary disputes over Johnsonian conversations in *Hebrides* and the *Life*. I focus in particular on Boswell's affronted insistence on rebutting in letters or in print those who offered divergent versions of Johnsonian conversation. Boswell used his battles over accuracy in his journal revisions for *Hebrides* and *Life* to set himself out as a new, different, and improved writer of Johnson's life, even conceiving of himself as a pioneer in methods of "authentick" biography as well.

Boswell's claims of his carefully preserved written memoranda's and journals' superior authenticity to old unwritten memories, in those cases for which contemporary journals or memoranda of keywords survived, have been subjected to criticism from his time to our own, but have generally survived this buffeting. He is especially contestable where he revised brief scraps into flamboyantly theatricalized dialogue, as in his well-known expansions of Johnson's conversations from memoranda or minutes. Nonetheless, from an obvious biological reality—that it is more difficult to remember the exact words in a conversation from decades or even years ago than to examine a piece of paper remembering them written that same number of decades or years ago—Boswell's claim to show Johnson "as he really was" by using evidence from his journals was more valid than the alternative, which would have been relying solely on his memories, in the way that Boswell's Johnsonian informants Bennet Langton, William Maxwell, George Steevens, William Seward, Isaac Reed, and Francis Barber did.[1] (As Boswell told Johnson in April 1775, "There are few [of Johnson's friends] from whom I can put down in writing your sayings [with confidence in their accuracy].")[2]

However, his putative opponents' accounts are not thereby rendered worthless, in the manner he claimed during his quarrels with them. His rivals' views are also typically accurate in their broad outlines of who was there, when and where, and the general broad outlines of the conversation in heads of discourse. Despite the often peculiarly bitter feuding of Boswell and his critics, with reference to reporting the words of Johnson in conversation, none of the contestants were deliberately mendacious or misleading, though some were muddled. There is not a sufficient degree of dissonance in their battles of words to declare any of them to be an unreliable narrator, or an outright liar. The question then arises, why did Boswell attack these mostly innocent rivals for inaccuracy with such energy and even viciousness, when their dissonances were so minor?

Boswell did not begin his literary career as overtly interested in biographical accuracy or obsessed with exactitude in reportage of conversations. Indeed, in the 1760s, he dabbled in publishing inventions and fabricated dialogues, and fake letters, often as literary pranks or antics.[3] Even the genuine letters that Boswell had exchanged with Andrew Erskine were heavily retouched, revised, and resequenced before their publication as a book in 1763.[4]

Accuracy first became a goal of Boswell's, and his "facts" began to outpace his "inventions," in the later 1760s. He began his legal career as an advocate in Edinburgh (1766), eventually married (1769), and began to think methodically of writing various biographies and editing historical documents with the scrupulousness a lawyer would bring to his legal papers. We see strong early evidence of a transformation around the time of his inferred contributions to the edition of the *Letters of the Right Honourable Lady Jane Douglas* (1767), and his sole authorship of the *Account of Corsica, the Journal of a Tour to That Island, and Memoirs of Pascal Paoli* (1768), the latter of which earned him his first real fame as "Corsica Boswell."

Samuel Johnson's life was only one among roughly twenty biographies that Boswell conceived of writing from 1773 to 1795, and he noted in 1780 that "biography is my favourite study."[5] He began saving materials on Johnson as an individual, but also on the Johnsonian Circle, and individuals within it such as James Oglethorpe, David Garrick, and Joshua Reynolds: as he noted in the title, the *Life* was not just a life of Johnson, but was "a View of Literature and Literary men in Great Britain for half a century."[6]

One of the first major incidents in which Boswell took umbrage at another's reporting of a Johnsonian conversation was with Arthur Murphy (later to be one of his rivals for the laurels of the greatest Johnsonian biographer). In March 1775, Murphy told a droll story about how he had heard "a Scotch gentleman" whose name he did not recollect being gently mocked by Johnson "at Tom Davies's" (the bookshop of Thomas Davies, where Boswell and Johnson first met) about his Scottishness. Boswell rankled, since "it was to me that this was said [on May 16, 1763], and Murphy was not present." Murphy then compounded his embroidery by saying "that the same gentleman then got the noted answer of the noble wild prospects," but "that was said to Ogilvie, the poet [on July 6, 1763]." Boswell did not say anything at the time, since "I could not contradict Murphy after he had said he was *present*, without being rather too hard upon him." To Boswell, Murphy's muddle proved "how difficult it is to get at the authenticity of Mr. Johnson's stories, or indeed at truth on almost any occasion."[7] But the next time Murphy dined out on the story, Boswell lost his temper: "Murphy again told his story of a Scotsman's introduction to Mr. Johnson . . . as if he had been present." Boswell "could not resist any longer correcting his inaccuracy," and told him he had not been there: "You are confounding what you have *heard* with what you have *seen*," he objected. Giuseppe Baretti just before that outburst had assured the company that it was actually Boswell in the story. Murphy, in response, "tried to escape by saying that I was not then of such consequence as to make him remember that I was the person." Later that day, when discussing the reliability of Johnson's friends Arthur Murphy, Bennet Langton, and Topham

Beauclerk as raconteurs, Boswell complained to Johnson that "it was hard to get at authenticity."[8]

The period of Boswell's greatest public fierceness about his accuracy versus that of his acquaintances, however, began just after Johnson's death in December 1784, when his friend and publisher Charles Dilly invited him to write a life of Johnson. The story of Boswell's painful struggle to complete that life with Edmond Malone's help is well told by Marshall Waingrow, Adam Sisman, and others.[9] In so many ways, certainly with respect to his bank balance and his mental health, Boswell would have been better off just tossing together the scissors-and-paste catchpenny work of four hundred or so pages of the fully-written-journal versions of Johnsonian conversations from his personal archives, the book that Dilly had offered to produce for him. Dilly had thought that such a publication, given the small amount of editing that it would require, could be on the booksellers' shops and stalls by February 1785. An edition of *Conversations with Samuel Johnson* or a collection of Boswellian *Johnsoniana* along the lines of Hester Thrale's *Anecdotes* would have been a relatively straightforward thing for Boswell to prepare, at least for those Johnsonian encounters for which Boswell had a fully written journal that was suitable for printing without significant revision.

Yet once that chance for a quick win had passed, the pressure for Boswell to do something recognizably and ostentatiously unique in his Johnsonian book built up from May 1785 to May 1786, and onward to May 1791, when he finally published the *Life* more or less according to his grand design. Like that other latecomer, Arthur Murphy, he faced a dilemma of how to set his Johnsonian life writing apart from the explosion on the book market from 1784 to 1792 of "anecdotes, apothegms, essays, and publications of every kind."[10] The longer Boswell waited to produce his magnum opus, the harder it would be to justify its intrusion into the crowded marketplace. Gradually, each avenue for making an original book of Johnsonian life writing was cut off, whether it was the quick biographical sketch for a magazine (Thomas Tyers, 1784), short books (William Cook and William Shaw, both 1785), Johnsoniana as bon mots (William Cook, 1785), Johnsoniana as "Dr. Johnson's Table Talk, or, Conversations" (attrib. Stephen Jones, 1785), some original letters to or from Johnson (William Shaw, 1785) scattered Anecdotes (Hester Piozzi, 1786), the dull but worthy set piece recital of the full scope of the life (John Hawkins, 1787), and the large collection of letters to or from Johnson (Hester Piozzi, 1788).

Boswell developed various strategies to deal with the gap between Dilly's offer to publish a book of Johnsonian conversations in December 1784, the completion of a first rough draft of the entire text in March 1789, and the actual publication of the *Life* in May 1791.

To begin with, he seems to have determined during the later 1780s that if he could not be the first in the contest, with a full-dress life, or even with a collection of all of his Johnsonian letters (he had some 340 relevant items of correspondence) or all of his Johnsonian anecdotes, he would have to prove himself first in "authentick Precision." Having been beaten of the distinction of being first to publish in category after category of Johnsonian lore, he could only say that his "Deliberation" in speed would grant "that authentick Precision which alone can render Biography valuable" and would "correct these erroneous Accounts" in his rivals.[11] In 1786, he wrote in a letter that "I have waited till I should first see Hawkins' compilation." He also opined in another letter that "I have solid reasons for delay . . . from the motive of having Sir John Hawkins to precede me that I might profit by his gross faults."[12]

One of the most strategically significant methods for gaining ground during the delay, and a costly one in time and effort, was to produce a working prototype of the *Life*, in the form of the *Tour to the Hebrides* published October 1785, in order to mark his territory as a trusted friend and confidante of Johnson's with "a Prelude to my large Work, The Life of Samuel Johnson."[13] As he noted on the title page, the book showed how he intended to present "A Series of his [Johnson's] Conversation, Literary Anecdotes, and Opinions of Men and Books." Although the boast of "Authentick Account," on that title page, was confined to the description of the adventures of the defeated Charles Edward Stuart in 1746, it could be taken to apply to the whole text.[14] It was in *Hebrides* that he first pushed forward his strident claims of attaining greater accuracy and authenticity than other writers. In the dedication to Edmond Malone, which prefaced *Tour to the Hebrides*, he wrote, "In every narrative, whether historical or biographical, authenticity is of the utmost consequence. Of this I ever been so firmly persuaded, that I inscribed a former work [*Corsica*, 1768] to that person who was the best judge of its truth [Pasquale Paoli]." A subsequent sentence could be read as a dare or challenge: "The friends of Dr. Johnson can best judge, from internal evidence, whether the numerous conversations which form the most valuable part of the ensuing pages are correctly related." To those friends he strove "to appeal for the accuracy of the portrait here exhibited to the World." Edmond Malone as reviser of the original journal could "vouch for the strict fidelity of the present publication."[15] He would later boast in May 1793 that King George III himself had endorsed this focus on accuracy over speed, saying to Boswell in May 1785, "'There will be many lives of Dr. Johnson: do you give the best.'"[16] *Hebrides* concluded with an advertisement for the *Life of Johnson*, "in one Volume Quarto," promising "the most authentick accounts that can be obtained from those who knew him best."[17]

The second of the methods was to put himself in the papers as impugning the veracity of his rivals and in effect, challenging them to a literary duel. He had early on demonstrated this authorial stratagem in 1768 in his public-private correspondence with Margaret Primerose about his book *The Essence of the Douglas Cause*.[18] There was more than a bit of pugnacity to Boswell's claims in the public prints of accurate and authentic reportage of Johnson's conversations.

This authorial combativeness seemed to have spilled over from other literary endeavors, and indeed from Boswell's general life struggles during the period of his permanent London residence which began in 1785–1786. If one looks at Boswell's other writings of the final years in London (1786–1795) and just beforehand, years that serve as the broader context of the battles over accuracy, one sees a pattern of scrappiness, fight picking, and competitiveness, which encouraged the squabbles over accuracy. The political *Letters* of 1780 and 1785 sniped at Henry Home, Lord Kames, and at Henry Dundas. Likewise, his vengeful poems *Ode by Dr. Samuel Johnson to Mrs. Thrale Upon Their Supposed Approaching Nuptials* (1781, published 1788), "Piozzian Rhymes" (April 1786), and the lines supposed to be written by Mrs. Piozzi in Italy (May 1786) all went for the jugular of Piozzi's romantic and marital difficulties in a way that had nothing to do with empiricism or authenticity, just snobbery and malice.[19]

On February 9, 1786, he printed an item claiming a method in his tardiness: "The truth is, that the competition between them [he and John Hawkins] is not who shall be *first*, but who shall be *last*; in short which shall *see the other's back*, so as to hold the lash of animadversion."[20] Surprisingly, Boswell did not seem to publish extensively against John Hawkins, until the *Life* first edition's underminings, perhaps because Hawkins died in May 1789, and even before his death was personally disinclined, unlike the more combative or defensive Hester Piozzi or Anna Seward, to enter a paper war in the mass media.

By contrast, Boswell sought a very public feud with Hester Piozzi, a former *frère ennemi* and after 1784 just an *ennemi*, whose postscript to the *Anecdotes* (2nd ed.) had impugned his veracity on the Mrs. Montagu story as reported in *Hebrides*.[21] Whereas Hawkins was not adept at recording conversation, or even much interested in reporting Johnsonian conversations, Piozzi was a brilliant and memorable *raconteuse*. Unlike Hawkins, she could not be attacked as pedantic or dull and was also fully immune to the charge made to Hawkins that he had never been an emotionally close friend of Johnson. Therefore, were she to be deemed by Boswell to be necessary to attack, she perforce would have to be attacked with regard to the truthfulness of her portrait of Johnson. Her work's truth value would be challenged both in terms of basic facts that Boswell contended were firmer in Boswell's journals than Piozzi's memory and even in her *Thraliana* and in terms of the more metaphysical truth of the validity of the lights and shadings of her sometimes unforgiving portrait of Johnson.[22]

Boswell or his allies' puff for the *Life* in the *Star* in March 1790 asserted his "inflexible love of truth" against the "perturbed spirit" of "Madam Piozzi," whose unflattering account of Johnson had made the sage "stink in the public nose." An item in the *Morning Post* in February 1790 claimed that "Mrs. Piozzi" was "taught to look with terror" on Boswell's forthcoming *Life* because "it will consist of facts only, Mr. Boswell being too honest and too benevolent a man to bring any charge but upon the most solid foundation and rational necessity."[23]

The steady drumbeat of boasting about Boswell's superior accuracy in remembering and recording the conversation of Johnson's circle eventually entered the world of the memes upon which newspaper writers could rely to get laughs. The *Morning Post* stated in June 1791 that "Bozzy's memory is astonishing, he has offered to lay [a bet of a] rump [roast] and dozen [of wine-bottles] that he will repeat, from the first to the last page, of his Life of Johnson, without missing a *syllable*!"[24]

However, there is a wide distance between boldly asserting accuracy in records of the conversations of Johnson and their wording and producing it. One way into thinking about how Boswell imagined accuracy or inaccuracy to work is by looking at cases during his own lifetime in which he disputed authenticity or accuracy with another "Johnsonian" reporter. Boswell's claims of accuracy in recording conversation can best be evaluated by reference to his contemporaries, measure for measure, by focusing on those reports of conversations in *Hebrides* and the *Life* for which both parties were present and both parties' accounts were available in Boswell's lifetime, and for which a dispute (whether public or private) between these reporters had resulted before Boswell's death. These contested conversations are not numerous, but they are revelatory. The verbal gaps one discovers by this method between Boswell's emphases and those of the alternative recounters are of historical interest, but they tend to reflect variations in focus and in emphasis, or in word choice, rather than some clever and nefarious conspiracy by Boswell to deprive the world of the true historical Samuel Johnson.

There are precious few instances in Boswell's *Tour to the Hebrides* (1785) or *Life of Johnson* (1791) for which the same conversation is preserved by Boswell and another person present at the time, whether it led to a clash of remembered facts during or after Boswell's lifetime, or not. There are even fewer recorded cases from 1785 to 1795 (the final decade of Boswell's life) in which someone called Boswell out on a published version of a conversation involving Johnson and he contested their version of the discussion in correspondence or in the press. In these few instances, readers of *Hebrides* and the *Life* told one of the same stories as Boswell did, and both parties agreed that they had been there at that same time and place and with those people, but a "battle of words" (literally) over quotations ensued. These debates tended to be over details that Boswell had purportedly (whether intentionally or inadvertently) suppressed or were false or inauthentic, and that sometimes led to a direct quarrel in the public prints between Boswell and the other raconteur.

The clashes over veracity in the text that were raised in print during Boswell's lifetime and counterblasted with published responses are the most useful conflicts of memory of Johnson's *ipsissima verba* for thinking about how Boswell meant his claim that he was authentic and accurate when he reported conversations. Boswell's clashes in the late 1780s with Thomas Blacklock and John Dun over the earlier *Tour to the Hebrides* and the quarrels in the early 1790s with Hester Lynch Piozzi, Anna Seward, and Mary Knowles over the *Life of Johnson* reveal much about the way in which he defined and defended his biographical methods, particularly with regard to the recounting of conversation. Some of these clashes (Dun, Seward, Knowles) have been analyzed individually by scholars, but their secondary accounts were "siloed" in separate publications, and this is the first essay setting them all in juxtaposition.

Boswell's responses to his antagonists offer us details about how and why he thought of his journals as recording the past precisely, as a careful historian would, rather than reshaping the past poetically, as a historical novelist in the tradition from Defoe to Scott to Mantel would. His explicit assertion to his readers and rivals of authorial precision over authorial invention runs counter to a current of Boswell and Johnson scholarship that for decades has stressed the novelistic and imaginative elements in Boswell's *Life*.

The earliest coherent attempt to examine how Boswell took the disorderly mess of his notes, memoranda, semi-completed journals, and fully-written-out journals and turned them into the *Life of Johnson* was undertaken by Geoffrey Scott in 1929 as volume 6 of the first attempt to publish the Boswell papers from Malahide Castle in Ireland.[25] Scott's successor in the editing of the Malahide texts, and one of the founders of the Yale Boswell Editions, Frederick Pottle, wrote an influential piece on Boswell's conscious use of the *ars memoriae* to capture keywords in a conversation. Boswell's memoranda and notes close to the events could later be expanded, the way a rehydrated bouillon cube expands (back) into soup, by the cued memory, into fully written journal.[26] In 1952, Louis Baldwin concluded a systematic comparison of Johnsonian conversation in and out of Boswell's *Life* by writing that "in the bulk of the conversation, if not all of it, the Dr. Johnson of the *Life* is quoting the real Dr. Johnson practically verbatim."[27] Frank Brady, a later Boswell Editions editor and the biographer of Boswell's "Later Years," wrote in 1984 a recension and summation on how Boswell's took his scattered notes and journals and made them into the *Life* that combined theories from Scott, Pottle, and others.[28] Brady's summary encapsulated the views most prevalent among of editors connected to the Yale Boswell Editions as to Boswell's methods and reliability.

Yet dissent from that "Boswellian" consensus had been brewing since the 1970s. Donald Greene was the least even-handed and most energetic of the critics, arguing that Boswell was a misleading biographer who was also gullible in accepting dubious anecdotes from Johnson's friends.[29] Both Pottle and Greene restated and reinforced their positions from the 1960s into the 1980s.[30] John A. Vance's volume in 1985 and Greg Clingham's in 1991 assembled disputants on both sides, including Paul Korshin on "Johnson's Conversation in Boswell's *Life of Johnson*."[31] Meanwhile,

William Siebenschuh in 1985 and 1989 deployed modern psychology of memory to suggest that Boswell might have perceived clear-cut memories in a way different from which they had occurred, without intending to distort or misrepresent Johnson as Greene, following Percy Fitzgerald's critique, had alleged.[32] Korshin presented a rival theory—more a questioning of Boswell's rhetorical resort to "Johnsonese" rather than his accuracy in recounting the matters discussed and positions taken—in which he alleged that Boswell's use of cued memory was influenced by Boswell's rendering Johnson's voice in the Latinate discourse of the formal essays rather than the rougher wit of the conversations.[33]

Leaving the debate on Boswell's accuracy in recording conversation aside, another element of dispute arose in the debate: that of the movement to portray Boswell as a genuine literary artist who reshaped his materials skillfully, rather than simply ripping out pages of the journals from their bindings and handing them to the printers as is. The project of a research edition of the manuscript of the *Life of Johnson*, begun by Marshall Waingrow, continued by Bruce Redford and Elizabeth Goldring, and now reaching its culmination under Thomas Bonnell, aimed to show that the old canard of Thomas Macaulay that Boswell was a dimwit whose sole merit was that he had jotted down the conversations of the Johnsonian Circle verbatim (as if he had been a courtroom stenographer) was false. Macaulay had argued in 1831, in an often-reprinted essay, that Boswell was "a dunce, a parasite, and a coxcomb" whose chief merit was "a quick observation and a retentive memory." "If he had not been a great fool," Macaulay opined, "he would never have been a great writer." Much of the Boswell scholarship published from the Victorian era until the 1960s was an effort to refute Macaulay, and has largely been a success in altering views of Boswell's intentional craft (or at worst, craftiness).[34]

Most of the work on the *Life* in the initial decades of Boswell studies was written in the period 1950 to 1990, by scholars trained as literary critics, who were usually employed as faculty in literature departments. In those departments, theoretical concepts promoted by the critics of the earlier decades in that period, particularly the high value placed on unity of form and artistic arrangement, had been advocated as the criteria of literary merit, and by implication determined a work like the *Life*'s canonicity and ability to be taught (usually abridged) in English or Scottish literature courses. For them, the question of Boswell's ability to create a unified and coherent work of literature became as important an argument, or more important, as his merits as a documentary recorder of Johnson's conversations.

Not all writers with a polished style judged to have literary merit are truthful in their autofictions (one thinks of the recent genre of "autofiction" novels melding fact and invention engaged in by Karl Ove Knausgård, Rachel Cusk, Chris Kraus, Edward St Aubyn, and others, and earlier works in that vein of fictionalized real-life by Thomas Wolfe, Truman Capote, and Hunter S. Thompson). Furthermore, the bulk of writers of accurate and truthful accounts of conversations are never seen as writing in a polished style judged to have literary merit (court depositions come to mind). Was Boswell writing "autofiction"? Was he simply recording Johnson's conversations mechanically as the tapes of presidents Johnson and Nixon recorded their discussions? Where was the "art" in his *Life*?

These scholars might have thought they were paying a high honor to Boswell in asserting, as Thomas Preston did in 1982, that Boswell was "primarily [a] literary artist."[35] Ralph Rader in 1968 arguably began this line of reasoning by analyzing Boswell's use of "Literary Form" in a "Factual Narrative."[36] The trend of emphasizing Boswell's artfulness above and beyond—or rather than—his truthfulness persisted despite Leo Damrosch's claim in 1973 that "the *Life of Johnson* is not a fully realized work of art"; it was "uneven but unique," and demonstrated "serious defects of structure and tone."[37] Richard Schwartz (writing in 1977) similarly complained that the *Life* in all its revised versions exhibited "stress [on] collection at the expense of systematic organization and shaping." (Although in the same critical study, Schwartz noted that Boswell made "attempts at compelling authenticity and accuracy.")[38] William Siebenschuh similarly juxtaposed Boswell's "Literary Art" and "Factual Accuracy," arguing that by 1977 "his abilities as a literary artist have become a 'given,' and it is his facts and his accuracy that are beginning to be suspect."[39] Robert Bell in 1977 argued even more broadly that Boswell created a "Supreme Fiction" in his unrevised and unpublished journals, as well as his revised and published ones.[40] In 1980, an editor associated with the Yale Boswell Editions, Irma Lustig, made the case that Boswell had transmuted "Fact into Art."[41]

But Boswell did not want to be known as a great writer of artful invention, at least after the little splash made in Edinburgh by his one and only novella, a *roman-à-clef* titled *Dorando* (published anonymously in 1767).[42] The advertisement for the *Life of Johnson* at the back of his *Tour to the Hebrides* (1785) announced that he had "interwoven the most authentick accounts that can be obtained from those who knew him best." He informed Anna Seward in a letter published in the *Gentleman's Magazine* for November 1793, "As my book was to be a *real history*, and not a *novel*, it was necessary to suppress all erroneous particulars, however entertaining."[43]

His battles over authenticity with Seward and others showed that he wanted to be known as an accurate portraitist and a provisioner of literal "authentick" truths about Johnson rather than mythistorical, metahistorical, or figurative truths. Had the concept of photography existed, Boswell would probably have used the documentary photograph as the metaphor for his book's aims rather than the concept of the "Flemish picture," a term which he borrowed from analyses of Low Countries genre painting. We can debate whether Boswell was delusional—or overestimated his powers of memory in his claim to preserve Johnsonian conversation in all its verbal nuance—once we have ventured past the boundaries of the relative guarantee of his initial keywords that he had jotted on the day of the events or soon after. Yet it is clear that his ambition was just such a truthful record, and he would have been affronted to be told by modern appraisers of his work that he was doing something other than that.

The common element in all of these debates of Boswell's version versus others' conflicting reports of Johnson's words is that

Boswell believed that his own written records compiled at the time or near the time of the conversation, even if they were fragmentary memoranda rather than fully written journals, were far more accurate than his opponents' later memories. He asserted this point not merely in private conversations and correspondences, but publicly in print. He developed the argument as a roster of specific instances of opponents' inaccuracy, but beyond that, he developed his defense of his mode of reportage as a general theoretical principle of how to record conversation. He maintained this point of accuracy in wording of salient moments or keywords in the conversation despite the fact that he knew—and he told his readers that he did this—that he commonly fleshed out or embellished the wording of later accounts by use of his memory, the technique of reconstruction that had been used by Thucydides and Xenophon.

The risk of the "friends of Doctor Johnson" contradicting his account of Johnson's sayings and actions during the *Tour* was minimal compared to the conversations in the *Life*, since Johnson's closest friends were in London, or at least in England, during 1773. For the most part, with the famous exception of Piozzi's disputing that she had reported her dislike of Elizabeth Montagu's *An Essay on the Writings and Genius of Shakepear* (1769) to Johnson, only Scots such as John Dun and Thomas Blacklock would be able to accuse Boswell of inaccurate records of Johnson's speech during the travels of Boswell and Johnson in Scotland as reported in the *Tour*.[44] Quarrels were, however, forthcoming.

The spat with John Dun, parish minister, was a tempest in a teacup about whether Johnson had said on November 5, 1773, "Sir, you know no more of our Church than a Hottentot" (Boswell's claim) or "Sir, you know nothing of the matter" (Dun's claim).[45] To most readers, that will be a distinction without much of a difference, since the point of Johnson's insult to Dun, that a Church of Scotland Presbyterian was ignorant of the Church of England's Episcopalian Anglicanism, was precisely the same in both versions. Yet because Boswell entrenched himself in a claim of being an *ipsissima verba* reporter of Johnson in key places in the dialogues, and he had a scrap of paper from around that time with the words

"Know no more of our Church than a Hottentot" on it, these trivialities of wording mattered, almost certainly too much, to him. He deleted Dun's name in future editions, but did not revise the conversation as Dun had asked him to.

Thomas Blacklock remembered differently aspects of Boswell's account of Blacklock's conversation with Johnson just before the Hebrides expedition, August 17, 1773, which he termed "my ideas of the conversation." He eirenically described it as "a little different from the delineation exhibited in the former edition of your *Journal*," rather than calling Boswell in error as Dun had.[46] Boswell's friend and wise counsel William Forbes reported Blacklock as saying "your [i.e., Boswell's] memory had not served you quite correctly as to a conversation between him and Dr. Johnston."[47] One point of contradiction was a matter of interpretation of why Blacklock had seemed so concerned during a discussion about skepticism, and there Boswell conceded Blacklock's gloss on the text, writing, "One may misconceive the motive by which a person is induced to discuss a particular topick (as in the case of Dr. Blacklock's speaking of Scepticism)." The other point, however, was on wording, and it was on keywords or main points in a conversation that Boswell was willing to fight. Boswell had written that Johnson said it "was *easier* to him to write poetry than to compose his Dictionary," whereas Blacklock remembered Johnson as saying "he could write a sheet of dictionary *with as much pleasure* as a sheet of poetry."[48] In this instance, Boswell offered to add an appendix offering Blacklock's version of the talk.[49] Privately, Boswell wrote to Forbes rather defensively about his methodology: "I have put Dr. Blacklock's letter into an appendix. I am glad that I misunderstood him as to scepticism. But he is undoubtedly wrong as to the other point, as I have shewn in a note. People must be satisfied to appear as they really did. Should they be allowed to improve and enlarge their conversations, upon *after thought*, the labour would be endless and the Book not authentick."[50] He tempered that harsh language in the published version, which was the final piece of prose in *Hebrides* before the announcement of the *Life of Johnson*: "If this book should again be reprinted, I shall with the utmost readiness correct any errours I may have committed, in stating conversations, provided it can be clearly shewn to me that I have been inaccurate. But I am slow to believe, (as I have elsewhere observed) that any man's memory, at the distance of several years, can preserve facts or sayings with such fidelity as may be done by writing them down when they are recent: and I beg it may be remembered, that it is not upon *memory*, but upon what was *written at the time*, that the authenticity of my *Journal* rests." His mention of what he had "elsewhere observed" was his statement, in opposition to Johnson's and William Robertson's praise of Voltaire's "wonderful memory" on November 11, 1773, that "no man's memory can preserve facts or sayings with such fidelity as may be done by writing them down when they are recent." His citing Robertson's mention of "Mr. Boswell's way, of writing down what he heard" was a somewhat immodest endorsement of his methods.[51]

We may contrast that stubborn assurance of the "authentick" and "the authenticity of my *Journal*" with Blacklock's genial and eirenic acceptance of the idea of various versions of a remembered event having value as mismatched sources. As Blacklock wrote to Boswell, "If every one concerned in the conversations related, were to send you what they can recollect of these colloquial entertainments, many curious and interesting particulars might be recovered, which the most assiduous attention could not observe, nor the most tenacious memory retain."[52]

Boswell, despite touting his accuracy, never claimed *Hebrides* was infallible. In the advertisement to the second edition (dated December 1785), he remarked that he had worked in "correcting the errours of the press in the former edition and some inaccuracies for which the authour alone is answerable." The third edition's advertisement (dated August 1786) announced that Boswell had been "correcting some inaccuracies which I discovered myself, and some which the kindness of friends or the scrutiny of adversaries pointed out." "A few notes," he told readers, "are added of which the principal object is to refute misrepresentation or calumny." He observed, "Any person who thinks it worth while to compare one edition with the other will find that the passages omitted [especially passages about Alexander Macdonald of Sleat, John Dun, Alexander Fraser Tytler, and, in an appendix, a clarification regarding Rev. Thomas Blacklock] were . . . the hasty effusion of momentary feelings, which the delicacy of politeness should have suppressed."[53]

The squabbles both in private letters and in published correspondence about veracity in *Hebrides* had prepared Boswell for a similar response of outrage when the *Life* finally appeared. As he wrote to one of his oldest friends, William Temple, "My 'Life of Johnson' is at last drawing to a close . . . I am at present in such bad spirits that I have every fear concerning it . . . I may make many enemies, and even have quarrels."[54] In the very beginning of the *Life*, he observed that "hard as it may be, I shall not be surprized if omissions or mistakes be pointed out with invidious severity."[55]

As he had done in *Hebrides*, Boswell used claims of the fuller accuracy of his reporting of conversation in order to place his records of Johnson's life and conversations in a higher plane of realism and authenticity than accounts by any of his rivals. As with *Hebrides*, the contests over details of conversation often seem to be over trivial bits of detail. In this excerpt from the *Life*, Boswell scores a point—a point that seems gratuitous, and a trivial victory—against Hester Thrale (later Hester Piozzi). On March 30, 1778, Boswell was recounting a "ridiculous story" that "an old man" had told him in the stage coach that day. She mentioned it later that day to Boswell as "the story told you by the old *woman*." He pounced on the slip-up: "Now, Madam, (said I,) give me leave to catch you in the fact: it was not an old *woman*, but an old *man*, whom I mentioned as having told me this." Boswell was eager—overeager—to "shew . . . this lively lady how ready she was, unintentionally, to deviate from exact authenticity of narration." It sweetened the rebuke that the correction was "in presence of Johnson."[56] Boswell was busily demonstrating, to his own satisfaction, that Piozzi will "deviate from exact authenticity of narration," albeit "unintentionally," calling her a muddled rememberer, not a liar. He presents himself in this dialogue as a master of "exact authenticity of narration" to a degree and at a level unmatched, and perhaps unmatchable, by his worthy opponents. This style of one-upmanship is highly characteristic of Boswell's forensic technique in the *Life of Johnson*. It was not enough for Boswell that he could prove that he is good at telling the truth of what actually happened. Instead, he must prove to his readers that he is better at "exact authenticity of narration," and will never "deviate" from it, even "unintentionally."

In the *Life*, Boswell attacked Piozzi's *Anecdotes* (1786) as being written down sometime after the events described, from far memory, as opposed to his preferred method of near memory. "I have had occasion," he wrote, "several times, in the course of this work, to point out the incorrectness of Mrs. Thrale, as to particulars which consisted with my own knowledge." "But indeed she has," he continued, "in flippant terms enough, expressed her disapprobation of that anxious desire of authenticity which prompts a person who is to record conversations, to write them down *at the moment*. Unquestionably, if they are to be recorded at all, the sooner it is done the better."[57] Boswell continued his critique of her method by noting that "she [Piozzi] boasts of her having kept a commonplace book; and we find she noted, at one time or other, in a very lively manner, specimens of the conversation of Dr. Johnson, and of those who talked with him; but had she done it recently, they probably would have been less erroneous; and we should have been relieved from those disagreeable doubts of their authenticity, with which we must now peruse them."[58]

His quarrel with her in the *Life* (an extended rant that Irma Lustig in her detailed analysis called the "Animadversions," but which might as easily be named the "Anti-Thraliad") runs for some five or so pages after the account of events dated June 30, 1784, quite close to Johnson's death on December 13, 1784. It was probably written near the end of 1788 or in 1789, and revised by John Courtenay, who aided Boswell in "lightening" the enraged critique in February 1791. Lustig observes that Boswell's set of animadversions energetically "climaxes scattered attacks in his work on the 'extreme inaccuracy' with which, he charged, all the *Anecdotes of Dr. Johnson* were 'discoloured and distorted.'"[59]

BOSWELL'S VERSION	PIOZZI'S VERSION
I at last had recourse to the maxim, ***in vino veritas***; a man who is well warmed with wine will speak truth. JOHNSON. "Why, Sir, that may be an argument for drinking, if you suppose men in general to be liars. But, Sir, I would not keep company with a fellow who **lyes** as long as **he** is **sober**, and whom you must make drunk before you can get a word of truth out of him."	You must allow me, Sir, at least that it produces truth; ***in vino veritas***, you know, Sir.—"That (replied Mr. Johnson) would be useless to a man who knew he was not a **liar** when **he** was **sober**."

FIGURE 5.1. The same conversation in Boswell and Piozzi's versions.

Many of Boswell's attacks on Piozzi might seem to modern readers to be frothed up and exaggerated. Their debates as often concern the setting, the company, or the date of an exchange, or whether Thrale was actually there, as the accuracy of the words employed, and while these facts do matter in the biographies, they are not architecturally crucial. In one instance, Boswell was able to aver that Thrale was not at the original conversation, but knew it only as hearsay, "communicated to her by me," and muddled: "Mrs. Piozzi . . . has given an erroneous account of this incident, as of many others. She pretends to relate it from recollection, as if she herself had been present."[60] Despite this, a comparison of the two texts, even if we presume that one version is Thrale's memory of a Boswell story and thus hearsay rather than an eyewitness account, shows a remarkable parity (figure 5.1).

We immediately, by means of this parallel of the rivals, see the common elements. The crux of both tales is the use, or abuse, of the proverb *in vino veritas*, the adage that under the influence of alcohol, one was more likely to tell unvarnished truths. The gist of the Johnsonian rebuttal differs, though. In Piozzi, a much shorter retort, Johnson says that a man who is truthful when he is sober does not need the benevolent influence of wine to get past the white lies characteristic of society. In Boswell, Johnson says the proverb would be of use only if the majority of humans lied. Boswell's version makes Johnson renounce fellowship with anyone whose tongue needed to be loosened with drink to get him to tell the truth. Stylistically, in Boswell, the Johnsonese "Sir" is placed with

Johnson, whereas in Piozzi, Boswell says it. Piozzi's Johnson is more often terse and laconic, like Xenophon's version of Socrates, whereas Boswell's Johnson is more often (though not always) flowery and euphuistic, like Plato's version of Socrates. The fundamental proposition that Johnson disliked the concept of *in vino veritas* is shared; there's a distinction with a difference in the direct opprobrium placed on the man who lies when sober in Boswell's Johnson as opposed to the chance at a sober truth teller held out in Piozzi's version. Yet it is not as if in one version Johnson praised the maxim's value and in the other version he damned it. It seems likely that the two biographers elevated their petty differences from a desire to carry on a paper war, rather than from any inherent magnitude of their divergences. Had they not been so very close to Johnson and so envious of each other's claims to be the key for readers who wanted to know the authentic Samuel Johnson, it seems improbable they should have bothered much about the very similar versions of Johnson they gave the public.

Typical of their nitpicking is an exchange in which Piozzi disagreed with a Boswell version of a Johnson story, making a mountain out of a molehill, or in this case, a mouse out of a flea. In her version in *Thraliana* (December 1777) and *Anecdotes*, Robert Vansittart talked an inordinately long time about a "Mouse," leading Johnson to wonder aloud what Vansittart would have said had he seen a "Lyon." In her revised version for *Anecdotes*, she simply said, "To a gentleman who had disserted some time about the natural history of the mouse—'I wonder what such a one would have said . . . if he had ever the luck to see a *lion*!'"[61] Boswell in the *Life* objected that "Mrs. Piozzi, to whom I told this anecdote, has related it, as if the gentleman had given 'the *natural history* of the *mouse*.'" In Boswell's version, Vansittart is explaining in an overly complex way (Boswell estimates it lasted seven or eight minutes in the telling) why the counsel attending the circuit court at Shrewsbury had been bitten by fleas. Johnson's punch line is, "It is a pity, Sir, that you have not seen a lion; for a flea has taken you such a time, that a lion must have served you a twelve-month." The "unusual carelessness" the editors of Boswell's rough notes for this period observe is important, but does not obviate the strong resemblance of the passages.[62]

The contest against Anna Seward was the most evenhanded spat over a conversation, since it involved two contemporary records of a conversation. Unlike Hester Piozzi, John Hawkins, or Arthur Murphy, Anna Seward's accounts of Johnson were brief miniatures or vignettes based on personal experience, rather than an attempt to show Johnson's life in full. Therefore, she was not a rival to Boswell in the way the other major biographers were. All the same, Boswell managed to take similar umbrage at her variant account of a conversation.

Boswell himself noted that three variant accounts survived of a dinner with Johnson which took place on April 15, 1778.[63] The first of these variant recollections was that in Boswell's own Journal for that day. The second was the "minutes . . . of this conversation," which Anna Seward supplied at Boswell's request—and which she later claimed he had "strangely mutilated, abridged, and changed." This quarrel between Seward and Boswell was carried out in the pages of the *Gentleman's Magazine* in 1793–1794, and was memorable enough to be republished in full by John Nichols in his *Illustrations of the Literary History of the Eighteenth Century* in the nineteenth century.[64] Additional letters by Seward published in 1811 revealed more details of the dispute.[65] James Clifford, James Wooley, and Donna Heiland have ably discussed the Seward dispute, and its deeper contexts in Seward's life, writings, and status as a Johnsonian informant.[66] As Heiland noted, their contretemps was preceded by a series of letters from Seward to Boswell dated 1784 to 1790, and various letters from Boswell to Seward in dialogue with her. Only two were included in the 1811 publication of Seward's letters, which had undergone successive pruning and reshaping by Seward and others.[67]

Unlike the John Dun or Hester Piozzi or Arthur Murphy quarrels discussed earlier in this essay, this conflict with Seward over what Johnson said does not involve weighing a rival's memory a decade or so after the events versus Boswell's account from memoranda or a journal written near or on the day. Boswell's journal "summarized the dialogue" by writing "probably the next day," and Seward had her own "record of the conversation [drawn up] at the time," which was known to Boswell as he wrote the *Life*.[68] In late March 1785, Seward referred to her evidence as "the minutes I made the time of that . . . tremendous conversation at Dilly's."[69]

After laboriously collating Boswell's account versus Seward's, Wooley remarked, "Her version does not necessarily contradict his in any significant way, and even if we grant his objections in the *Life* to Mrs. Knowles's account [of the same conversation], it is far from obvious that the same objections pertain to Miss Seward's." Neither in his long quarrel with her in the *Gentleman's Magazine* in 1793 and 1794 nor in any other place does Boswell ever attempt to impeach her report of this particular conversation. Nonetheless, he appears to search out every possible evidence of the worthlessness of her information, and asserts that before burning her "Johnsonian Narratives," he "first extracted from those sheets all that I could possibly consider to be authentic."[70]

Not only do we have a dispute between Boswell and Seward and Boswell and Knowles about this conversation, but we also have a dispute between Seward and Mary Knowles.[71] The most insistent issue between Knowles and Boswell and Knowles and Seward is regarding what was left out, rather than how what was said was said. Knowles's account is generally seen as one of the most artificial and repolished of any Johnsonian dialogues written by those who had spoken with Johnson personally. Judith Jennings has written four very thorough, if distinctly *parti pris*, discussions of the quarrel.[72]

These controversies over conversations in *Hebrides* and *Life* follow a broad general pattern of *parturient montes, nascetur ridiculus mus*: a massive destructive earthquake giving birth to a mouse. The debates on Johnson's conversations with Dun, Blacklock, Piozzi, Seward, and Knowles typically hinge either on segments of a long conversation that assumed a strong importance in Narrator A, but were not emphasized by Narrator B. Or they involve a word or words supposed by Narrator A to be salient or essential to the conversation, but considered to be marginal or forgettable by

Narrator B. Yet the conversations, for all that, read very much alike. They corroborate far more than they contradict, except in those instances in Piozzi where the company, venue, and presence of the storyteller can be contradicted. That consonance speaks to the relative veracity in main points not only of Boswell, but of Dun, Piozzi, Seward, and (less so) Knowles as well.

There is an unsavory degree of one-upmanship in Boswell's desire to serve Murphy, Tytler, Blacklock, Dun, Hawkins, Piozzi, Seward, and Knowles with a slightly more accurate, or slightly differently weighted, version of a conversation. Sometimes, as with Piozzi and Seward, his opponents could slang back at him as hard as he had done to him. Yet elsewhere, as with Hawkins, Blacklock, Dun, Tytler, and Knowles, he was dealing with people who were too meek, too obscure to pick on, or even, like Hawkins, dead and unable to respond. Perhaps some of the "Johnsonian Æther" Boswell said he had been infused with from 1763 to 1783 was the absurd desire exhibited by Johnson to seek victory even in trivial debates, and to score points against real or perceived opponents, even at the risk of brutalizing them.[73]

The debate over whether Boswell was an accurate or an inaccurate biographer of Johnson will continue on, as it has since the 1970s, and I cannot and do not hope here to have offered a definitive answer to that seemingly endless scholars' feud. Instead, I have demonstrated that Boswell's aggressive and pugnacious obsession with accuracy was not inherent to his earlier ideas of prose writing, but rather evolved after he matured away from his initial post-adolescent fascination in the 1760s with inventions, forgeries, and made-up characters. The transition took place in part from his seeing how, in incidents such as his disagreement with Murphy in 1775, the journals that he had kept on and off since the early 1760s often contradicted amusing-dinner-party-story accounts of Johnson's sayings. What Boswell chose to portray as a race from 1784 to 1793 to be the best biographer of Johnson was a historical happenstance dependent on the accidents of the timing of Johnson's death at the age of seventy-five, and on Hawkins's and Piozzi's speed in issuing their own books on Johnson before Boswell could complete his work. Another catalyst was the discussion of the contest by the newspapers, by satirists like Peter Pindar, and by caricatures that presented Hawkins, Piozzi, and Boswell as rivals for the crown of best biographer of Johnson. That contest, as the years wore on and the completion of the *Life* by Boswell and Malone was delayed, catalyzed Boswell's prior fascination with accurate and authentic conversation into an *idée fixe*. His campaign in the newspapers (and in the text of the *Life* itself) to show that he was the most authentic of them all—by demeaning his opponents as inauthentic—brought out the most jealous, competitive, and combative side of his personality.

Notes

In this essay, I cite as *Life* or *Hebrides* in *Life* the standard edition: George Birkbeck Hill, ed., Lawrence Fitzroy Powell, rev. and enl., *Boswell's Life of Johnson, Together with Boswell's Journal of a Tour to the Hebrides and Johnson's Diary of a Journey into North Wales*, vols. 5–6, 1st ed. (Oxford: Clarendon, 1964), 134–150. Paul Tankard, ed., *Facts and Inventions: Selections from the Journalism of James Boswell* (New Haven, CT: Yale University Press, 2014) is cited as "Tankard." "Journal" refers to the journals of James Boswell; the texts are cited from the "trade edition" of the journals since the research editions of the journals for these years have not yet been published.

1. Maxwelliana (*Life*, 3:116–133), Langtoniana, (*Life*, 4:2–33), and anecdotes by Steevens and Seward. James Boswell to Edmond Malone, November 17, 1788, cited in Marshall Waingrow, ed., *The Correspondence and Other Papers of James Boswell Relating to the Making of the Life of Johnson*, 2nd ed. (Edinburgh: Edinburgh University Press; New Haven, CT: Yale University Press, 2001), lix. For the Barber Questionnaire, see James J. Caudle and Michael Bundock, *The Runaway and the Apothecary: Francis Barber, Edward Ferrand, and the Life of Johnson—With a New Text of James Boswell's Francis Barber Questionnaire, 1786* (Norwich, CT: Thames, 2011).
2. Journal, April 1, 1775, in Charles Ryskamp and Frederick A. Pottle, eds., *Boswell: The Ominous Years 1774–1776* (London: Heinemann, 1963),

113; cf. Boswell's clarification in *Life*, 2:333: "There were very few of his friends so accurate as that I could venture to put down in writing what they told me as his sayings."

3. Tankard, 430, s.v. "inventions."
4. For a comparison of the surviving Erskine-Boswell letters in manuscript and as revised for Boswell's edition of them, see David Hankins and James J. Caudle, eds., *The General Correspondence of James Boswell, 1757–1763* (Edinburgh: Edinburgh University Press, 2006).
5. Journal, January 11, 1780, in Joseph W. Reed and Frederick A. Pottle, eds., *Boswell: Laird of Auchinleck 1778–1782* (London: Heinemann, 1977), 165.
6. The phrase appears before the *Life* was published in James Boswell to Robert Boswell, September 28, 1790, cited in Marlies K. Danziger and Frank Brady, eds., *Boswell: The Great Biographer 1789–1795* (London: Heinemann, 1989), 110.
7. Journal, March 30, 1775, in Ryskamp and Pottle, *Boswell*, 108–109.
8. Journal, April 1, 1775, in ibid., 113.
9. Adam Sisman, *Boswell's Presumptuous Task* (London: Harper, 2006); Waingrow, *Correspondence*.
10. George Birkbeck Hill, ed., *Johnsonian Miscellanies*, 2 vols. (Oxford: Clarendon, 1897). Hill reprinted Piozzi and Murphy in vol. 1 and Tyers, along with selections from Hawkins and Cooke, in vol. 2. O. M. Brack and Robert E. Kelley, eds., *The Early Biographies of Samuel Johnson* (Iowa City: University of Iowa Press, 1974) included fourteen biographies, six of them from before Johnson's death.
11. Frederick Pottle, *The Literary Career of James Boswell, Esq. Being the Bibliographical Materials for a Life of Boswell*, 2nd ed. (Oxford: Clarendon, 1966), 163.
12. Pat Rogers, "Introduction," in R. W. Chapman, ed., *James Boswell, Life of Johnson* (Oxford: Oxford University Press, 1980, 1998), xxv.
13. James Boswell to Bishop Barnard, March 20, 1785, quoted in Waingrow, *Correspondence*, li.
14. *Hebrides* in *Life*, 5:xxvii.
15. *Hebrides* in *Life*, 5:1.
16. J. M. Osborn, *By Appointment to His Majesty Biographer of Johnson* (New Haven, CT: Yale University Press, 1964).

17. *Hebrides* in *Life*, 5:421.

18. *Edinburgh Advertiser*, July 22, August 12, November 1, 1768; *Scots Magazine*, June, July, August 1768.

19. The sniping at Kames and Dundas occurred in Boswell's anonymous *A Letter to Robert Macqueen Lord Braxfield, on His Promotion to Be One of the Judges of the High Court of Justiciary* (Edinburgh: n.p., 1780) and *Letter to the People of Scotland, on the Alarming Attempt to Infringe the Articles of the Union* (London: Printed for Charles Dilly, 1785). The attacks on Piozzi were the anonymous "Piozzian Rhymes" in *London Chronicle*, April 20, 1786; his unpublished "Lines Supposed to Be Written by Mrs. Piozzi in Italy," May 1786, in Yale MS M310; and *Ode by Dr. Samuel Johnson to Mrs. Thrale Upon Their Supposed Approaching Nuptials* (London: Printed for R. Faulder, 1784 [presumed to be a false imprint for 1788]). The two published poems abovementioned may be read in Tankard, 235–237, 241–248.

20. Attrib. Boswell, "Johnson's Biographers," *Public Advertiser*, February 9, 1787; in Tankard, 239.

21. *Public Advertiser*, April 18, 1786; in Tankard, 233–235.

22. Judicious accounts may be found focused both more on Boswell—Frederick A. Pottle and Charles H. Bennett, "Boswell and Mrs. Piozzi," *Modern Philology* 39, no. 4 (1942): 421–30, 423–27—and more on Thrale/Piozzi—Mary Hyde, *The Impossible Friendship: Boswell and Mrs. Thrale* (Cambridge, MA: Harvard University Press, 1972).

23. *Morning Post*, February 22, 1790, *Star*, March 3, 1790; *Morning Post*, clipping from early 1790 currently undated (three items from Boswell's newspaper cuttings file at Yale MS P100: 3–5); in Tankard, 250, 257.

24. *Morning Post and Daily Advertiser*, June 25, 1791.

25. Geoffrey Scott, "The First Records," *Boswell Papers* 6 (1929): 15–27, reprinted in "The Making of the Life of Johnson as Shown in Boswell's First Notes," in James L. Clifford, ed., *Twentieth Century Interpretations of Boswell's Life of Johnson* (Englewood Cliffs, NJ: Prentice Hall, 1970), 27–39.

26. F. A. Pottle, "The Power of Memory in Boswell and Scott," in *Essays on the Eighteenth Century: Presented to David Nichol Smith in Honour of His Seventieth Birthday* (Oxford: Clarendon, 1945), 168–189.

27. Louis Baldwin, "The Conversation in Boswell's 'Life of Johnson,'" *Journal of English and Germanic Philology* 51, no. 4 (1952): 492–506, 506.
28. Frank Brady, *James Boswell: The Later Years* (New York: McGraw-Hill, 1984), 329–333.
29. Donald Greene, "The World's Worst Biography," *American Scholar* 62, no. 3 (Summer 1993): 365–382.
30. Donald Greene, "'Tis a Pretty Book, Mr. Boswell" (orig. 1978); Greene, "Boswell's *Life* as 'Literary Biography'"; and Frederick A. Pottle, "The Adequacy as Biography of Boswell's *Life of Johnson*" (orig. 1974); all in John A. Vance, ed., *Boswell's Life of Johnson: New Questions, New Answers* (Athens: University of Georgia Press, 1985), 110–171. The theoretical slant of Vance's collection may be inferred from his allowing Greene an initial statement, Pottle a peculiar sort of rebuttal given that his piece was published before Greene's was, and then giving Greene a chance at a rebuttal of Pottle's rebuttal.
31. Paul J. Korshin, "Johnson's Conversation in Boswell's *Life of Johnson*," and Greg Clingham, "Truth and Artifice in Boswell's Life of Johnson," both in *New Light on Boswell: Critical and Historical Essays on the Occasion of the Bicentenary of the Life of Johnson*, ed. Greg Clingham (Cambridge: Cambridge University Press, 1991, 1993), 174–193, 207–230.
32. William R. Siebenschuh, "Boswell's Second Crop of Memory: A New Look at the Role of Memory in the Making of the Life," in Vance, *Boswell's Life of Johnson*, 25–52; William R. Siebenschuh, "Cognitive Processes and Autobiographical Acts," *Biography* 12, no. 2 (1989): 142–153.
33. Korshin, "Johnson's Conversation."
34. Thomas Babington Macaulay, "Croker's Edition of Boswell's *Life of Johnson*," *Edinburgh Review* 54 (September 1831): 1–38.
35. Thomas R. Preston, "From Typology to Literature: Hermeneutics and Historical Narrative in Eighteenth-Century England," *Eighteenth Century* 23, no. 3 (1982): 181.
36. Ralph Rader, "Literary Form in Factual Narrative," in *Essays in Eighteenth-Century Biography*, ed. Philip P. Daghlian (Bloomington: Indiana University Press, 1968), 3–42.
37. Leopold Damrosch, "The Life of Johnson: An Anti-theory," *Eighteenth-Century Studies* 6, no. 4 (1973): 486–505, 486–487, 504.

38. Richard Schwartz, *Boswell's Johnson: A Preface to the Life* (Madison: University of Wisconsin Press, 1978), 31.
39. William R. Siebenschuh, "The Relationship between Factual Accuracy and Literary Art in the 'Life of Johnson,'" *Modern Philology* 74, no. 3 (1977): 273–288.
40. Robert H. Bell, "Boswell's Notes toward a Supreme Fiction. From *London Journal* to *Life of Johnson*," *Modern Language Quarterly* 38 (1977): 132–148.
41. Irma Lustig, "Fact into Art: James Boswell's Notes, Journals, and the Life of Johnson," in *Biography in the 18th Century*, ed. John H. Browning (New York: Garland, 1980), 112–146.
42. *Dorando: A Spanish Tale* (London: printed for J. Wilkie. Sold also by J. Dodsley, T. Davies, and by the Booksellers of Scotland, 1767). Tankard includes many of Boswell's shorter fictions, not properly "short stories," but outright fictions nonetheless.
43. *Gentleman's Magazine*, November 1793, 63:1009–1011; Tankard, 277.
44. Edward G. Fletcher, "Mrs. Piozzi on Boswell and Johnson's Tour," *University of Texas Studies in English* 32 (1953): 45–58; *Public Advertiser*, April 18, 1786, as "Boswell's Reply to the Postscript of Mrs. Piozzi's *Anecdotes*," in Tankard, 233–235.
45. James J. Caudle, "The Case of the Missing Hottentot: John Dun's Conversation with Samuel Johnson in James Boswell's *Tour to the Hebrides*, as Reported by Boswell and Dun," in Anthony W. Lee, ed., *Community and Solitude (Transits: Literature, Thought & Culture 1650–1850)* (Lewisburg, PA: Bucknell University Press, 2019), 53–76.
46. Thomas Blacklock to James Boswell, November 12, 1785; Yale MS C152; *Life*, 5:47, 417–418.
47. William Forbes to James Boswell, December 6, 1785; Yale MS C1276.
48. Thomas Blacklock to James Boswell, November 12, 1785; Yale MS C152; *Life*, 5:47, 417–418, emphasis added.
49. First printed in the second edition of the *Tour*. See *Life*, 5:417–418.
50. James Boswell to William Forbes, December 20, 1785.
51. *Hebrides* in *Life*, 5:418–419, 393.
52. Thomas Blacklock to James Boswell, November 12, 1785; Yale MS C152; *Life*, 5:47, 417–418.

53. *Journal of a Tour to the Hebrides*, 3rd ed. (1786), 435n[?]. See also Richard B. Sher, "Appendix: Boswell, Forbes, and the Quarrel with 'Young Mr. Tytler,'" in *The Correspondence of James Boswell with Sir William Forbes* (Edinburgh: Edinburgh University Press, forthcoming); Claire Lamont, "James Boswell and Alexander Fraser Tytler," *Bibliotheck* 6 (1971): 1–16.
54. James Boswell to William Temple, April 6, 1791, in Chauncey Brewster Tinker, ed., *Letters of James Boswell*, 2 vols. (Oxford: Clarendon, 1924), 2:432.
55. James Boswell, "Advertisement," *Life*, 1:7.
56. *Life*, 3:226 and n. 3.
57. *Life*, 4:343–347.
58. Ibid.
59. Irma S. Lustig, "Boswell at Work: The Animadversions on Mrs Piozzi," *Modern Language Review* 67 (1972): 11–30; *Life*, 1:416, n. 1.
60. Katharine C. Balderston, *Thraliana: The Diary of Mrs. Hester Lynch Thrale (Later Mrs. Piozzi), 1776–1809* (Oxford: Clarendon, 1942), 195–196. The corresponding passage is in the original *Anecdotes of the Late Samuel Johnson, LL.D. during the Last Twenty Years of His Life. By Hester Lynch Piozzi* (London: Printed for T. Cadell, 1786), 261. See also Journal, April 15, 1772, in William K. Wimsatt Jr. and Frederick A. Pottle, eds., *Boswell for the Defence 1769–1774* (London: Heinemann, 1959), 127–128.
61. Balderston, *Thraliana*, 1:202; Piozzi, *Anecdotes*, 191.
62. *Life*, 2:194 and n. 2; Wimsatt and Pottle, *Boswell for the Defence*, 133.
63. *Life*, 3:298–299.
64. John Nichols and John Bowyer Nichols, *Illustrations of the Literary History of the Eighteenth Century: Consisting of Authentic Memoirs and Original Letters of Eminent Persons; and Intended as a Sequel to the Literary Anecdotes*, 8 vols. (London: J.B. Nichols and Son, 1817–1858), 7:321–364.
65. Anna Seward to Mary Knowles, March 27, 1785, and Seward To Mrs. Mompesson, December 31, 1785, in *Letters of Anna Seward, Written between the Years 1784 and 1807*, 6 vols. (Edinburgh: George Ramsay, 1811), 1:47–48, 97–104.
66. James L. Clifford, "The Authenticity of Anna Seward's Published Correspondence," *Modern Philology* 39, no. 2 (1941), 113–122; James D. Wooley, "Johnson as Despot: Anna Seward's Rejected Contribution to

Boswell's Life," *Modern Philology* 70 (1972): 140–145; Donna Heiland, "Swan Songs: The Correspondence of Anna Seward and James Boswell," *Modern Philology* 90, no. 3 (1993), 381–391.

67. Heiland, "Swan Songs," discusses Seward to Boswell (Yale Boswell MSS C2461–2474) dated 1784–1790, and Boswell to Seward (Yale Boswell MSS L1142–1153), dated 1784–1788. Two of Seward to Boswell appeared in a revised form as Letters X and XXVII in *Letters of Anna Seward*, 1:39–45, 129–133. The discussions between Boswell and Seward have been discussed by Teresa Barnard, in her *Anna Seward: A Constructed Life—A Critical Biography* (Farnham: Ashgate, 2009), 2–4, 41–42.
68. Wooley, "Johnson as Despot," 140.
69. Seward to Mary Knowles, March 27, 1785, in *Letters of Anna Seward*, 1:46–48.
70. Wooley, "Johnson as Despot," 144nn14–15.
71. [Mary Knowles], "An Interesting DIALOGUE between the Late Dr. SAMUEL JOHNSON and Mrs. KNOWLES," *Gentleman's Magazine* 61 (1791): 500–502; [Knowles], *Dialogue between Dr. Johnson and Mrs. Knowles* (London: Printed for J. and A. Arch, 1799); [Knowles], *Dialogue between Mrs. Knowles and Dr. Johnson* (London: Printed by C. Stower, 1805); [Knowles], "Notes of a Conversation between Dr. Johnson and Mary Knowles in a Letter to Boswell," London Library of the Religious Society of Friends, Portfolio MSS 3/126.
72. Judith Jennings, "A Trio of Talented Women: Abolition, Gender and Political Participation 1780–91," *Slavery and Abolition* 26, no. 1 (2005,): 55–70; Jennings, "Confronting Samuel Johnson" and "Defying James Boswell," both in *Gender, Religion, and Radicalism in the Long Eighteenth Century: The "Ingenious Quaker" and Her Contemporaries*, ed. Jennings (Aldershot: Ashgate, 2006), 49–72, 99–120; Jennings, "'By No Means in a Liberal Style': Mary Morris Knowles versus James Boswell," in *Women Editing/Editing Women: Early Modern Women Writers and the New Textualism*, ed. Ann Hollinshead Hurley and Chanita Goodblatt (Newcastle-upon-Tyne: Cambridge Scholars, 2009), 227–255; Jennings, "Jane Harry Thresher and Mary Morris Knowles Speak Out for Liberty in Jamaica and England," in *Free at Last? Reflections on Freedom and the Abolition of the British Transatlantic*

Slave Trade, ed. Amar Wahab and Cecily Jones (Newcastle upon Tyne: Cambridge Scholars, 2011), 61–84, esp. "Mary Morris Knowles's Debate with Samuel Johnson," 70–73.

73. Felicity A. Nussbaum, "Boswell's Treatment of Johnson's Temper: 'A Warm West-Indian Climate,'" *Studies in English Literature, 1500–1900* 14, no. 3 (1974): 421–433.

6

Charles Burney's Handel Reconsidered

TODD GILMAN

Truth like beauty varies its fashion, and is best recommended by different dresses to different minds.
—Samuel Johnson, *Idler* 85

If the writer respects his hero, the reader will respect the writer.
—André Maurois, "Ethics of Biography"

The opening sentence of William Weber's 2009 biographical entry on the eminent eighteenth-century English critic and historian of music Dr. Charles Burney (1726–1814) in the *Cambridge Handel Encyclopedia* identifies the subject as a "musician, historian and author who held conflicting feelings about Handel."[1] Though he cites neither Roger Lonsdale nor Kerry S. Grant, both scholars who devoted considerable energy to their research on Burney, Weber is clearly indebted to them here. Yet, his statement misrepresents Burney's feelings by stressing conflict. That three leading scholars could remain unchallenged for so long raises key issues concerning biographical writing as it is theorized and practiced both in the eighteenth century and today.

In 1965, in his literary biography of Burney, Roger Lonsdale, a young, Oxford-educated scholar, slaughtered one of Great Britain's sacred cows.[2] Burney had been characterized as almost saintly, according to his daughter Frances's portrait.[3] In a massive, two-volume biography penned in the middle of the last century, Percy Scholes dubbed him *The Great Dr. Burney*;[4] and one of Lonsdale's reviewers reflected, "Perhaps no figure of the eighteenth-century scene was so universally liked as Doctor Burney. Amiable, talented, graceful in person and manner, he was welcomed in every circle. . . . Everyone regarded him as a model of charm and virtue, and it is a view that posterity has endorsed."[5] Dr. Samuel Johnson numbered among the more celebrated of his friends and associates. Frances Burney quoted Johnson rhapsodizing during a visit to Streatham: "I love Burney! my heart, as I told him—goes out to meet Burney! . . . Dr. Burney is a man for every body to love" (*Mem.*, 2:175–176). She also reported that Johnson had earlier claimed to have read the whole of her father's *German Tour* (1773), "except, perhaps, the description of the great pipes in the organs of Germany and the Netherlands," and that he had modeled his *Journey to the Western Islands of Scotland* (1775) on it for "size and form" (2:78–79). Similarly, in his *Life of Johnson*, James Boswell remarked that Johnson gave "much praise" to Burney's "elegant and entertaining travels," which he had "in his eye" when writing his own *Journey*.[6] Boswell also affirmed Johnson's regard for Burney as a combination of esteem as a fellow professional writer and filial affection, inserting this "last token of [Johnson's] remembrance of that ingenious and amiable man, . . . :- 'MR. JOHNSON, who came home last night, sends his respects to dear Dr. Burney, and all the dear Burneys, little and great'" (*Life of Johnson*, 974). For his part, Burney proudly reported Johnson's last words to him: "this impressive precept—'Do all the good you can'" (*DCB*, 287).[7] In contrast, Lonsdale disclosed that this consistently kind, charming, good-humored man could, unfortunately, also be "intensely ambitious" and behave in a manner that was "almost . . . ruthless" (*DCB*, viii).

In the 1950s, several large collections of Burney family papers had been discovered and acquired by collectors.[8] Lonsdale was among the first scholars to mine this treasure trove: he traveled great distances and pored over materials on both sides of the Atlantic. In the most egregious example Lonsdale adduced—hereafter the Bewley/Hawkins incident—Charles Burney audaciously but covertly sabotaged the *General History of the Science and Practice of Music* of his rival, Sir John Hawkins,[9] as though he were the wicked stepsibling from a classic fairy tale.[10] Perhaps cautious of reactions to his disclosure, Lonsdale soft-pedaled it. He maintained in his prefatory remarks that "the charm which his daughter attributes to him will still I trust be apparent in this book," and while this other side of Burney's character "must also now emerge," it might only "make him more recognizably human" and "need not diminish the affection with which he is usually regarded" (*DCB*, viii). Yet few writers on Burney since Lonsdale have failed to mention it—even those claiming still to hold him in high esteem.

Furthermore, in concluding his biography, Lonsdale offers less flattering assessments that counter the idealized portraits by Frances Burney and Scholes. Lonsdale considered Frances Burney's rendering to be "affectionate but emasculated" (*DCB*, 480), as many others had before him. He gave little more credence to Scholes's Charles Burney: "it is hardly fair to describe him as 'The Great Dr. Burney'": he was "not a great man, for he was limited by his pursuit of social and literary success." Burney "is now remembered by the literary historian only as a by no means dominating member of the Johnsonian and Streatham circles, who occasionally crosses the pages of [*Boswell's Life*] and of *Thraliana*" (*DCB*, 478, 481, 480). Still, *faute de mieux*, before 1965, Scholes came far closer than Frances Burney did to achieving general recognition as a credible biographer of her father. With only about a hundred Charles Burney letters known to exist in 1948, though, *Dr. Charles Burney* was poised to supersede *The Great Dr. Burney* from the moment Lonsdale set pen to paper.

Lonsdale wraps up his decidedly more sober, revisionist biography of Burney with the following eulogy: "Yet his intelligence, charm, and energy, the almost unremitting vitality of his response to life and to the demands he made upon himself, the diversity of his interests and the impressive range of his friendships, make him *a unique, if not a profound, personality in his own right*" (*DCB*, 481, emphasis added).[11] With rhetorical aplomb, Lonsdale lavishes praise on Burney with one hand while taking it away with the other.

Margaret Anne Doody, though no booster of Burney, drew the line at Lonsdale's pronouncement on his personality: "We do our subjects an injustice if we avoid clues to their complexities."[12] Others have simply accepted this assessment and many more besides, even to the point of echoing Lonsdale's use of *litotes* or ironic understatement (e.g., "need not diminish," above). An early reviewer of *Dr. Charles Burney*, for example, at first affirms Burney's conventional image "as a model of charm and virtue."[13] Then, insisting that Lonsdale "has not reversed this verdict" and that his subject "still emerges as an uncommonly nice man," the reviewer allows only that Burney "is no longer almost too good to be true" ("Sets Out to Please," 310). By contrast, Lawrence Lipking subjects Burney to a thorough drubbing, deeming the Bewley/Hawkins incident "perhaps the darkest page in his career" and suggesting that Burney's charm and good nature were "manufactured by the will" in order to disguise "pride and fear and turmoil."[14] Similarly, Alvaro Ribeiro, S. J., a former student of Lonsdale's, simply accepts his mentor's interpretation of this incident (*LBURNEY*, xxiv–xxv).

Christopher Hogwood likewise condemns the incident as Burney's "own disgracefully implemented critical attack on [Hawkins]."[15] Hogwood claims the attack had the effect of eclipsing Hawkins's *General History of the Science and Practice of Music* soon after its publication, with the unfortunate result that Burney's views as expressed in his own *GHM* "have been taken not only as representative of his true opinions but also of eighteenth-century critical thought in general." According to the fallacious (either/or) reasoning that follows, Hogwood wishes that Burney's surviving manuscripts had been available before now specifically in order that he could have dismissed the man's published views as fabrications whenever Burney's manuscript "true opinions" contradict them

("Burney Revealed," 10). An attendant benefit, Hogwood implies, is that the hypocrisy and duplicity to which the published versus manuscript Burney attests would by now have been established, the more convincingly to pigeonhole Burney as "scurrilous" for his attack on Hawkins ("Burney Revealed," 10).

In a famous *Rambler* essay on biography, Johnson cautioned that most biographies are "barren and useless," offering the reader "little intelligence," because most of their writers lack the aptitude to "portray a living acquaintance, except by his most prominent and observable particularities, and the grosser features of his mind."[16] As a consequence, he warns, "it may easily be imagined how much of this little knowledge may be lost in imparting it, and how soon a succession of copies will lose all resemblance to the original." Similarly, we can see the consequences of Lonsdale's positivistic use of unpublished sources to expose Burney's attack on Hawkins. Lonsdale interpreted these sources in such a way as to present a caricature of Burney at once misleading and shocking enough to ensure its own longevity. With each retelling by other writers, the portrait grew increasingly sensational and more distorted, sadly affirming Johnson's precept.

Whatever his intentions or aspirations were, Lonsdale shattered Burney's reputation and enhanced his own. Young Lonsdale wielded such power because he was in the right place at the right time. Burney's amiable personal style served him well to balance the intimidating professional persona he cultivated as an occasionally peremptory and idiosyncratic critic in his published opinions on music. Burney's contempt for French music generally, and for French opera in particular (see *GHM*, 2:7 and 2:966–967), stands as one notorious example. In his harsh criticism of French music, as in his opinions on many other musical topics, Burney follows Rousseau. As Burney's friend Samuel Crisp, a critic he much admired, wrote in a review of Burney's *Present State of Music in France and Italy* (1771; hereafter *Italian Tour*), Burney's attitude to French music reflected the fashionable point of view in the "severity with which he treats [it] . . . especially since Rousseau's [*Lettre sur la musique française* (1753)]."[17] But Burney was also cautious of alienating his readers by appearing too peremptory, as evidenced in his *Essay on Music Criticism* that prefaces volume 3 of *GHM*. Because Burney was aware that in all his published judgments on music he relied on and advocated a subjective, ineffable evaluative criterion, that is, "taste," the *Essay* clearly attempted to instill confidence in his readers in his impartiality as a critic and "to explain and apologize for the critical remarks which have been made in the course of this History . . . [in order to] prevent their being construed into pedantry and arrogance" (*GHM*, 2:7). Burney attempts to appeal to all his readers via a modest apology for his own taste that recalls his personal style. Still, he has no qualms about dictating the precepts by which his taste should be considered superior, distinguishing between an unskilled listener and a "prudent" critic who requires "not only extensive knowledge, and long experience, but a liberal, enlarged and candid mind" (2:7–8).

Similarly, Lonsdale used his access to Burney's papers to position himself as the man who knew the truth about his subject. Robert Ketton-Cremer momentarily wondered aloud whether there was room "so soon" for another biography of Burney after Joyce Hemlow's *History of Fanny Burney* and *GDB*, only to reassure his readers that Lonsdale had proven "abundantly" there was ("Sets Out to Please," 310). Indeed, carefully maneuvering (it appears) between Hemlow and Scholes in order to ensure his own marketability, Lonsdale had chosen a singular focus: Burney's ambition to be accepted, in Frances Burney's coinage, as a "man of letters" rather than as a "mere musician" (*DCB*, viii).

Far from meaning to deface a national monument for professional gain, Lonsdale insists he has a more altruistic motive: "to use the new material which has been made available to me in such a way as to enable [Burney] for the first time to tell his own story as far as possible, with the assistance of his friends and with the minimum of interference of his daughter" (*DCB*, ix). Moreover, as many students of eighteenth-century English literature will recognize, by adopting the principle of letting Burney speak for himself, Lonsdale was emulating no less a biographer than James Boswell. Introducing his *Life of Samuel Johnson* (1791), Boswell had stated that "instead of melting down my materials into one mass, and constantly speaking in my own person, by which I might have appeared to have more merit in the execution of the work," he had resolved to let Johnson himself speak via "his own minutes, letters or conversation" (*Life of Johnson*, 21). Lonsdale's stated aim was to empower Burney by giving voice to more of his private thoughts than had previously been possible, filling in the context with quotations from letters written by his friends, and by removing Frances Burney's (and other biographers') editorial excrescences. Indeed, for Boswell, writing biography should not mean indulging in facile "panegyrick," but ultimately, honoring one's subject, a precept for which he cannily offered Johnson's own endorsement: the biographer strives to "lay open to posterity the private and familiar character of [a] man . . . whose candor and genius will to the end of time be by his writings preserved in admiration" (*Life of Johnson*, 21, 22–23).

So Burney's case raises a thorny ethical issue: one that had occupied other English literary biographers' minds at least since Johnson published his biography of Richard Savage (1744). Many of Johnson's contemporaries questioned the biographer's decision to include unflattering details of Savage's life; and the debate continues. However, Richard Holmes has shown that Johnson so identified with his subject that he often revealed a strong bias toward him, even suppressing evidence of guilt.[18] Soon after *DCB* appeared, James L. Clifford, widely recognized for his "standard" biography of Johnson's early years,[19] published a related volume of his thoughts on "the operative concerns [of a] practicing biographer."[20] Although he does not mention Lonsdale specifically, Clifford quotes Charles Burney Jr.'s censorious comments on Hester Lynch Thrale's *Anecdotes of Dr. Johnson* in raising a question central to Lonsdale's biography: "How much should a biographer tell?"[21]

So highly nuanced is Clifford's discussion that he declines to proffer definitive or even provisional answers, particularly when considering the ethical dimensions of the question—only this eminently sensible tenet: "If what is hidden shows the subject to be very different from his professed character or conventional image, then the importance of truth may override any obligations of confidence. Each matter must be judged on its own merits. What is vital is that it be judged fairly, and that there be a balancing of pressures and contingencies" (*From Puzzles to Portraits*, 125). Clifford, a leading contemporary figure in Lonsdale's subfield, had been addressing this question since at least the late 1950s,[22] and Burney raised it due to concerns over his own legacy.

Ironically, we find Clifford himself opining, in a survey of Johnson studies published the same year as *From Puzzles to Portraits*, that Lonsdale's biography "can surely be called definitive."[23] Yet, a decade earlier, in a review of Hemlow's *HFB*, a book that in this survey shares the "definitive" moniker with *DCB*, Clifford explicitly praised Hemlow's discretion in treating "without lurid emphasis" delicate matters like the "whole sensational scandal" surrounding Frances Burney's brother James's elopement with his half-sister (review of *HFB*, 646). Clifford more likely took *DCB* to be definitive because, like Hemlow, Lonsdale had benefited (as the reviewer remarked) from "access to a wealth of new evidence contained in Burney family papers now in the British Museum, [Berg], and [Osborn]" (Clifford and Greene, *Johnson*, 16).

For that matter, it may have been the sheer aggregation of prestigious repositories containing the source material that clinched the "definitive" designation for Clifford: Hermione Lee identifies a political motive behind the use of this adjective when it is "attached to biographies by hopeful publishers or enthusiastic reviewers."[24] In such cases, she opines, it does not matter that biography is actually "a mixed, unstable genre, whose rules keep coming undone" with the result that its only rule is "that there is no such thing as a definitive biography" (*Biography*, 18). All that matters (at least to their writers) is how certain books come to be so designated. In the case of Lonsdale and Hemlow taken together, then, we can surmise that Clifford valued the fact that they incorporated new primary source material, and that this material is housed in prestigious repositories, which can often be counted on to endorse scholarly publications that make extensive use of their holdings. That one early reviewer of *DCB* had classed the book with Clifford's own biographies of Hester Thrale and Johnson along with *HFB* can only have augmented Clifford's ardor.[25]

Lonsdale set a new precedent for how Burney would be viewed for the foreseeable future—or until such time as another cache of Burney's papers turns up. Precisely because of this precedent, our understanding of certain aspects of Burney's personality, and especially of its apparent effect on his writing and editing practices, was profoundly changed. Nowhere has Lonsdale's work brought about a more pervasive effect than on a question central to Burney's intellectual legacy: the sincerity of his published opinions concerning George Frideric Handel, the baroque composer long assumed to be Burney's hero because of the voluminous and high praise lavished on him in Burney's published works.

Before *DCB*, music historians regarded Burney as Handel's greatest champion, as measured primarily by the sheer number of words he devoted to exalting the composer generally and to praising his individual works, and secondarily by the multiplicity and prominence of Burney's publications in which these featured. Yet, since Lonsdale, the question of the relative degrees of candor and dishonesty evident in Burney's published and unpublished writings on Handel has become vexed. To all appearances, Lonsdale had no qualms about using his access to the new Burney materials to alter drastically his subject's conventional image for his readers; and he proved to be the first scholar able to make extensive and sophisticated enough use of these materials to produce a biography that Oxford University Press deemed worthy of its imprimatur. Subsequent commentators accepted his claims without question.[26]

Previously, nearly all commentators saw Burney as amiable, judicious, and good-humored. Lonsdale alone convinced them that the same man harbored numerous prejudices while holding forth as the self-appointed arbiter of British musical taste; and that Burney made a habit of deceiving his readers for petty, self-serving reasons. Even more destructive is the fact that so many commentators uncritically accepted Lonsdale's claim that Burney's affinity for duplicity pervaded his published writing. For Burney's deceptions seemed plausible to them, as did the idea that these could manifest themselves so promiscuously: in the form of insincere praise or flattery, anonymous denunciations—sometimes by proxy—and in the appropriation of others' writing as his own. So those who wished to have a fuller insight into any issue about which Burney wrote would now have to consider his unpublished works as well and adjudicate any apparent inconsistencies between these and their published versions.[27]

In the case of Burney's writings on Handel, Lonsdale discovered significant discrepancies between the published and unpublished writings. Burney's unpublished papers reveal that by 1784, Burney also came to resent King George III, the conductor Joah Bates, who had led the five performances of London's first great Handel Commemoration that year,[28] and the faction of nobility and gentry whom Burney's confidant Thomas Twining referred to as "Handelomaniacs," those "partisans of what is called the *old* Music" who rejected all post-Handelian musical trends.[29] In Burney's mind, all these men were guilty of suppressing native English and modern Italian and German composers in favor of the Saxon baroque composer Handel, who had towered over the London musical world for half a century until his death in 1759. They were also guilty of forcing Burney to publicly and posthumously exalt Handel to the exclusion of all other composers living or dead.

On the strength of this exciting new evidence, Lonsdale ventured a giant critical leap, concluding that by the time of the 1784 commemoration, Burney had decidedly mixed feelings about Handel's supremacy as a composer. Lonsdale's argument ran counter to the received wisdom of Burney's ideas on Handel, which was based on his published writings: to cite the two most obvious examples, both Burney's *Account* and *GHM* lavishly praise him. As Claudia L. Johnson, apparently innocent of Lonsdale's or Grant's revisionist stance, once opined of the latter publication, "Handel so dominates [Burney's *GHM*] that he almost appears to be the motive for writing it to begin with."[30]

Moreover, in 1983, Grant, in *Dr. Burney as Critic and Historian of Music*,[31] quoting from the same sources Lonsdale had, adduces even further evidence of Burney's duplicitous hostility and hidden motives, thereby consolidating Lonsdale's portrait of the man ambivalent about Handel.[32] He states that Burney, "often afflicted with melancholy, and narrow-minded and jealous in pursuit of his profession," could not overcome the source of his conflicts: his "intense desire to be liked" (11). Grant later adds, "Judging him in the harshest light, it may be said that his impulse to be agreeable led him to sacrifice objective criticism for praise" (305). Grant goes so far as to condemn Burney's high praise of Handel as "the most extensive prevarication in his work"; for the truth of the matter was that "the model of the 'good Handelian' [Joseph Kerman's coinage] held Handel largely responsible for the stagnation of English music" (305, 304). Grant surely hyperbolizes for rhetorical effect here: "The point is not Kerman's perception, but [Burney's] deception. In responding to the forces around him, and in shaping his work to meet the narrow taste of some of his patrons, he produced a work [that has] misled scholars for 200 years" (303). Grant even claims that so intently did Burney disdain Handel, he eventually allowed this judgment to color his final published statement on the composer: his entry on Handel in Abraham Rees's *Cyclopaedia* (1811).[33]

Finally, in 1991, Father Ribeiro published the first volume of a projected four-volume edition of Burney's letters.[34] This magisterial tome complemented (even as it dwarfed by comparison) a recent collection of surviving fragments of Burney's "Memoirs" covering the years 1726 to 1769—painstakingly de-redacted, arranged, and annotated—that managed to escape Frances Burney's most sedulous efforts at censorship.[35] Now readers could judge for themselves the accuracy of the portrait that Lonsdale and Grant had drawn based on the new manuscript material, but only through the end of 1784, thirty years before Burney's death. After 1991, due to a series of unfortunate events, the fate of the rest of the volumes remained uncertain.

The editorial project has resumed under Peter Sabor, but none of the subsequent volumes has yet appeared.[36] The bulk of Burney's papers, written in a hand not easily deciphered, scattered in public and private repositories across the globe,[37] have yet to be published and continue to be generally inaccessible. These include nearly all materials that could be used to shed light on Burney's true opinion of Handel after the coerced paean that Lonsdale and Grant claim appeared in the *Account*—especially on Burney's thinking as he completed volumes three and four of his *GHM* and prepared his contributions to Rees's *Cyclopaedia*. We have been forced instead to rely on Lonsdale's and Grant's opinions, often based on selective quotation, and on two edited volumes of papers, for far too long.

I would like, then, to redress Lonsdale's and Grant's conclusions by resituating Burney's attitude toward Handel within the larger context of Burney's whole output. My goal is to update our notion of the evolution of Burney's attitude toward Handel's accomplishments as a composer and musician. I concentrate on the surviving unpublished letters and manuscripts from January 1785 (*LBURNEY* ends in December 1784) to 1811, the year Burney's "Handel" entry in Rees appeared in print. A reconsideration of the evidence will reveal that to the end of his life, Burney held a higher opinion of Handel than Lonsdale and Grant claimed he did, in spite of Handel's adherence to his "ancient," high baroque style even while his contemporaries had long since adopted the "modern," Neapolitan, galant, or pre-Classical style.[38] Indeed, it is clear that for Burney, Handel always remained a "Colossus"[39] possessed of "original genius" or "great fire,"[40] a talent unrivalled even decades after his death.

Neither Lonsdale nor Grant acknowledged Burney's rationale for many of the differences evident in the manuscript versus print versions of his writings: that he thought it inappropriate to display the degree of bias he felt was demanded of him in some of his published works. Because Burney in his private documents tended to shade distinctions he offered in more black-and-white terms in these published works, Lonsdale and Grant questioned his sincerity in certain instances to such a degree that they rejected it entirely.

My case relies on three reinterpretations of Burney's actions and writings. First, we should remember that Burney repeatedly stated both privately and publicly that he was a man of integrity in the sense that he would not and did not publish statements that he did not believe to be true. I have concluded, based on my own survey of the surviving manuscripts and letters,[41] that with the exception of a few passages in his *Account*—passages that Burney himself admitted he was politically pressured into publishing (Burney to Twining, July 31, 1784, in *LBURNEY*, 423–431)—Burney's commitment to truth in print is sincere.

For his part, although he adduces irrefutable evidence of Burney's duplicity on certain occasions, even Lonsdale finds himself forced to concede Burney's basic strength of character. Citing a letter Burney wrote to Edmund Burke expressing intense relief that his friend is not angry with him for refusing to cast a vote against his conscience, Lonsdale remarks that a surviving draft of this letter shows even more clearly how troubled Burney had been at the possibility of alienating an old friend, and thus, that "beneath his invariably genial manner and in spite of his intense desire always to please, [Burney] possessed a tough core of integrity" (*DCB*, 336). Lonsdale adds to this the example of Mrs. Thrale believing Burney "to be the only man whose pardon [Johnson] had ever begged, after [Burney] had taken offence at an apparent aspersion against his veracity" (*DCB*, 336).

Second, even when he had no reprisals to fear, Burney ultimately refrained from publishing the comments critical of Handel that he had formerly hinted he would, and that Grant tries—unconvincingly, for lack of evidence—to demonstrate that he did. In the letter to Twining cited above (July 31, 1784), Burney had vowed, "I will not write like an Apostate. . . . Some time or other I'll shew you a passage or two that I have been obliged to expunge, or render utterly insipid" (*DCB*, 425–427). Similarly, in the preface to the *Account*, Burney had offered dissociation from "bigotry in favor of Handel": "As it amounts not to bigotry, or the preclusion of all respect or admiration of excellence in others, wherever I can find it, my narrative will be less likely to excite suspicions of improbability, or hyperbole" (xvi).

Yet Burney's portrait of Handel in Rees cannot reasonably be read even as "mildly censorious," despite Grant's claim in his argument that Burney "set the record straight in print" (*DBCHM*, 289). For Burney's final treatment of Handel actually reads as quite laudatory, suggesting instead that Burney came to appreciate his merits *more* over time, not *less*. Even Grant himself is forced to acknowledge that this is true: "Notwithstanding his objections to some aspects of Handel's style, [Burney] genuinely admired the composer's tremendous genius. As he undertook the minute examination of Handel's works [according to one of his manuscript notebooks in Osborn], [Burney] uncovered even 'more reason' for the 'long duration of national partiality'" (*DBCHM*, 241). Thus, as Grant further concedes, "'Indeed [says Burney], I have lately discovered beauties of composition which perhaps I formerly did not see'" (241). Moreover, in spite of Burney's praise of the Neapolitan opera composer Johann Adolphe Hasse's arias as the height of perfection, Grant allows (correctly, in my view) that Burney "was most impressed with Handel's variety of design (form) in aria compositions" (241). Indeed, Burney maintained in the *Account* that in "variety of style and ingenuity of accompaniment [the form of Handel's arias transcended] those of all preceding and cotemporary [*sic*] Composers throughout Europe" (*Account*, 40). Finally, I believe that, taken together, Burney's unpublished private correspondence and notebooks—in which he seldom had occasion to be deceptive and tended to speak unguardedly—portray a man full of admiration for Handel even as he acknowledges certain imperfections.

Lonsdale and Grant were correct in noting that Burney long favored the opera arias of Hasse to those of Handel, owing to Burney's appreciation for Hasse's more modern, pre-Classical style. Writing to Christoph Daniel Ebeling (1741–1817, a German scholar, librarian, and devotee of Handel) twelve years after Handel's death, Burney rhapsodizes, "I confess to you, that of all the Composers of songs that have ever existed in any Country, Hasse stands the highest in my opinion. He is possessed of grace, invention, propriety beyond all others. The Poet & the singer are equally respected by him, & he never sacrifices either to the pedantry of crowding his Score, or the vanity of Instrumental Performers. He has not perhaps the nervous grandeur, I had almost called it martial grandeur of Handel, which so well suited his age & the English nation; but he has more Melody, more simplicity, more taste, & more happiness in the expression of words" (Burney to Ebeling, 1771, in *LBURNEY*, 103). Moreover, Burney resented being pressured by the king and Joah Bates to offer unstinting praise of the king's favorite composer in the *Account* he was writing, and worried about the consequences if he resisted. As he wrote to Twining on July 31, 1784, "*Entre nous*, I wish there was any other mediator than [Joah] B[ates]—whom I perceive no praise either of himself or Handel can satisfy—& the K. is full as *intoleratingly* fond of the old Saxon as B[ates].—so that, if I was to act *politically* & *wisely*, I shd openly abuse all other Music, Musicians, & lovers of Music in all parts of the world, but Handel & his insatiable & exclusive admirers" (*LBURNEY*, 425). Putting aside the gratuitous snide reference to Handel as "the old Saxon," Burney's objection appears to be both the coercive nature of the so-called request and the need to praise Handel *exclusively*, not just to praise him. The next sentence reads, "And in that Case shd not you think me a very fit person to write a *general Histy* of Music—to do justice to Genius & Talents in every Time & Country where I cd find them?" (*LBURNEY*, 425). It is worth repeating that Burney remains adamant that he will not misrepresent himself: "But I will not write like an Apostate—I will not deny my liberal principles—I will not abuse the lovers of the best Music of Italy & Germany, & say that they are only admired *through fashion*, & want of good taste & judgment.—I will ransack the language for terms of praise, in speaking of his [i.e., Handel's] best works—& the Manner in wch they have been lately performed; but cannot, will not say that there is no other Music fit to be heard, or as well performed. . . . My heart & pen are locked up.—I wrote the Preface, Life of Handel—Introduction & 3 1st Days wth my heart *au bout de la langue*"

(*LBURNEY*, 425, 428).[42] Still, during the course of this letter, Burney concedes that he has no choice but to capitulate in certain instances, even while protesting the affront to his integrity:

> *One Key* of Panegyric is all they want.—fine!—very fine!—charming! exquisite! grand!! sublime!!!—These are all the notes . . . I must use—Some time or other I'll shew you a passage or two that I have been obliged to expunge, or render utterly insipid, because they [objected]—Into what a Scrape am I got?—I may do myself irreparable mischief—& *can* I fear derive no good—considering the hands I am in. I set out with the design of praising honestly & heartily what I felt deserving—& to be silent as to the rest. . . . But now, I am terrified at every word I write—my playful . . . way of expressing myself taken from me, reduces me to the state of a hireling ministerial Scribler, without the Pay—(*LBURNEY*, 427–428)

Yet when we read Burney's published preface to his *Account*, we see that the critic has openly dissociated himself from "bigotry" in favor of Handel: "However my mind may be impressed with a reverence for HANDEL, by an early and long acquaintance with his person and works, yet, as it amounts not to bigotry, or the preclusion of all respect or admiration of excellence in others, wherever I can find it, my narrative will be less likely to excite suspicions of improbability, or hyperbole, in such readers as were not so fortunate as to participate of the surprize and rapture of all that were present at these magnificent performances, and are able to judge of the reality of the sensations described" (Burney, preface to *Account*, xv). Indeed, Burney tells his readers that he wishes to be seen as fair-minded by extolling the virtues of certain specific aspects of the commemoration while saving a more penetrating and critical examination of Handel's works for the fourth installment of his *General History of Music*: "And though I reserve the critical examination of the entire works of HANDEL for the last volume of my History, yet, as indiscriminate praise is little better than censure, I shall [here] specify such beauties of composition and effect as I felt most forcibly in attending the performance of each day, and for which, by a careful perusal of the score, I have been since enabled to assign reasons" (xvi).

Commenting on Burney's general critical integrity, Richard Luckett noted that "Burney's difficulty was in being constant to his feelings or allowing them the weight they deserved, yet it is his great merit that he could not disguise what he felt."[43] By contrast, Lonsdale pointed to these same passages, and to Burney's subsequent private comments to Twining (September 1, 1784) on this subject, to justify the opposite conclusion: that the critic is not only biased, but seeking revenge. Burney writes to Twining, "I have reserved to myself, for the sequel of my History, the critical examination of Handel's works in general, and then shall 'extenuate nothing, nor set down aught in malice'" (*LBURNEY*, 437).

Lonsdale adduces the evidence above to make the case that in his preface, Burney "hinted that, as he had already told Twining, he would be less tactful and confined in his remarks on Handel when he could escape the scrutiny of the 'Royal Eye'" (*DCB*, 308). I agree with Lonsdale that Burney's use of this quote from the distraught Othello—just before he commits suicide after discovering he has been tricked into murdering the innocent Desdemona—to describe himself can be interpreted as significantly more pointed than the published version. Yet Burney asserts in the same sentence that although he will excuse no faults ("extenuate nothing"), he explicitly does *not* seek revenge ("nor set down aught in malice").

Thus Lonsdale's comment quoted above, in combination with his editorial gloss that during the 1784 Handel Commemoration Burney's "only consolation was the thought of what he would say about Handel in his uncensored *History*" (*DCB*, 305), amount in my view to both a case of special pleading on Burney's behalf and a compromise of Lonsdale's expressed commitment to let the subject "tell his own story as far as possible." Indeed, in the next sentence, Burney expresses to Twining his praise of the king's musical judgment, even if it *is* focused exclusively on Handel: "I must do his Maj. the justice to say that he is much better acquainted with

Handels works & merit than any of the noble or gentle Directors. Right or wrong, he gives reasons for his admiration; & the great crime of *exclusive liking*, (particularly in a King) excepted, I can heartily subscribe to most of his notions" (September 1, 1784, in *LBURNEY*, 437). In affirming the king's musical judgment as sound, which he does because he recognizes it as built upon a solid foundation of knowledge, and because he admires royalty, Burney clearly abandons his former reservations and endorses ("heartily subscribe[s] to") Handel into the bargain.

Moreover, in a letter two months later (November 9, 1784) to Sir Robert Murray Keith, British envoy extraordinary and plenipotentiary to the Imperial Court at Vienna, Burney admits to being pleasantly surprised by the high quality of the performances and how they showcased Handel's music to so great an effect as to exceed his and everyone else's expectations:

> You must long have observed, Sir, that there are partisans for every kind of music as well as Sectaries of every religion, and that the followers of Handel are very numerous in England: indeed the belief in his infalibility [*sic*] & *supremacy* forms a part of our national musical creed. But even those who being accustomed to more modern, and, as they contend, more graceful, elegant and fanciful music; & who call his style of composition Gothic, inelegant & clumsy, readily allowed that the effects in performance by a band of voices & instruments in Westminster-Abbey, amounting to 525, were such as they had never experienced, & excited sensations of delight for which they were wholly unable to account. (*LBURNEY*, 446)

Indeed, it is as if Burney is relieved to have been proven wrong that he now allows himself a candid admission of his former skepticism concerning the whole concept of the Handel Commemoration: "I own that previous to performance . . . I had not allowed imagination to run riot, or anticipate many great & good effects, unless from the aggregate of sound in the Choruses. The Solo parts, I thought would be lost in the expanse through wch they had to travel to a great Part of the company, unless very coursely [*sic*] performed; and with the *ensemble* I expected to be stunned" (446). In a final rhetorical flourish, Burney uses the voicing of his reservations as a foil to set off a second burst of enthusiasm featuring a catalog of merits each of which expressly quells the earlier doubt: "But incredulity is silenced, and experience & speculation overturned. The loud was *not* course [*sic*], nor the soft *inaudible*. The general Mass of Harmony attracted & impelled, with a kind of centripetal power, all the parts of this immense band to keep together; &, from the happy construction of the building, the most gentle vocal breathing and inflexion of sound was augmented without reverberation, & conveyed to the most distant hearers more sweet & full than it was delivered" (446). Burney's admission that his fears proved to be unfounded, combined with his awestruck report of the success of the event, thus offers further evidence that he was openly and dynamically impressed by Handel and his music in ways he had not been before. What is more, it registers a new affirmation of his interest in listening to and studying Handel that could easily justify his decision to devote so much real estate in the fourth book of *GHM* to Handel, and with such undeniable care and conviction.

Writing in the mid-1950s, Eric David Mackerness, later author of *A Social History of English Music*, in which he deemed the 1784 Handel Commemoration "in some ways the most important single event in the history of English music in the eighteenth century,"[44] offered high praise for Burney's talent as a biographer. Mackerness was particularly impressed by the capsule composer biographies Burney contributed to Rees: "It would be no exaggeration to say that his biographical articles make up a body of writing comparable in excellence with [Johnson's] *Lives of the Poets*. . . . As examples of effective prose expression, many of his 'lives' have the trenchancy and authoritative tone which are dominant characteristics of [Johnson's] more celebrated biographies."[45] Mackerness acknowledged that many of the lives of composers and performers given in Rees constitute "little more than transcripts" from those in *GHM* (e.g., the biographies of Purcell, Blow, and

J. C. Bach), but added that others are entirely new, or considerably enlarged from their earlier versions ("Dr. Burney, Biographer," 353–354). The entry on Handel is one such case, for although it is mainly condensed from the *Account*, Burney also revised and augmented it. So impressed was Mackerness with the version in Rees that he singled it out both for comparison with Johnson and as exemplary music criticism: "Like [Johnson], [Burney] had well defined standards of what constitutes artistic merit. And his qualities as a biographer and music critic are seen at their best, perhaps, in his life of Handel, which occupies eleven columns of print—as against Haydn's two, Mozart's one and a quarter, and J. S. Bach's one and a half. However much of this may have been derived from other sources, the Handel article as it stands in [Rees] is a miniature masterpiece, and forms an effective tribute to a genius about whom [Burney] obviously had no reservations" (356). Mackerness then emphasizes how when Burney sums up Handel's qualities as a musician, he adamantly defends his powers of invention by refuting his alleged lack of originality, "a critical principle dear to [Burney] and other musical aestheticians of his day" (356). After slightly misquoting Burney's eloquent defense,[46] Mackerness concludes by noting that he finds Burney persuasive because of his sheer erudition: "Behind a pronouncement of that kind stands a whole system of critical valuations" (356). Although Burney copied this passage from his own *Account*, he composed the paragraph directly following it (see below: "We will not assert . . .") specifically for Rees. Taken together, then, the two paragraphs suggest that around 1803, Burney carefully considered and repeated the passage Mackerness quotes because he still believed it to be true of Handel, as the subsequent qualifying paragraph confirms.

In stark contrast to Mackerness, Grant claimed that in the *Cyclopaedia* entry on Handel, Burney "finally set the record straight in print" concerning "Handel's ranking against other composers in every style," and "belatedly reasserted his integrity, though many of his original readers were no longer alive to witness the rectification" (*DBCHM*, 289). Yet the passage to which Grant points consists of two sentences appended to the same superlative assessment of Handel that Mackerness had earlier quoted ("Dr. Burney, Biographer," 356) in order to demonstrate that Burney adamantly defended Handel: "We will not assert that his vocal melodies were more polished and graceful than those of his countryman and contemporary Hasse; or his recitatives, or musical declamation, superior to that of his rivals, Bononcini and Porpora. But in his instrumental compositions there is a vigour, a spirit, a variety, a learning, and invention, superior to every other composer that can be named; and in his organ fugues, and organ playing, there is learning always free from pedantry; and, in his choruses, a grandeur and sublimity which we believe has never been equaled since the invention of counterpoint" (Burney, "Handel"). These words conclude an entry that opened with yet another sentence penned expressly for the *Cyclopaedia*, in which Burney identifies Handel as "the greatest musical composer of his time, and in some particulars, of any time or country in Europe" (*ibid.*). Yet Grant continues pushing, eliding the all-important distinction between the Handelians and Handel's music when speculating on the cause of Burney's misgivings about disclosing his true feelings:

> The Handelians exerted an overpowering influence on [Burney]'s criticism. Yet even the [passage in the *Cyclopaedia*] does not fully reveal the stifling force the devotees of Handel wielded over musical life in England. To [Burney], it was a pernicious influence, affecting far more than his writings; at the bottom of a page in one of his notebooks [in Osborn] there is a passage written for no eyes but his own:
>
> "I dare not say what I have long thought. That it is our reverence for old authors and bigotry to Handel, that has prevented us from keeping pace with the rest of Europe in the cultivation of Music." (*DBCHM*, 289)

Even if we accept Grant's claim as true, that is, that Burney feared the consequences of speaking truth to power, we should remember that in this passage, Burney expresses nothing more than frustration over the pervasive influence of Handel's zealous devotees—whom he mainly regarded as obstructive philistines. Burney wrote in April 1800 to Christian Latrobe expressing contempt for "the Handelians, who are most of them utterly unable to judge of Handel's real merit; and all jealous of that of others—as well as pert & flippant soi-disant Connoisseurs" (Osborn). Burney does not express contempt for Handel's music itself, nor does Grant claim otherwise, in spite of the context.

Thus we have cause to doubt Lonsdale's claim that Burney's bloated chapter on Handel at the end of *GHM* was essentially an act of pandering on a par with his *Account*. Lonsdale writes, "When [Burney] came to write his chapter on the rise and progress of Italian opera in England during the eighteenth century, his gratitude for the King's generosity in permitting him to use the Handel Manuscripts in the Royal Collection obliged him to deal with that composer's theatrical works at enormous length. Earlier threats about the uncensored criticism of Handel which would appear in [*GHM*] were now forgotten and his lengthy and detailed discussion of the operas was obviously written primarily for the delectation of the King: for once Burney hardly cared about his general readers" (*DCB*, 337). Yet, as Grant notes, Burney's general audience comprised those most likely to be familiar with these works. The works of Handel were constantly before the public. Many of his readers would remember seeing the operas, which (though none had not been performed in decades) were soon to be made available in Arnold's edition. Thus, "the availability of the music was even more decisive in shaping this chapter than were the preferences of the king" (286).

Lonsdale continues, "[Burney] included, indeed, a direct compliment to the King's taste which, in July 1784, would have seemed inconceivable: 'happy for the art, when a sovereign's favour is founded on so firm a basis as the works of Handel! Indeed, our country would certainly now be less sensible of their worth, were it not for the royal countenance and patronage with which they have been long and steadily honoured'" (*DCB*, 337–338). Lonsdale opines in conclusion that Burney "himself, we may suspect, might have been 'less sensible of their worth' in other circumstances," meaning, that is, if Burney had not felt the need to praise the king's prejudiced devotion to Handel (338).

Yet Burney's thanking the king for providing him access to the Royal Collection can scarcely be dismissed as mere pandering, given that this access enabled Burney's all-important reassessment of the vast bulk of Handel's compositions up close; and it follows that we cannot attribute Burney's extensive focus on Handel to any obvious motive but an acknowledgment of their value, merit, and importance. Even Grant felt obligated to take Lonsdale to task on this point, arguing that "had [Burney] been so solicitous of the king's pleasure at this time, he most certainly would not have curtailed his discussion of the king's favorite Handelian music, the oratorios, for which he provides only a brief list of dates and a reference to the *Account*" (*DBCHM*, 286–287).

On February 17, 1805, just shy of age eighty, Burney wrote to his protégé William Crotch, formerly a child prodigy and now a formidable critic in his own right.[47] Irving reads the letter and its crotchety reply as revealing "a tendency on the part of both respected authorities to view their art in terms of a deep, bitter and persistent ancient-modern division," that is, a preoccupation with music's quarrel over ancients versus moderns (*Ancients and Moderns*, 28). In arguing that Franz Joseph Haydn, despite some "oddities" in his music, "remain[s] serious, beautiful & sublime [enough], to constitute a truly great man," Burney praises Haydn's achievements as comparable to Handel's insofar as the two composers share the distinction—common to all "original writers"—of being "at first regarded as innovators" (Gerald Coke Handel Collection; the letter is reprinted in Burney, *GHM*, 2:1032–1036).

Burney elaborates on the similarity between the two by insisting that Handel's famous *Utrecht Te Deum* of 1713 was for decades considered so "odd" that it was never performed at St. Paul's Cathedral, but instead confined to the Chapel Royal at St. James's Palace. "The first concert of Anc[t] Music established in this country in 1711 or 12 was set up against Handel, whose style had so much more force & variety than what our nation had been accustomed to[,] that the Te Deum which he composed for the peace of Utrecht in 1713, was not performed at St Pauls, or anywhere but in the Chapel Royal at St James's, till 1732" (*GHM*, 2:1032–1036).[48] And yet, Burney argues, it was that very oddity that made him realize how far superior Handel's instrumental style was to Purcell's, whom he had until then considered unsurpassed among English composers of secular vocal and instrumental music: "No one ever loved the memory & melody of Purcell and his powers of making Englishmen feel English words, with more enthusiasm than I have always done. . . . But it was not till I heard the instrumental effects of Handel's Utrecht Te Deum that I made this discovery [i.e., how far superior Handel's force and variety of style were even to Purcell's]" (*GHM*, 2:1032–1036). While it may seem strange that Burney ranks him among English composers, especially in light of the Saxon's long association with Italian opera, Handel became a British citizen in 1727, and his English oratorios further naturalized him from then on.

Similarly, although as an auto-didact, Burney had also studied many of Handel's published scores, he notes that it was not "till I had heard [Handel's] Oratorios performed that I preferred his sacred Music *in general* to that of our Doctors Blow, Crofts [*sic*], and Greene," that is, to the pantheon of Purcell's English contemporaries and immediate successors (*GHM*, 2:1032–1036, emphasis added).[49] The implication is that just as what were at first widely considered "odd" emanations from the pen of that original genius, Handel, ultimately distinguished him in Burney's mind as superior even to Purcell—and just as hearing Handel's oratorios made him regard the sacred music of Blow, Croft, and Greene as inferior—so, too, will Haydn's supposed oddities set him apart from *his* predecessors. All this by way of emphasizing *the profundity of Burney's regard for Handel as superior to all the other composers of distinction he names here*, even as he implies that Haydn might well eventually supersede Handel.

Continuing almost like a sinner unburdening himself in confession, Burney at last arrives at the crucial point of his reservations: that praising Handel to the exclusion of all other composers undermines his own credibility as the most authoritative arbiter of taste. He reflects,

> Whoever writes or speaks to the public must not indulge favouritism. In writing my general Hist. of Music, if I had only gratified the exclusive admirers of Handel, I should have celebrated the genius and abilities of no other Musician. And what sort of general history would it have been? *In my account of his commemoration he was my sole Hero, & I have stuck close to him, as his faithful 'Squire. I was nursed in Handel's music, and have revered it & praised it more fully than that of any other, but not exclusively.* I have endeavored to discriminate & point out the peculiar merit of other great Masters in every country. (Burney to Crotch, February 17, 1805, emphasis added)

Hence we see the central importance of Burney's final surviving private statement on the matter, written to his friend Dr. Parry in 1807:

> I own as I am not always an exclusive admirer of the Great Handel, I do wish you to see what pains I have taken to blazon his great abilities, by not only pointing out the beauties of his best compositions, but by assigning reasons for their effects. In writing a General History of Music I was to praise good music wherever I found it, and Italy, which Handel made his model in his youth in vocal music, & Germany which he has made our model in Instrumental, have produced great composers before and since his time; *but I must repeat what I have already said in print*, that there is a force and spirit in his Oratorio Choruses, and in his Hautbois Concertos, which I meet with in no other music of any other country.[50]

Thus, rather than contradict himself—as Lonsdale and Grant have led us to expect—Burney finally affirms the truth of what he has said in print.

Readers may be curious to know whether, after publishing *DCB* nearly fifty-five years ago, Lonsdale ever revisited Burney's opinion of Handel. In fact, he did publish an article evaluating Burney's music-related contributions to Rees. Lonsdale wished to determine the extent to which the essays—of which he estimates Burney penned some two thousand—reflect the critic and historian's most mature thoughts on these subjects versus the extent to which they are a pastiche of his earlier writings.[51] Lonsdale offers lively new insights into Burney's thinking on a variety of subjects. Yet when he arrives at the Handel entry, the biographer invokes Mackerness's effusive commentary only to contradict him, insisting that the entry contains nothing new at all: "Alas, the biography of Handel is in fact only a somewhat compressed and occasionally slightly rephrased transcription of the 'Sketch' of the composer's life [from Burney's *Account*] in 1785" ("Dr. Burney's 'Dictionary of Music,'" 163). As we have seen—and as Grant would later demonstrate (inadvertently, by placing the passages in question side by side precisely in order to gainsay this very point)—this is not true (*DBCHM*, 288–289). Ribeiro also recognized the significance of Burney's "Handel" entry, twice calling readers' attention to it. First he referred to Burney's "great and genuine admiration for Handel in his [*GHM*] and [*Account*] *and in his article 'Handel' in Rees*"; later, he directed readers to see "especially Rees, for [Burney's] *final assessment of Handel*" (*LBURNEY*, 11n12, 425n12, emphasis added).

By contrast with Lonsdale, Grant appears to acknowledge, if only tacitly, the extent to which his earlier pronouncement on Burney's opinions of Handel had been misleading. In the biography of Burney he contributed to the second edition of *The New Grove* (2001), Grant states, "The extensive treatment of Handel in the fourth volume of the [*GHM*] is the result both of [Burney] being granted access to the king's great collection of Handel manuscripts and of his catering to the general enthusiasm for Handel's music that dominated English taste for many years. [Burney] himself was a modernist who, *though capable of admiring what was exceptional about Handel's music*, was unprepared to accept Handel *or any other composer* as the greatest that ever lived or ever would live."[52] Just how much Grant's perspective mellowed may be judged by comparison with Weber's more recent, less nuanced biographical entry on Burney in the *Cambridge Handel Encyclopedia*, with which we began.

Once raised, the question of the extent to which Burney should be taken at his word versus dismissed as a prevaricator will not be quelled in some minds, no matter how effectively it can be and has been settled, not just concerning Handel, but in general. The fact that Burney behaved deceptively toward Hawkins and others, that Lonsdale exaggerated the impact of this behavior, and that when it came to Handel, the die was cast by those with the greatest access to the evidence (i.e., Lonsdale and Grant), ensures that many will continue to believe Burney's obvious, sustained, amply demonstrated and documented admiration for Handel was nothing but a politically motivated and self-serving fabrication perpetrated on an unsuspecting public. For this reason among many others, Hunter's recent *Lives of Handel* (2015) offers a welcome antidote to some of the distortions surrounding Handel by his biographers since the eighteenth century. Hunter's book can be read as an early entrant in a new subgenre of biography that Holmes has named comparative biography. Yet instead of a subgenre of biography properly so-called, Holmes sees comparative biography as "virtually a new discipline": based on the premise that every biography is the interpretation of a life, and that many different interpretations are always possible; the student examines the handling of one subject by a number of different biographers, and over several different historical periods.[53]

His ideas on this subject having been adumbrated more than a decade before Hunter published his *Lives of Handel*, Holmes originally identified the following studies as worthy examples of comparative biography: Sylvia Norman's book on the "strange shifts in Shelley's posthumous reputation," *Flight of the Skylark* (1954); Ian Hamilton's book about "the cumulative influence of literary executors," *Keepers of the Flame* (1992); Geoffrey Cantor's work on "changing 'public images' of scientific heroism in the Victorian biographies of Michael Faraday";[54] and Lucasta Miller's study of "the increasingly exotic literary cult of Haworth Parsonage," *The Brontë Myth* (2001). In a similar vein, Hunter's *Lives of Handel*, a sort of metabiography, critically analyzes the ways in which Handel has been portrayed over the centuries. The objective that motivates such a large-scale effort is to carefully expose the underlying ideologies that have impeded our ability to regard the composer neutrally, on his own terms. I hope this essay further demonstrates the need for such agnostic investigations.

Notes

1. Annette Landgraf and David Vickers, eds., *The Cambridge Handel Encyclopedia* (Cambridge: Cambridge University Press, 2009), s.v. "Burney, Charles." The entry is signed by William Weber.
2. Roger Lonsdale, *Dr. Charles Burney: A Literary Biography* (Oxford: Clarendon, 1965) (hereafter *DCB*).
3. Frances Burney d'Arblay, *Memoirs of Doctor Burney* (London: Edward Moxon, 1832) (hereafter *Mem.*).
4. Percy A. Scholes, *The Great Dr. Burney* (London: Oxford University Press, 1948) (hereafter *GDB*).
5. Robert Wyndham Ketton-Cremer, "Dr. Burney Sets Out to Please," review of *DCB*, *Times Literary Supplement*, April 22, 1965, 310.
6. James Boswell, *The Life of Samuel Johnson*, ed. David Womersley (London, 1791; London: Penguin, 2008), 867 (hereafter *Life of Johnson*).
7. See also Lonsdale, "Johnson and Dr. Burney," in *Johnson, Boswell and Their Circle* (Oxford: Clarendon, 1965), 21–40; Peter Sabor, "'I Dearly Love to Praise Old Friends': Dr. Burney and Dr. Johnson," *Johnsonian News Letter* 66 (2015): 6–17; and Sabor, "'The March of Intimacy': Dr. Burney and Dr. Johnson," *Eighteenth-Century Life* 42, no. 2 (2018): 38–55.
8. These collections contain more than two thousand letters and manuscripts held mainly at the British Library; the Berg Collection, NYPL (hereafter Berg); and the Burney Family Collection, James and Marie

Osborn Collection, Beinecke Rare Book and Manuscript Library, Yale University (hereafter Osborn). They comprise some fifteen hundred letters between Burney and his relatives and friends; notebooks Burney penned while working on his massive *General History of Music* and other books; and around a hundred fifty fragments of the twelve notebooks of Memoirs he composed ca. 1806. Charles Burney, *A General History of Music*, 4 vols. 1776–1789; modern ed. by Frank Mercer, 4 vols. in 2 (London: Foulis, 1935; repr., Dover, 1957) (hereafter *GHM*). For the provenance of Burney's papers, see Joyce Hemlow et al., eds., *A Catalogue of the Burney Family Correspondence, 1749–1878* (New York: New York Public Library, 1971), x–xviii; and *The Letters of Dr. Charles Burney*, vol. 1: *1751–1784*, ed. Alvaro Ribeiro, S. J. (Oxford: Clarendon, 1991), xxx–xxxi (hereafter *LBURNEY*). Some of the letters had been printed after Burney's death in *Mem.* and in the *Diary and Letters of Madame d'Arblay (1778–1840)*, ed. Austin Dobson (London: Macmillan, 1904–1905), nearly always censored: see Kerry S. Grant, *Dr. Burney as Critic and Historian of Music* (Ann Arbor, MI: UMI Research Press, 1983), xii–6 (hereafter *DBCHM*); Lonsdale, *DCB*, 432–455; and Hemlow, *The History of Fanny Burney* (Oxford: Clarendon, 1958), 446–466 (hereafter *HFB*). Mercer transcribed and included additional letters in his appendix to the second volume of *GHM*.

9. John Hawkins, *A General History of the Science and Practice of Music* (London, 1776; repr., New York: Dover, 1963).
10. Lonsdale details the Bewley/Hawkins incident in *DCB*, 208–219.
11. Lonsdale was not the first to balk at Scholes's bias. Robert Stevenson, "'The Rivals'—Hawkins, Burney, and Boswell," *Musical Quarterly* 36, no. 1 (1950): 67–82, pointed to a pattern in *GDB* of favoritism matched by a strong prejudice against Hawkins. In stark contrast, Lonsdale's evaluation of Burney's personality as "unique, if not . . . profound" clashes with the preceding encomium and diminishes it.
12. Margaret Anne Doody, *Frances Burney: The Life in the Works* (New Brunswick, NJ: Rutgers University Press, 1988), 10.
13. Ketton-Cremer, "Sets Out to Please," 310.
14. Lawrence Lipking, *The Ordering of the Arts in Eighteenth-Century England* (Princeton, NJ: Princeton University Press, 1970), 272.

15. Christopher Hogwood, "Burney Revealed," review of *LBURNEY*, *Times Literary Supplement*, Nov. 13, 1992, 10.

16. Samuel Johnson, *Rambler*, no. 60 (October 13, 1750), repr. in *Johnson on Savage*, ed. Richard Holmes (London: Harper Perennial, 2005), 115.

17. Samuel Crisp, review of *Italian Tour*, by Burney, *Contemporary Review* 31 (1771): 421–432.

18. Richard Holmes, *Dr. Johnson & Mr. Savage* (London: Hodder & Stoughton, 1993), esp. 100–125.

19. James L. Clifford, *Young Samuel Johnson* (London: Heinemann, 1955); as *Young Sam Johnson* (New York: McGraw-Hill, 1955). It would be another fourteen years before Clifford's sequel appeared: *Dictionary Johnson* (New York: McGraw-Hill, 1979). Pat Rogers describes Clifford's achievement as "a sober, factual, but never boring narrative that constitutes the 'standard' account for [Samuel Johnson] in these decades preceding his first acquaintance with [James Boswell]." "Johnson, Samuel," in *St. James Guide to Biography*, ed. Paul E. Schellinger (Chicago: St. James Press, 1991), 415–416.

20. James L. Clifford, *From Puzzles to Portraits* (Chapel Hill: University of North Carolina Press, 1970), vii.

21. Clifford mistakes Charles Burney, Jr.'s review of Hester Lynch Thrale's *Anecdotes* for a review by Burney of *Boswell's Life*. (Thanks to Peter Sabor for alerting me to the fact that the true reviewer of the *Anecdotes* was not Burney himself but his son.)

22. See, for example, Clifford, review of *HFB*, by Hemlow, *Modern Language Notes* 74, no. 7 (1959): 644–646; and the introduction to *Biography as an Art*, ed. Clifford (New York: Oxford University Press, 1962), ix–xx.

23. Clifford and Donald J. Greene, *Samuel Johnson: A Survey and Bibliography of Critical Studies* (Minneapolis: University of Minnesota Press, 1970), 16.

24. Hermione Lee, *Biography* (Oxford: Oxford University Press, 2009), 18.

25. Philip M. Griffith, "A Man of Talent and Literature," review of *DCB* by Lonsdale, *Burke Newsletter* 8, no. 2 (1966): 667–668, writes that the biography "may stand on the same shelf, unembarrassed, with James L.

Clifford's *Piozzi*, with the same author's *Young Sam Johnson*, and with [*HFB*]."

26. Griffith, ibid., 668, is the only reviewer of *DCB* to openly resist the notion that Lonsdale told everything one might wish to know.
27. That said, Laura Marcus observes that Lytton Strachey, for one, suggested that the "'inner truth' of confessional writings is no more reliable as evidence than 'outward seeming,'" and thus questioned the popular notion, "beloved of biographers, that the more 'private' the document, the closer to the truth of the self the biographer reaches." Marcus, *Auto/Biographical Discourses* (Manchester: Manchester University Press, 1994), 115.
28. For a concise modern description of this event, see Howard Smither, *A History of the Oratorio*, vol. 3 (Chapel Hill: University of North Carolina Press, 1987), 222–237. Robert Manson Myers, *Handel's Messiah: A Touchstone of Taste* (New York: Macmillan, 1948), 187–231, documents the 1784 commemoration using contemporary sources.
29. Twining coined the term "Handelomaniacs" in a footnote to his anonymous review of Burney's *Account of the Musical Performances in Westminster-Abbey . . . in Commemoration of Handel* (London: 1785; repr. [New York: Da Capo Press, 1979]) (hereafter *Account*). [Thomas Twining], review of *An Account of the Musical Performances in Westminster-Abbey . . . in Commemoration of Handel*, by Charles Burney, *Contemporary Review* 59 (1785): 130–138. See note on p. 131.
30. Claudia L. Johnson, "'Giant HANDEL' and the Musical Sublime," *Eighteenth-Century Studies* 19, no. 4 (1986): 515–532, 522. Johnson cites neither Lonsdale nor Grant.
31. See note 8 for the complete citation.
32. Echoing Lonsdale, Grant, *DBCHM*, 304, reminds us that "the agreeable [Burney], under cloak of anonymity, wrote sharp and often biting reviews in the [*MR*], contrived reviews of [John Hawkins's] work, and composed malicious poetry."
33. Burney, "Handel," in *The Cyclopaedia; or Universal Dictionary of Arts, Sciences, and Literature*, ed. Abraham Rees, 45 vols. (London: Longman, Hurst, Rees, Orme, and Brown, 1802–1820), vol. 17, unpaginated. As Grant, *DBCHM*, 289, notes, Burney wrote this passage earlier,

although it was not published until 1811. *DCB*, 430, adds that Burney completed all the *Cyclopaedia* work between 1801 and 1805, or from the age of seventy-five to seventy-nine; we can surmise, then, that he completed the Handel article ca. 1803, around age seventy-seven.

34. Ribeiro, *LBURNEY*. Ribeiro brought together 191 letters in chronological order, 154 of which had never been printed before.
35. *Memoirs of Dr. Charles Burney, 1726–1769*, ed. Slava Klima et al. (Lincoln: University of Nebraska Press, 1988).
36. The complete set will add four more volumes: vol. 2 (1785–1793), ed. Lorna Clark; vol. 3 (1794–1801), ed. Stewart Cooke; vol. 4 (1802–1807), ed. Stewart Cooke; vol. 5 (1808–1814), ed. Peter Sabor. See https://www.mcgill.ca/burneycentre/publications/current-projects#Charles%20Burney.
37. *DCB*, 495–497, lists the surviving letters and manuscripts of Burney that had been identified as of ca. 1964. Hemlow et al., *Catalogue of the Burney Family Correspondence*, 3–62, which claims to list the location of all of Burney's letters that the editors had seen or known to be extant as of 1971, cites holdings as widely dispersed as the United Kingdom, the United States, Canada, and Italy.
38. Howard Irving, *Ancients and Moderns* (Aldershot: Ashgate, 1999), provides the most thorough recent discussion of the quarrel of the "ancients" versus "moderns" in music as it pertains to Burney and Handel. See also Todd Gilman, "Arne, Handel, the Beautiful, and the Sublime," *Eighteenth-Century Studies* 42, no. 4 (2009): 529–555, and Johnson, "'Giant HANDEL' and the Musical Sublime," 515–533.
39. Burney, *Frag. Mem.* (B.L. Add. MS. 48345, f. 8).
40. This is implied in Burney's notebook, "Materials towards a History of German Music," of ca. 1772–1790 (Osborn).
41. I was fortunate to do this thanks to a month-long McGill-ASECS Fellowship in the archives of the Burney Centre. See https://mcgill.ca/burneycentre/mcgill-asecs-fellowship. For an account of the origins and development of this repository to 1988, see Lars Troide, "History and Description of the Burney Project," *Fontanus* 1 (1988): 38–49, http://fontanus.mcgill.ca/article/view/2/2.
42. The phrase "with my heart *au bout de la langue*" (literally "at the end of the tongue") means "sincerely."

43. Richard Luckett, "'Or Rather Our Musical Shakespeare': Charles Burney's Purcell," in *Music in Eighteenth-Century England*, ed. Christopher Hogwood and Richard Luckett (Cambridge: Cambridge University Press, 1983), 73.
44. Eric David Mackerness, *A Social History of English Music* (London: Routledge, 1964), 127.
45. Eric David Mackerness, "Dr. Burney, Biographer," *Contemporary Review* 189 (1956): 352–357.
46. The original reads: "All that the greatest and boldest musical inventor *can* do, is to avail himself of the best effusions, combinations, and effects of his predecessors; to arrange and apply them in a new manner; and to add, from his own source, whatever he can draw, that is grand, graceful, gay, pathetic, or in any other way pleasing. This Handel did in a most ample and superior manner." Burney, "Handel."
47. Irving, *Ancients and Moderns*, provides an incisive exploration of Burney and Crotch's relationship, and of the younger man's development and achievements as a musician-critic.
48. This statement is not quite accurate; for as Burney himself earlier noted (*GHM*, 2:388), by order of Queen Anne, Handel's *Utrecht Te Deum* was performed biannually at St. Paul's on the feast of the Sons of the Clergy, alternating with Purcell's *Te Deum and Jubilate*, which had until then been the featured work. Thirty years later, Handel's *Dettingen Te Deum* superseded both.
49. While Burney omits mention of the younger generation of English composers (e.g., Arne, Boyce, and Stanley), he leaves no doubt here and in *GHM* that he does not consider them to be on par with Handel, either. Concerning Arne in particular, see Todd Gilman, "Polemical Introduction," in *The Theatre Career of Thomas Arne* (Newark: University of Delaware Press, 2013), 1–30, esp. 12.
50. Burney to Dr. Caleb Hillier Parry of Bath, 1807, in Osborn, emphasis added.
51. Roger Lonsdale, "Dr. Burney's 'Dictionary of Music,'" *Musicology Australia* 5, no. 1 (1979): 159–171.
52. "Burney, Charles," in *The New Grove Dictionary of Music and Musicians*, 2nd ed., ed. Stanley Sadie and John Tyrrell (London: Macmillan, 2001), 4:642, emphasis added.

53. Richard Holmes, "The Proper Study?" in *Mapping Lives*, ed. Peter France and William St. Clair (Oxford: Oxford University Press for the British Academy, 2002), 16. See also his related essay, "Biography: Inventing the Truth," in *The Art of Literary Biography*, ed. John Batchelor (Oxford: Clarendon, 1995), 15–25.
54. Geoffrey Cantor, "The Scientist as Hero: Public Images of Michael Faraday," in *Telling Lives in Science: Essays on Scientific Biography*, ed. Michael Shortland and Richard Yeo (Cambridge: Cambridge University Press, 1996), 171–194.

Bibliography

Anderson, David D. "Another Biography? For God's Sake, Why?" *Georgia Review* 35, no. 2 (1981): 401–406.

Anonymous. *The Life and Adventures of Bampfylde-Moore Carew, the Noted Devonshire Stroller and Dog Stealer; as Related by Himself.* London, 1749.

Arblay, Alexander d'. Alexander d'Arblay to Alexandre d'Arblay, May 19, 1813. Archives Nationales, Paris.

———. Alexander d'Arblay to Alexandre d'Arblay, March 7, 1817. Berg Collection. New York Public Library.

———. "On the Subject of My Entering Orders." Berg Collection. New York Public Library.

Arblay, Frances Burney d'. *Diary and Letters of Madame d'Arblay (1778–1840).* Edited by Austin Dobson. London: Macmillan, 1904–1905.

———. *Memoirs of Doctor Burney.* London: Edward Moxon, 1832.

Austen, Henry. "Biographical Notice of the Author (1818)." In *A Memoir of Jane Austen and Other Family Recollections*, edited by Kathryn Sutherland, 135–143. Oxford: Oxford University Press, 2002.

Austen, Jane. *Jane Austen's Letters.* 4th ed. Edited by Deirdre Le Faye. Oxford: Oxford University Press, 2011.

Backscheider, Paula. "Sex, Sin and Ideology: The Drama's Gift to the Genesis of the Novel." *Lumen: Selected Proceedings from the Canadian Society for Eighteenth-Century Studies* 12 (1993): 1–15.

———. *Spectacular Politics: Theatrical Power and Mass Culture in Early Modern England.* Baltimore: Johns Hopkins University Press, 1993.

Balderston, Katherine C., ed. *Thraliana: The Diary of Mrs. Hester Lynch Thrale (Later Mrs. Piozzi), 1776–1809.* Vol. 2, *1784–1809.* Oxford: Clarendon, 1942.

Baldwin, Louis. "The Conversation in Boswell's 'Life of Johnson.'" *Journal of English and Germanic Philology* 51, no. 4 (October 1952): 492–506.

Barnard, Teresa. *Anna Seward: A Constructed Life—A Critical Biography*. Farnham: Ashgate, 2009.

Barrett, Charlotte. Charlotte Barrett to Marianne Francis, August 24, 1812. Barrett Collection. British Library.

Beauvoir, Simone de. *Le deuxieme sexe* [The Second Sex]. 2 vols. Paris: Gallimard, 1949.

Bell, Robert H. "Boswell's Notes toward a Supreme Fiction. From *London Journal* to *Life of Johnson*." *Modern Language Quarterly* 38 (1977): 132–148.

Benger, Elizabeth. *Memoirs of the Late Mrs. Elizabeth Hamilton*. 2 vols. London: Longman, 1818.

———. *Memoirs of Mr. John Tobin, Author of the Honey-moon, with a Selection of His Unpublished Writings*. London: Longman, Hurst, Rees, Orme, 1820.

Benkovitz, Miriam. "Dr. Burney's Memoirs." *Review of English Studies* 10, no. 39 (1959): 257–268.

Benton, Michael. "Literary Biography: The Cinderella Story of Literary Studies." *Journal of Aesthetic Education* 39, no. 3 (2005): 44–57.

Berglund, Lisa. "Why Should Hester Lynch Piozzi Be Doctor Johnson's Mrs. Thrale?" *Names: A Journal of Onomastics* 64, no. 4 (December 2016): 189–201.

Bloom, Edward A., and Lillian D. Bloom, eds. *The Piozzi Letters: Correspondence of Hester Lynch Piozzi, 1784–1821*. Vol. 1, *1784–1791*. Newark: University of Delaware Press, 1989.

Bostic, Heidi. *The Fiction of Enlightenment: Women of Reason in the French Eighteenth Century*. Newark: University of Delaware Press, 2010.

Boswell, James. *Boswell in Holland, 1763–1764, Including His Correspondence with Belle de Zuylen (Zélide)*. Edited by Frederick A. Pottle. New York: McGraw-Hill, 1928, 1952.

———. *Boswell in Search of a Wife*. Edited by Frank Brady and Frederick A. Pottle. New York: McGraw-Hill, 1956.

———. *Letter to the People of Scotland, on the Alarming Attempt to Infringe the Articles of the Union*. London: Printed for Charles Dilly, 1785.

———. *A Letter to Robert Macqueen Lord Braxfield, on His Promotion to Be One of the Judges of the High Court of Justiciary*. Edinburgh: n.p., 1780.

———. *Life of Samuel Johnson*. Edited by David Womersley. 1791. New York: Penguin, 2008.

———. *The Life of Samuel Johnson, LL.D.* 2 vols. London, 1791.

———. *The Life of Samuel Johnson LLD. Comprehending an Account of His Studies and Numerous Works, in Chronological Order; a Series of His Epistolary Correspondence and Conversations with Many Eminent Persons; and Various Original Pieces of His Composition*. London, 1791.

———. "Lines Supposed to Be Written by Mrs. Piozzi in Italy." May 1786. Yale MS M310.

———. *London Journal 1762–1763*. Edited by Gordon Turnbull. New York: Penguin, 2010.

———. *Ode by Dr. Samuel Johnson to Mrs. Thrale upon Their Supposed Approaching Nuptials*. London: Printed for R. Faulder, New-Bond-street, 1784. Presumed to be a false imprint for 1788.

———. "Piozzian Rhymes." *London Chronicle*, April 20, 1786.

Boswell, James, and Samuel Johnson. *A Journey to the Western Islands of Scotland and the Journal of a Tour to the Hebrides*. Edited by Peter Levi. New York: Penguin, 1984.

Brack, O. M., and Robert E. Kelley, eds. *The Early Biographies of Samuel Johnson*. Iowa City: University of Iowa Press, 1974.

Bradford, Richard, ed. *Life Writing: Essays on Autobiography, Biography and Literature*. Basingstoke: Palgrave Macmillan, 2010.

Brady, Frank. *James Boswell: The Later Years*. New York: McGraw-Hill, 1984.

Brant, Clare. *Eighteenth-Century Letters and British Culture*. New York: Palgrave Macmillan, 2006.

Brunström, Conrad. *Thomas Sheridan's Career and Influence: An Actor in Earnest*. Lewisburg, PA: Bucknell University Press, 2011.

"Burney, Charles." In *The New Grove Dictionary of Music and Musicians*, edited by Stanley Sadie and John Tyrrell, 2nd ed., 4:642. London: Macmillan, 2001.

Burney, Charles. Charles Burney to Frances d'Arblay, July 30, 1806. Osborn Collection. Beinecke Library, Yale University.

———. *A General History of Music*. London, 1776–1789. Modern ed. by Frank Mercer. London: Foulis, 1935. Reprint, Dover, 1957.

———. "Handel." In *The Cyclopaedia; or Universal Dictionary of Arts, Sciences, and Literature*, edited by Abraham Rees, vol. 17, unpaginated. London: Longman, Hurst, Rees, Orme, and Brown, 1802–1820.

———. *The Letters of Dr. Charles Burney*. Vol. 1, *1751–1784*. Edited by Alvaro Ribeiro, S. J. Oxford: Clarendon, 1991.

———. *Memoirs of Dr. Charles Burney, 1726–1769*. Edited by Slava Klima et al. Lincoln: University of Nebraska Press, 1988.

Burney, Frances. *The Additional Journals and Letters of Frances Burney*. Vol. 2, *1791–1840*. Edited by Peter Sabor. Oxford: Oxford University Press, 2018.

———. *The Complete Plays of Frances Burney*. 2 vols. Edited by Peter Sabor et al. London: Pickering and Chatto, 1995.

———. *Journals and Letters*. Selected with an introduction by Peter Sabor and Lars Troide. New York: Penguin, 2001.

———. *The Journals and Letters of Fanny Burney (Madame d'Arblay)*. 12 vols. Edited by Joyce Hemlow, Curtis D. Cecil, Althea Douglas, Patricia Hawkins, George G. Falle, Edward A. Bloom, Lilian D. Bloom, Peter Hughes, and Warren Derry. Oxford: Clarendon, 1972–1984.

Cantor, Geoffrey. "The Scientist as Hero: Public Images of Michael Faraday." In *Telling Lives in Science: Essays on Scientific Biography*, edited by Michael Shortland and Richard Yeo, 171–194. Cambridge: Cambridge University Press, 1996.

Caudle, James J. "The Case of the Missing Hottentot: John Dun's Conversation with Samuel Johnson in James Boswell's *Tour to the Hebrides*, as Reported by Boswell and Dun." In *Community and Solitude (Transits: Literature, Thought & Culture 1650–1850)*, edited by Anthony W. Lee, 53–76. Lewisburg, PA: Bucknell University Press, 2019.

Caudle, James J., and Michael Bundock. *The Runaway and the Apothecary: Francis Barber, Edward Ferrand, and the Life of Johnson—With a New Text of James Boswell's Francis Barber Questionnaire, 1786*. Norwich, CT: Thames, 2011.

Chapman, R. W. *Johnson, Boswell and Mrs. Piozzi: A Suppressed Passage Restored*. London: Oxford University Press, 1929.

———, ed. *The Letters of Samuel Johnson, with Mrs. Thrale's Genuine Letters to Him*. Vol. 3, *1783–1784, Letters 821.2–1174*. Oxford: Clarendon, 1952.

———. "Mrs. Piozzi's Omissions from Johnson's Letters to the Thrales." *Review of English Studies* 22, no. 85 (January 1946): 17–28.

———. "Mrs. Thrale's Letters to Johnson Published by Mrs. Piozzi in 1788." *Review of English Studies* 24, no. 93 (January 1948): 58–61.

Charrière, Isabelle de. *Bien-Né* [Well-Born]. In *Observations et conjectures politiques*. Les Verrières: Jérémie Witel, 1787–1788. See also entry for *Observations*.

———. *Caliste* [*Caliste, ou suite des Lettres écrites de Lausanne*, 1787]. In *Four Tales*, translated by S[ybil] M. S[cott], 165–263. 1926. Freeport, NY: Books for Libraries Press, 1970.

———. "Constance's Story" [L'Histoire de Constance]. In *The Nobleman and Other Romances*, translated by Caroline Warman, 285–315. New York: Penguin, 2012.

———. *Éclaircissements relatifs à la publication des Confessions de Rousseau* [1790]. In *Oeuvres complètes d'Isabelle de Charrière/Belle de Zuylen*, 10:183–194.

———. *Éloge de Jean-Jacques Rousseau* [In Praise (& Critique) of Jean-Jacques Rousseau; Paris: Grégoire, 1791]. In *Oeuvres complètes d'Isabelle de Charrière/Belle de Zuylen*, 10:195–211.

———. *Émigré Letters* [*Lettres trouvées dans des portefeuilles d'émigrés*, 1793]. In *The Nobleman and Other Romances*, translated by Caroline Warman, 183–255. New York: Penguin, 2012.

———. *Letters from Neuchâtel* [*Lettres neuchâteloises*, 1784]. In *The Nobleman and Other Romances*, translated by Caroline Warman, 23–74. New York: Penguin, 2012.

———. *Letters of Mistress Henley Published by Her Friend* [*Lettres de Mistriss Henley publiées par son amie*, 1784]. Translated by Philip Stewart and Jean Vache. New York: MLA, 1993.

———. Letters to Comte de Dönhoff [in French]. "Les Lettres," printed in Kees van Strien and Madeleine van Strien-Chardonneau, "Belle de Zuylen/Isabelle de Charrière et le Comte de Dönhoff: Deux lettres inédites." *Revue d'histoire littéraire de la France* 104, no. 2 (2004): 473–483. Utrechts Archief, 347–1: Archives Van Hardenbroek, inv. Nr. 457-c-29.

———. *Letters Written from Lausanne: Cécile* [*Lettres écrites de Lausanne*, 1785]. In *The Nobleman and Other Romances*, translated by Caroline Warman, 103–172. New York: Penguin, 2012.

———. *Lettres d'un évêque français à la nation* [Letters from a French Bishop to the Nation, 1789]. In *Oeuvres complètes d'Isabelle de Charrière/Belle de Zuylen*, 10:127–160.

———. *Lettres trouvées dans la neige* [Letters Found in the Snow, 1793]. In *Oeuvres Complètes d'Isabelle de Charrière/Belle de Zuylen*, 10:223–254.

———. *L'incognito* [The Incognito, a libretto, 1784]. The piece is not extant but is confirmed in various letters (*Oeuvres complètes*).

———. *The Nobleman* [*Le Noble*, 1762]~~, 1–22~~. In *The Nobleman and Other Romances*, translated by Caroline Warman, 1–22. New York: Penguin, 2012.

———. *Observations et conjectures politiques* [Political Observations and Conjectures, 1787–1788]. In *Oeuvres complètes d'Isabelle de Charrière/Belle de Zuylen*, 10:57–110.

———. *Oeuvres complètes d'Isabelle de Charrière/Belle de Zuylen*. 10 vols. Edited by Jean-Daniel Candaux, C. P. Courtney, Pierre H. Dubois, Simone Dubois-De Bruyn, Patrice Thompson, Jeroom Vercruysse, and Dennis M. Wood. Amsterdam: G.A. van Oorschot. Geneva: Slatkine, 1979–1984.

———. "Portrait de M.lle de Z . . . Sous le nom de Zélide" [Portrait of Zélide]. In *Oeuvres complètes d'Isabelle de Charrière/Belle de Zuylen*, 10:37–39.

———. *There Are No Letters Like Yours: The Correspondence of Isabelle de Charrière and Constant d'Hermenches*. Translated and edited by Janet Whatley and Malcolm Whatley. Lincoln: University of Nebraska Press, 2000.

———. *Three Women, a Novel by the Abbé de la Tour* [*Trois Femmes* and, in German, *Drei Weiber*, 1795]. Translated by Emma Rooksby. New York: MLA, 2007.

Chisholm, Kate. *Fanny Burney: Her Life, 1752–1840*. London: Chatto and Windus, 1998.

Cixous, Hélène. "The Laugh of the Medusa" (1975). In *Feminism*, edited by Robyn R. Warhol and Diane Price Herndl, 334–335. New Brunswick, NJ: Rutgers University Press, 1991.

Clifford, James L. "The Authenticity of Anna Seward's Published Correspondence." *Modern Philology* 39, no. 2 (1941): 113–122.

———. *From Puzzles to Portraits*. Chapel Hill: University of North Carolina Press, 1970.

———. *Hester Lynch Piozzi (Mrs. Thrale)*. 2nd ed. New York: Columbia University Press, 1987.

———. *Young Samuel Johnson*. London: Heinemann, 1955.

Clifford, James L., and Donald J. Greene. *Samuel Johnson: A Survey and Bibliography of Critical Studies*. Minneapolis: University of Minnesota Press, 1970.

Clingham, Greg. "Truth and Artifice in Boswell's Life of Johnson." In *New Light on Boswell: Critical and Historical Essays on the Occasion of the Bicentenary of the Life of Johnson*, edited by Greg Clingham, 207–230. Cambridge: Cambridge University Press, 1991, 1993.

Coleman, Jenny. "Vested Interests: The Con Artist, the Historian, and the Feminist Biographer." *a/b: Auto/Biography Studies* 25, no. 1 (Summer 2010): 18–31.

Constant, Benjamin. *Le Cahier Rouge*. Paris, 1907.

Constant, Samuel de. *Le Mari sentimental, ou le mariage comme il y en a quelques-uns: Lettres d'un homme du pays de Vaud*. Edited by Giovanni Riccioli. 1783. Milan: Cisalpino-Goliardica, 1975.

Cook, Daniel, and Amy Culley, eds. *Women's Life Writing, 1700–1850: Gender, Genre and Authorship*. Basingstoke: Palgrave Macmillan, 2012.

Coulombeau, Sophie. "Introduction." *Eighteenth-Century Life* 42, no. 2 (2018): 1–11.

Courtney, C. P. *Isabelle de Charrière (Belle de Zuylen): A Biography*. Oxford: Voltaire Foundation, 1993.

———. *A Preliminary Bibliography of Isabelle de Charrière. Studies on Voltaire and the Eighteenth Century*. Oxford: Voltaire Foundation, 1980.

Crisp, Samuel. Review of *Italian Tour*, by Charles Burney. *Contemporary Review* 31 (1771): 421–432.

Croker, John Wilson. Review of *Memoirs of Dr. Burney*. *Quarterly Review* (April 1833): 97–125.

Culley, Amy, ed. *British Women's Life Writing, 1760–1840: Friendship, Community, and Collaboration*. Basingstoke: Palgrave Macmillan, 2014.

———. "Women's Life Writing in the Long 18th Century: A Critical Survey." *Literature Compass* 12, no. 1 (January 2015): 1–11.

Damrosch, Leo. *The Club: Johnson, Boswell, and the Friends Who Shaped an Age*. New Haven, CT: Yale University Press, 2019.

———. "The Life of Johnson: An Anti-theory." *Eighteenth-Century Studies* 6, no. 4 (1973): 486–505.

Danziger, Marlies K., and Frank Brady, eds. *Boswell: The Great Biographer 1789–1795*. London: Heinemann, 1989.

Doody, Margaret Anne. *Frances Burney: The Life in the Works*. New Brunswick, NJ: Rutgers University Press, 1988.

Dowd, Michelle M., and Julie Eckerle, eds. *Genre and Women's Life Writing in Early Modern England*. Farnham: Ashgate, 2007.

Durant, Jack D. "*Truth* for Sheridan: A Biographical Dilemma." In *A Fair Day in the Affections*, edited by Jack D. Durant and M. Thomas Hester, 119–130. Raleigh, NC: Winston Press, 1980.

Edel, Leon. "Biography: A Manifesto." *Biography* 1, no. 1 (Winter 1978): 1–3.

Equiano, Olaudah. *The Interesting Narrative of the Life of Olaudah Equiano, or Gustavus Vassa, the African*. London, 1789.

European Magazine. Unsigned review of *Letters to and from the Late Samuel Johnson, LL.D.*, by Hester Lynch Piozzi. Vol. 13 (March 1788): 164–166.

Examiner. Unsigned review of "The Memoirs of Dr. Burney. By His Daughter, Madame D'Arblay." December 2, 1832, 774.

Faraday, Michael. *Telling Lives in Science*. Edited by Michael Shortland and Richard Yeo. Cambridge: Cambridge University Press, 1996.

Farnum, Dorothy. *The Dutch Divinity: A Biography of Madame de Charrière, 1740–1805*. London: Jarrolds, 1959.

Fitzer, Anna. "Relating a Life: Alicia LeFanu's *Memoirs of the Life of Frances Sheridan*." *Women's Writing* 15, no. 1 (2008): 32–54.

Fletcher, Edward G. "Mrs. Piozzi on Boswell and Johnson's Tour." *University of Texas Studies in English* 32 (1953): 45–58.

France, Peter, and William St. Clair, eds. *Mapping Lives: The Uses of Biography*. Oxford: Oxford University Press for the British Academy, 2002.

"Frances Sheridan." In *New and General Biographical Dictionary*, 13:376. 1798.

Francus, Marilyn. *Monstrous Motherhood: 18th-Century Culture and the Ideology of Domesticity*. Baltimore: Johns Hopkins University Press, 2012.

———. "Shaping a Legacy: Alicia LeFanu's *Memoirs of the Life and Writings of Mrs. Frances Sheridan*." *Female Spectator* 17, no. 1 (2013): 6–7.

Fuchs, Miriam, and Craig Howes. "Introduction." In *Teaching Life Writing Texts*, edited by Miriam Fuchs and Craig Howes, 1–22. New York: MLA, 2008.

Geiger, Ludwig. *Therese Huber, 1764–1829, Leben and Briefe einer deutschen Frau*. Stuttgart: Cotta, 1901.

Gentleman's Magazine. Unsigned review of "The Memoirs of Dr. Burney, Arranged from His Own Manuscripts, &c by His Daughter, Madame D'Arblay." February 1833, 142–147.

Gentleman's Magazine. Unsigned review of "The Memoirs of the Life and Writings of Mrs. Frances Sheridan." June 1824, 532–534.

Gilman, Todd. "Arne, Handel, the Beautiful, and the Sublime." *Eighteenth-Century Studies* 42, no. 4 (2009): 529–555.

———. "Polemical Introduction." In *The Theatre Career of Thomas Arne*, 1–30. Newark: University of Delaware Press, 2013.

Godet, Philippe. *Madame de Charrière et ses amis, d'après de nombreux documents inédits*. 2 vols. Geneva: Jullien, 1906. Slatkine Reprints, 1973.

Godwin, William. "Of History and Romance" (1797). In *Political and Philosophical Writings of William Godwin*, edited by Mark Philip, 5:292–295. London: Pickering & Chatto, 1993.

———. *Memoirs of the Author of a Vindication of the Rights of Woman*. London: J. Johnson, and G.G. and J. Robinson, 1798.

Grant, Kerry S. *Dr. Burney as Critic and Historian of Music*. Ann Arbor, MI: UMI Research Press, 1983.

Greene, Donald. "The World's Worst Biography." *American Scholar* 62, no. 3 (Summer 1993): 365–382.

Hamilton, Ian. *Keepers of the Flame: Literary Estates and the Rise of the Biography*. London: Faber & Faber, 1992.

Hankins, David, and James J. Caudle, eds. *The General Correspondence of James Boswell, 1757–1763*. Edinburgh: Edinburgh University Press, 2006.

Harman, Claire. *Fanny Burney: A Biography*. London: HarperCollins, 2000.

Harris, Jocelyn. *Satire, Celebrity, and Politics in Jane Austen*. Lewisburg, PA: Bucknell University Press, 2017.

Hawkins, John. *A General History of the Science and Practice of Music.* London, 1776. Reprint, Dover, 1963.

Hays, Mary. *Female Biography or Memoirs of Illustrious and Celebrated Women, of All Ages and Countries. Alphabetically Arranged.* 6 vols. London: Printed for Richard Phillips, 1803.

Heiland, Donna. "Swan Songs: The Correspondence of Anna Seward and James Boswell." *Modern Philology* 90, no. 3 (1993): 381–391.

Hemlow, Joyce, ed. *A Catalogue of the Burney Family Correspondence, 1749–1878.* New York: New York Public Library, 1971.

———. *The History of Fanny Burney.* Oxford: Clarendon, 1958.

Hill, George Birkbeck, ed. *Johnsonian Miscellanies.* 2 vols. Oxford: Clarendon, 1897.

Hill, George Birkbeck, and Lawrence Fitzroy Powell, eds. *Rev. Boswell's Life of Johnson, Together with Boswell's Journal of a Tour to the Hebrides and Johnson's Diary of a Journey into North Wales.* Vols. 5–6. Oxford: Clarendon, 1934–1950, 1964.

Hitchings, Henry. *The World in Thirty-Eight Chapters, or Dr. Johnson's Guide to Life.* London: Macmillan, 2018.

Hogwood, Christopher. "Burney Revealed." Review of *The Letters of Charles Burney. Times Literary Supplement*, November 13, 1992.

Holmes, Richard. *Dr. Johnson & Mr. Savage.* London: Hodder & Stoughton, 1993.

———. "The Proper Study?" In *Mapping Lives: The Uses of Biography*, edited by Peter France and William St. Clair, 7–18. Oxford: Oxford University Press for the British Academy, 2002.

Hunter, David. *The Lives of George Frideric Handel.* Suffolk, UK: The Boydell Press, 2015.

Hyde, Mary. *The Impossible Friendship: Boswell and Mrs. Thrale.* Cambridge, MA: Harvard University Press, 1972.

Irving, Howard. *Ancients and Moderns.* Aldershot: Ashgate, 1999.

Jennings, Judith. "'By No Means in a Liberal Style': Mary Morris Knowles versus James Boswell." In *Women Editing/Editing Women: Early Modern Women Writers and the New Textualism*, edited by Ann Hollinshead Hurley and Chanita Goodblatt, 227–255. Newcastle-upon-Tyne: Cambridge Scholars, 2009.

———. "Confronting Samuel Johnson" and "Defying James Boswell." In

Gender, Religion, and Radicalism in the Long Eighteenth Century: The "Ingenious Quaker" and Her Contemporaries, edited by Judith Jennings, 49–72, 99–102. Aldershot: Ashgate, 2006.

———. "Jane Harry Thresher and Mary Morris Knowles Speak Out for Liberty in Jamaica and England." In *Free at Last? Reflections on Freedom and the Abolition of the British Transatlantic Slave Trade*, edited by Amar Wahab and Cecily Jones, 61–84. Newcastle upon Tyne: Cambridge Scholars, 2011.

———. "A Trio of Talented Women: Abolition, Gender and Political Participation 1780–91." *Slavery and Abolition* 26, no. 1 (2005): 55–70.

Jensen, Meg. "Separated by a Common Language: The (Differing) Discourses of Life Writing in Theory and Practice," *a/b: Auto/Biography Studies* 24, no. 2 (2009): 299–314.

Johnson, Claudia L. "'Giant HANDEL' and the Musical Sublime." *Eighteenth-Century Studies* 19, no. 4 (1986): 515–532.

"Johnson, Samuel." In *St. James Guide to Biography*, edited by Paul E. Schellinger, 415–416. Chicago: St. James Press, 1991.

Johnson, Samuel. *The History of Rasselas, Prince of Abyssinia*. 1759. London: Penguin, 1985.

———. *The Idler and the Adventurer*. Edited by W. J. Bate, John M. Bullitt, and L. F. Powell. New Haven, CT: Yale University Press, 1963.

———. *Rambler*, no. 60 (October 13, 1750).

———. *The Rambler*. Edited by W. J. Bate and Albrecht Strauss. New Haven, CT: Yale University Press, 1969.

———. *The Yale Edition of the Works of Samuel Johnson III*. Edited by W. J. Bate and Albrecht B. Strauss. New Haven, CT: Yale University Press, 1969.

Kant, Immanuel. *The Cambridge Edition of the Works of Immanuel Kant*. 3 vols. Translated and edited by Peter Heath and J. B. Schneewind. Cambridge: Cambridge University Press, 1997.

Karl, Frederick R. *Art into Life: The Craft of Literary Biography*. Youngstown, OH: Etruscan Press, 2005.

Ketton-Cremer, Robert Wyndham. "Dr. Burney Sets Out to Please." Review of *Dr. Charles Burney*. *Times Literary Supplement*, April 22, 1965, 310.

[Knowles, Mary]. *Dialogue between Dr. Johnson and Mrs. Knowles*. London, 1799, 1805.

———. *Dialogue between Mrs. Knowles and Dr. Johnson*. London: Printed by C. Stower, 1805.

———. "An Interesting DIALOGUE between the Late Dr. SAMUEL JOHNSON and Mrs. KNOWLES." *Gentleman's Magazine* 61 (1791): 500–502.

———. "Notes of a Conversation between Dr. Johnson and Mary Knowles in a Letter to Boswell." London Library of the Religious Society of Friends. Portfolio MSS 3/126.

Korshin, Paul J. "Johnson's Conversation in Boswell's *Life of Johnson*." In *New Light on Boswell: Critical and Historical Essays on the Occasion of the Bicentenary of the Life of Johnson*, edited by Greg Clingham, 174–193. Cambridge: Cambridge University Press, 1991, 1993.

Lamont, Claire. "James Boswell and Alexander Fraser Tytler." *Bibliotheck* 6 (1971): 1–16.

Landgraf, Annette, and David Vickers, eds. *The Cambridge Handel Encyclopedia*. Cambridge: Cambridge University Press, 2009.

Lansdowne, The Marquis of, ed. *The Queeney Letters, Being Letters Addressed to Hester Maria Thrale by Doctor Johnson, Fanny Burney and Mrs. Thrale-Piozzi*. New York: Farrar & Rinehart, 1934.

Lee, Hermione. *Biography*. Oxford: Oxford University Press, 2009.

LeFanu, Alicia. *Memoirs of the Life and Writings of Mrs. Sheridan*. London: G. and W. B. Whitaker, 1824.

———. *Strathallan*. Edited by Anna Fitzer. London: Pickering and Chatto, 2008.

Le Faye, Deirdre. *Jane Austen's Letters*. 3rd ed. New York: Oxford University Press, 1995.

Letzter, Jacqueline, and Robert Adelson. "Isabelle de Charrière's Parisian Sojourn of 1786–87: A Turning Point in Her Operatic Career." In *Isabelle de Charrière: Proceedings of the International Conference Held at Yale University in April 2002*, edited by Vincent Giroud and Janet Whatley, 115–129. New Haven, CT: Beinecke Rare Book and Manuscript Library, 2004.

Lipking, Lawrence. *The Ordering of the Arts in Eighteenth-Century England*. Princeton, NJ: Princeton University Press, 1970.

Literary Chronicle. Unsigned review of "The Memoirs of the Life and Writings of Mrs. Frances Sheridan." Vol. 253 (March 20, 1824): 177–179.

Lonsdale, Roger. "Dr. Burney's 'Dictionary of Music.'" *Musicology Australia* 5, no. 1 (1979): 159–171.

———. *Dr. Charles Burney: A Literary Biography*. Oxford: Clarendon, 1965.

———. "Johnson and Dr. Burney." In *Johnson, Boswell and Their Circle*, 210–240. Oxford: Clarendon, 1965.

Looser, Devoney. "'Her Later Works Happily Forgotten': Rewriting Frances Burney and Old Age." *Eighteenth-Century Life* 37, no. 3 (Fall 2013): 1–28.

———. *Women Writers and Old Age in Great Britain, 1750–1850*. Baltimore: Johns Hopkins University Press, 2008.

Luckett, Richard. "'Or Rather Our Musical Shakespeare': Charles Burney's Purcell." In *Music in Eighteenth-Century England*, edited by Christopher Hogwood and Richard Luckett, 59–78. Cambridge: Cambridge University Press, 1983.

Lustig, Irma S. "Boswell at Work: The Animadversions on Mrs Piozzi." *Modern Language Review* 67 (1972): 11–30.

———. "Fact into Art: James Boswell's Notes, Journals, and the Life of Johnson." In *Biography in the 18th Century*, edited by John H. Browning, 112–146. New York: Garland, 1980.

MacArthur, Elizabeth. "Devious Narratives: Refusal of Closure in Two Eighteenth-Century Epistolary Novels." *Eighteenth-Century Studies* 21 (Fall 1987): 1–20.

Macaulay, Thomas Babington. "Croker's Edition of Boswell's *Life of Johnson*." *Edinburgh Review* 54 (September 1831): 1–38.

Mackerness, Eric David. "Dr. Burney, Biographer." *Contemporary Review* 189 (1956): 352–357.

———. *A Social History of English Music*. London: Routledge, 1964.

Marcus, Laura. *Auto/Biographical Discourses*. Manchester: Manchester University Press, 1994.

McCarthy, William. *Hester Thrale Piozzi: Portrait of a Literary Woman*. Chapel Hill: University of North Carolina Press, 1985.

Miller, Lucasta. *The Brontë Myth*. New York: First Anchor Books, 2001.

Monthly Review. Unsigned review of "The Memoirs of the Life and Writings of Mrs. Frances Sheridan." July 1824, 257–265.

Moore, Thomas. *Memoirs of the Life of the Right Honourable Richard Brinsley Sheridan*. London: Longman, 1825.

Moser-Verrey, Monique. "Isabelle de Charrière en quète d'une meilleure entente." *Stanford French Review* 11 (Spring 1987): 63–76.

[Murphy, Arthur]. Review of *Letters to and from the Late Samuel Johnson, LL.D.*, by Hester Lynch Piozzi. *Monthly Review* 78 (March 1788): 324–331.

Myers, Robert Manson. *Handel's Messiah: A Touchstone of Taste*. New York: Macmillan, 1948.

New Annual Register. Unsigned review of "The Memoirs of the Life and Writings of Mrs. Frances Sheridan." January 1824, 10–12.

Nichols, John, and John Bowyer Nichols. *Illustrations of the Literary History of the Eighteenth Century: Consisting of Authentic Memoirs and Original Letters of Eminent Persons; and Intended as a Sequel to the Literary Anecdotes*. 8 vols. London: J. B. Nichols and Son, 1817–1858.

Norman, Sylvia. *Flight of the Skylark: The Development of Shelley's Reputation*. Norman: University of Oklahoma Press, 1954.

Nussbaum, Felicity. *The Autobiographical Subject: Gender and Ideology in Eighteenth-Century England*. Baltimore: Johns Hopkins University Press, 1989.

———. "Boswell's Treatment of Johnson's Temper: 'A Warm West-Indian Climate.'" *Studies in English Literature, 1500–1900* 14, no. 3 (1974): 421–433.

Oliphant, Margaret. *Sheridan*. New York: Harper & Brothers, 1883.

Osborn, J. M. *By Appointment to His Majesty Biographer of Johnson*. New Haven, CT: Yale University Press, 1964.

O'Toole, Fintan. *A Traitor's Kiss: The Life of Richard Brinsley Sheridan*. London: Granta Books, 1997.

Parke, Catherine N. *Biography: Writing Lives*. New York: Twayne, 1996.

———. "Johnson and the Arts of Conversation." In *The Cambridge Companion to Samuel Johnson*, edited by Greg Clingham, 18–33. Cambridge: Cambridge University Press, 1997.

Pennington, Montagu. *Memoirs of the Life of Mrs. Elizabeth Carter, with a New Edition of Her Poems*. 2 vols., 2nd ed. London: F.C. and J. Rivington, 1808.

———, ed. *A Series of Letters between Mrs. Elizabeth Carter and Miss Catherine Talbot from the Year 1741 to 1770. To Which Are Added, Letters from Mrs. Elizabeth Carter to Mrs. Vesey between the Years 1763 and 1787*. 4 vols. London: F.C. and J. Rivington, 1809.

Pilkington, Mary. *Biography for Boys*. London: Vernor and Hood, 1799.

Piozzi, Hester Lynch. *Anecdotes of the Late Samuel Johnson LL.D. during the Last Twenty Years of His Life*. 1786. Edited by Arthur Sherbo. New York: Oxford University Press, 1974.

———. *Letters to and from the Late Samuel Johnson, LL.D. to Which Are Added Some Poems Never Before Printed, Published from the Original Mss. in Her Possession*. 2 vols. London: A. Strahan and T. Cadell, 1788.

Pittock, Murray. *James Boswell*. Aberdeen: Aberdeen Introductions to Irish and Scottish Culture, 2007.

Podnieks, Elizabeth. "Introduction: 'New Biography' for a New Millennium." *a/b: Auto/Biography Studies* 24, no. 1 (Summer 2009): 1–14.

Pope, Alexander. "An Essay on Man: Epistle II." In *The Poems of Alexander Pope*, edited by John Butt, 515–525. New Haven, CT: Yale University Press, 1963.

Popkin, Jeremy. "Life Writing in the Family." *a/b: Auto/Biography Studies* 25, no. 2 (2010): 172–185.

Pottle, Frederick A. *The Literary Career of James Boswell, Esq. Being the Bibliographical Materials for a Life of Boswell*. Oxford: Clarendon, 1929. Reprinted 1966.

———. "The Power of Memory in Boswell and Scott." In *Essays on the Eighteenth Century: Presented to David Nichol Smith in Honour of His Seventieth Birthday*, 168–189. Oxford: Clarendon, 1945.

Pottle, Frederick A., and Charles H. Bennett. "Boswell and Mrs. Piozzi." *Modern Philology* 39, no. 4 (1942): 421–430.

Preston, Thomas R. "From Typology to Literature: Hermeneutics and Historical Narrative in Eighteenth-Century England." *Eighteenth Century* 23, no. 3 (1982): 181–196.

Radcliffe, Mary Ann. *The Memoirs of Mrs. Mary Ann Radcliffe, in Familiar Letters to Her Female Friend*. Edinburgh: Manners and Miller, 1810.

Rader, Ralph. "Literary Form in Factual Narrative." In *Essays in Eighteenth-Century Biography*, edited by Philip P. Daghlian, 3–42. Bloomington: Indiana University Press, 1968.

Radner, John B. *Johnson and Boswell: A Biography of Friendship*. New Haven, CT: Yale University Press, 2013.

Rae, W. Fraser. *Sheridan: A Biography*. New York: Henry Holt, 1896.

Redford, Bruce. *The Converse of the Pen: Acts of Intimacy in the Eighteenth-Century Familiar Letter*. Chicago: University of Chicago Press, 1986.

———, ed. *The Letters of Samuel Johnson*. 5 vols. Princeton, NJ: Princeton University Press, 1992–1994.

Reed, Joseph W., and Frederick A. Pottle, eds. *Boswell: Laird of Auchinleck 1778–1782*. London: Heinemann, 1977.

Reitter, Paul. "Fin de Siecle Vienna and the Challenge of Family Biography." *American Imago* 68, no. 4 (2011): 665–678.

Roberts, Mary. *Select Female Biography, Comprising Memoirs of Eminent British Ladies*. London: Harvey & Darton, 1829.

Robinson, Mary. *Memoirs of the Late Mrs. Robinson*. 4 vols. London: Phillips, 1801.

Rogers, Pat. "Introduction." In James Boswell, *Life of Johnson*, edited by R. W. Chapman, v–xxxiv. Oxford: Oxford University Press, 1980, 1998.

Rooksby, Emma. "Introduction." In Isabelle de Charrière, *Three Women*, translated by Emma Rooksby, ix–xxxiii. New York: MLA, 2007.

Rosenthal, Laura, ed. *Nightwalkers: Prostitute Narratives from the Eighteenth Century*. Peterborough, ON: Broadview Press, 2008.

Rousseau, Jean-Jacques. *Discours sur* [the Moral Effects of] *les sciences et les arts*. Paris, 1750.

Ryskamp, Charles, and Frederick A. Pottle, eds. *Boswell: The Ominous Years 1774–1776*. London: Heinemann, 1963.

Sabor, Peter. "Creative and Uncreative Gloom: Frances Burney and Alexander d'Arblay." *European Spectator* 11 (2010): 19–41.

———. "'I Dearly Love to Praise Old Friends': Dr. Burney and Dr. Johnson." *Johnsonian News Letter* 66 (2015): 6–17.

———. "'The March of Intimacy': Dr. Burney and Dr. Johnson." *Eighteenth-Century Life* 42, no. 2 (2018): 38–55.

Scholes, Percy A. *The Great Dr. Burney*. London: Oxford University Press, 1948.

Schwartz, Richard. *Boswell's Johnson: A Preface to the Life*. Madison: University of Wisconsin Press, 1978.

Scott, Geoffrey. "The First Records." *Boswell Papers* 6 (1929): 15–27. Reprinted in "The *Making of the Life* of Johnson as Shown in Boswell's First Notes." In *Twentieth Century Interpretations of Boswell's Life of Johnson*, edited by James L. Clifford, 27–39. Englewood Cliffs, NJ: Prentice Hall, 1970.

———. *The Portrait of Zélide*. 1925. New York: Scribner's, 1959.

Seelig, Sharon Cadman, ed. *Autobiography and Gender in Early Modern Literature*. Cambridge: Cambridge University Press, 2006.

Sévery, William de, and Clara de Charrière de Sévery. *La Vie de society dans le pays de Vaud à la fin du dix-huitième siècle*. 2 vols. Lausanne: Bridel. Paris: Fischbucher, 1911–1912.

Seward, Anna. *Letters of Anna Seward: Written between the Years 1784 and 1807*. 6 vols. Edinburgh: George Ramsay, 1811.

———. *Memoirs of the Life of Dr. Darwin*. London: J. Johnson, 1804.

Seymour, Miranda. "Shaping the Truth." In *Mapping Lives: The Uses of Biography*, edited by Peter France and William St. Clair, 253–266. Oxford: Oxford University Press, 2002.

Sher, Richard B. "Appendix: Boswell, Forbes, and the Quarrel with 'Young Mr. Tytler.'" In *The Correspondence of James Boswell with Sir William Forbes*. Edinburgh: Edinburgh University Press, forthcoming.

Sichel, Walter. *Sheridan, from New and Original Material; Including a Manuscript Diary by Georgiana Duchess of Devonshire*. Boston: Houghton Mifflin, 1909.

Siebenschuh, William R. "Boswell's Second Crop of Memory: A New Look at the Role of Memory in the Making of the Life." In *Boswell's Life of Johnson: New Questions, New Answers*, edited by John A. Vance, 25–52. Athens: University of Georgia Press, 1985.

———. "Cognitive Processes and Autobiographical Acts." *Biography* 12, no. 2 (1989): 142–153.

———. "The Relationship between Factual Accuracy and Literary Art in the 'Life of Johnson.'" *Modern Philology* 74, no. 3 (1977): 273–288.

Sisman, Adam. *Boswell's Presumptuous Task*. London: Hamish Hamilton, 2000. New York: Farrar Straus Giroux, 2001. Revised, Penguin, 2001, 2002. Reprint, Harper Perennial, 2006.

Smith, Sidonie, and Julia Watson. *Reading Autobiography: A Guide for Interpreting Life Narratives*. Minneapolis: University of Minnesota Press, 2001.

Smither, Howard. *A History of the Oratorio*. Vol. 3. Chapel Hill: University of North Carolina Press, 1987.

Staël, Madame [Germaine] de. *Corinne, ou l'Italie*. Paris, H. Nicolle, 1807.

Standage, Tom. *The Turk: The Life and Times of the Famous Eighteenth-Century Chess-Playing Machine*. New York: Walker, 2002.

St. Clair, William. "The Biographer as Archeologist." In *Mapping Lives: The Uses of Biography*, edited by Peter France and William St. Clair, 219–234. Oxford: Oxford University Press, 2002.

Steel, Anthony. *The Custom of the Room: Early Wine-Books of Christ's College, Cambridge*. Cambridge: Heffer, 1949.

Stevenson, Robert. "'The Rivals'—Hawkins, Burney, and Boswell." *Musical Quarterly* 36, no. 1 (1950): 67–82.

Stewart, Joan Hinde. *The Enlightenment of Age: Women, Letters and Growing Old in Eighteenth-Century France*. Oxford: Voltaire Foundation, 2010.

Still, Judith. "Isabelle de Charrière's *Three Women*—Adopting and Adapting Hospitality after Kant." *German Life and Letters* 64 (2011): 19–30.

Strien, Kees van, and Madeleine van Strien-Chardonneau. "Belle de Zuylen/Isabelle de Charrière et le Comte de Dönhoff: Deux lettres inédites." *Revue d'histoire littéraire de la France* 104, no. 2 (2004): 475–483.

Tankard, Paul, ed. *Facts and Inventions: Selections from the Journalism of James Boswell*. New Haven, CT: Yale University Press, 2014.

Thaddeus, Janice Farrar. *Frances Burney: A Literary Life*. New York: St. Martin's, 2000.

"Thomas Sheridan." *A New and General Biographical Dictionary* 8 (1795): 172–176.

Tinker, Chauncey Brewster, ed. *Letters of James Boswell*. 2 vols. Oxford: Clarendon, 1924.

Troide, Lars. "History and Description of the Burney Project." *Fontanus* 1 (1988): 38–49, http://fontanus.mcgill.ca/article/view/2/2.

Turnbull, Gordon. "Boswell and Belle de Zuylen: Language and Legislation." In *Isabelle de Charrière: Proceedings of the International Conference Held at Yale University in April 2002*, edited by Vincent Giroud and Janet Whatley, 87–100. New Haven, CT: Beinecke Rare Book and Manuscript Library, 2004.

[Twining, Thomas]. Review of *An Account of the Musical Performances in Westminster-Abbey . . . in Commemoration of Handel*, by Charles Burney. *Contemporary Review* 59 (1785): 130–138.

Ulph, Cassandra. "Authoring the 'Author of My Being' in *Memoirs of Doctor Burney*." *Eighteenth-Century Life* 42, no. 2 (2018): 152–169.

Vance, John A., ed. *Boswell's Life of Johnson: New Questions, New Answers.* Athens: University of Georgia Press, 1985.

van Strien, Kees. *Isabelle de Charrière (Belle de Zuylen) Early Writings: New Material from Dutch Archives.* Leuven: Peeters, 2005.

Vissière, Isabelle. "La Correspondance d'Isabelle de Charrière et Benjamin Constant: Un Théâtre de Société." In *Isabelle de Charrière: Proceedings of the International Conference Held at Yale University in April 2002*, edited by Vincent Giroud and Janet Whatley, 55–67. New Haven, CT: Beinecke Rare Book and Manuscript Library, 2004.

———. "Une intellectuelle face au mariage: Belle de Zuylen (Madame de Charrière)." In *Femmes savantes et femmes d'esprit: Women Intellectuals of the French Eighteenth Century*, edited by Roland Bonnel and Catherine Rubinger, 273–295. New York: Peter Lang, 1994.

Voltaire [François-Marie Arouet]. *Candide, ou l'optimisme.* Geneva, 1759.

Waingrow, Marshall, ed. *The Correspondence and Other Papers of James Boswell Relating to the Making of the Life of Johnson.* London: Heinemann; New York: McGraw-Hill, 1969. 2nd ed., Edinburgh: Edinburgh University Press; New Haven, CT: Yale University Press, 2001.

Walkden, Andrea. *Private Lives Made Public: The Invention of Biography in Early Modern England.* Pittsburgh: Duquesne University Press, 2016.

Walter, James. "'The Solace of Doubt'? Biographical Methodology after the Short Twentieth Century." In *Mapping Lives: The Uses of Biography*, edited by Peter France and William St. Clair, 321–335. Oxford: Oxford University Press for the British Academy, 2002.

Watkins, John. *Memoirs of the Public and Private Life of the Right Honorable Richard Brinsley Sheridan, with a Particular Account of His Family and Connexions.* London: Printed for Henry Colburn, 1817.

West, Anthony. *Mortal Wounds.* New York: McGraw-Hill, 1973.

Whatley, Janet. "The Engaged Life of a Quiet Man: Charles-Emmanuel de Charrière." *Cahiers Isabelle de Charrière / Belle de Zuylen Papers* 3 (2008): 11–23.

———. "Reading the Life of Isabelle de Charrière." In *Isabelle de Charrière: Proceedings of the International Conference Held at Yale University in April 2002*, edited by Vincent Giroud and Janet Whatley, 131–148. New Haven, CT: Beinecke Rare Book and Manuscript Library, 2004.

Whyte, Samuel. *Miscellanea Nova.* New ed. Dublin: Robert Marchbank, 1800.

Wimsatt, William K., Jr., and Frederick A. Pottle, eds. *Boswell for the Defence, 1769–1774.* New York: McGraw-Hill; London, Heinemann, 1959.

Winiker, Rolf. *Madame de Charrière: Essai d'un Itineraire spiritual.* Lausanne: Editions l'Age d'Homme, 1971.

Wolff, Elisabeth, and Agatha Deken. *Sara Burgerhart.* Original Dutch 1782. French translation 1787.

Wood, Dennis. *Benjamin Constant: A Biography.* New York: Routledge, 1993.

Wooley, James D. "Johnson as Despot: Anna Seward's Rejected Contribution to Boswell's Life." *Modern Philology* 70 (1972): 140–145.

Notes on Contributors

LISA BERGLUND is a professor of English at Buffalo State College, where she teaches lexicography, book history, Shakespeare, and the extremely long eighteenth century. Since 2017 she has served as executive director of the American Society for Eighteenth-Century Studies (ASECS). Her scholarship on Hester Lynch Piozzi has been published in the *Journal of Eighteenth-Century Studies*, *Dictionaries: The Journal of the Dictionary Society of North America*, *The Age of Johnson*, *Names: A Journal of Onomastics*, and *Living in the Eighteenth Century: A Festschrift in Honor of Betty Rizzo*.

TANYA M. CALDWELL is a professor and associate graduate director in the Department of English at Georgia State University. She teaches and has published on various aspects of late seventeenth- and eighteenth-century literature and culture, with a particular focus on translation from the ancients, drama, and life writing. Her books include an edited anthology of plays, *Popular Plays by Women in the Restoration and Eighteenth Century* (2011); *Virgil Made English: The Decline of Ancient Authority* (2008); and *Time to Begin Anew: Dryden's Georgics and Aeneis* (2000). She is currently working on a biography of the playwright Hannah Cowley (1743–1809).

JAMES J. CAUDLE is a research associate at the Centre for Robert Burns Studies at the University of Glasgow, currently working with the team creating the first-ever edition of Burns's complete correspondence for the *Oxford Edition of the Works of Robert Burns*. He has published many articles on James Boswell and is the author of several chapters on him in forthcoming multiauthor collections. As the associate editor of the Yale Boswell Editions from 2000 to 2017, he was coeditor of a volume of Boswell's earliest correspondence and more recently worked on a forthcoming volume of Boswell's correspondence with Sir William Forbes of Pitsligo. He also writes on the history of the book, political thought in media such as sermons, and the role of social verse in Georgian culture.

MARILYN FRANCUS is a professor of English at West Virginia University. She is the author of *Monstrous Motherhood: 18th-Century Culture and the Ideology of Domesticity* (2012) and *The Converting Imagination: Linguistic Theory and Swift's Satiric Prose* (1994), and editor of the *Burney Journal*. Her current research focuses on the origins of the mommy wars in the eighteenth century.

TODD GILMAN taught literature and writing at the University of Toronto, Boston University, and MIT before embarking on a career in academic librarianship. Since 2001 he has served as a librarian for literature in English at Yale University. In 2013, he published the only modern biography of eighteenth-century London's preeminent native-born composer for the stage, *The Theatre Career of Thomas Arne*, the culmination of nearly two decades of research. In 2018, at the University of Rochester, he codirected the first complete performance since the eighteenth century of Arne's once-famous 1762 comic opera *Love in a Village*. He holds a bachelor's degree in English from the University of Michigan–Ann Arbor, a master's and PhD in English from the University of Toronto, and a master's in library and information science from Simmons College.

PETER SABOR is Canada Research Chair and a professor of English at McGill University, where he is also director of the Burney Centre. His publications on Frances Burney include *The Cambridge Companion to Frances Burney* and coedited editions of Burney's *Cecilia*, *The Wanderer*, her selected journals and letters, and her collected plays. He is general editor of *The Court Journals and Letters of Frances Burney*, with five of six volumes published to date, and the two-volume *Additional Journals and Letters of Frances Burney*, of which the second volume was published in 2018. He is also general editor of *The Letters of Dr. Charles Burney*, begun in 1991, which will be completed in six volumes.

VICTORIA WARREN received her PhD from Binghamton University, specializing in eighteenth-century studies and focusing on British literature and culture. Her published articles in peer-reviewed journals are on a variety of historical and literary topics, including on playwright Susanna Centlivre in *Studies in English Literature*. Her most recent publication is "Maria Edgeworth's *Belinda*: A Dialogue with Alexander Pope" in *Eighteenth-Century Fiction* (Summer 2018). At Binghamton, she has created and taught courses devoted to studying life writing. Her current scholarship aims to emphasize Charrière's importance to our views of the (international) eighteenth century and of life writing as a field.

Index